Also by Nat Hentoff

NONFICTION

Hear Me Talkin' to Ya (edited with Nat Shapiro)

The Jazz Makers (edited with Nat Shapiro)

Jazz (edited with Albert McCarthy)

The Jazz Life

Peace Agitator: The Story of A. J. Muste

The New Equality

Our Children Are Dying

The Collected Essays of A. J. Muste

A Doctor Among the Addicts

A Political Life: The Education of John V. Lindsay

State Secrets: Police Surveillance in America
(with Paul Cowan and Nick Egleson)

Jazz Is

Does Anybody Give a Damn? Nat Hentoff on Education

*The First Freedom: The Tumultuous History of
Free Speech in America*

FICTION FOR ADULTS

Call the Keeper

Onwards!

Blues for Charlie Darwin

The Man from Internal Affairs

FICTION FOR YOUNG READERS

Jazz Country

I'm Really Dragged but Nothing Gets Me Down

Journey into Jazz

In the Country of Ourselves

This School Is Driving Me Crazy

Does This School Have Capital Punishment?

The Day They Came to Arrest the Book

NONFICTION FOR YOUNG READERS

American Heroes: In and Out of School

JOHN
CARDINAL
O'CONNOR

John Cardinal O'Connor trying on his new biretta in Rome after his elevation to cardinal, May 25, 1985. *Photograph by Chris Sheridan/*Catholic New York.

JOHN CARDINAL O'CONNOR

At the Storm Center of a Changing
American Catholic Church

NAT HENTOFF

Charles Scribner's Sons

NEW YORK

Charles Scribner's Sons
Macmillan Publishing Company
866 Third Avenue, New York, NY 10022
Collier Macmillan Canada, Inc.

Library of Congress Cataloging-in-Publication Data
Hentoff, Nat.
John Cardinal O'Connor : at the storm center of a changing
American Catholic Church / by Nat Hentoff.
p. cm.
"From the speeches and writings of John Cardinal
O'Connor": p.
1. O'Connor, John Joseph, 1920– . 2. Catholic Church—United
States—History—20th century. I. O'Connor, John Joseph, 1920–
Selections. 1988. II. Title.
BX4705.O335H46 1988
282'.092'4—dc19
[B]
ISBN 0-684-18944-5   87-31790
CIP

Macmillan books are available at special discounts for bulk purchases for
sales promotions, premiums, fund-raising, or educational use. For details,
contact:

Special Sales Director
Macmillan Publishing Company
866 Third Avenue
New York, NY 10022

10 9 8 7 6 5 4 3 2 1

Designed by Jack Meserole

PRINTED IN THE UNITED STATES OF AMERICA

In memory of CELIA MCCOY,
for whom the Church was life itself—
and much more

There's no point in simply talking to people about filling their souls if you don't fill their bellies.

—JOHN CARDINAL O'CONNOR,
Christmas 1986

CONTENTS

ACKNOWLEDGMENTS

I wish to express my gratitude to William Shawn, who encouraged me to begin a profile of Cardinal O'Connor, and to Robert Gottlieb, the current editor of *The New Yorker,* for his advice in the completion of the project, which is part of this book.

My thanks, too, to Chris Sheridan, of *Catholic New York,* for his extraordinarily generous help in putting together the section of photographs, many of which are his own exemplary work.

And to Martin Baron, who is in charge of fact-checking at *The New Yorker,* my appreciation—and awe.

JOHN CARDINAL O'CONNOR

I

A CHICAGO LAWYER, a Catholic, quotes a friend asking him: "How can you stand to be in the same Church with Cardinal O'Connor?"

The lawyer answers: "Hacks are always in, holy men are always out."

In the fall of 1986, the Vatican moved to make an example of variously straying members of the American Church. Father Charles Curran, for one, was banned from teaching theology at the Catholic University of America because he disagrees, in part, with some of the official teachings concerning homosexuality, divorce, and birth control. Curran was exiled even though the particular teachings with which he differs have *not* been revealed to the Pope, through the Holy Spirit, as divinely infallible and therefore unchangeable.

And Archbishop Raymond Hunthausen of Seattle was, for a time, stripped of much of his authority. Although held in great affection and respect by Catholics and non-Catholics in that city, Hunthausen was publicly humiliated because the Holy See decided he had been lax in fulfilling some of his responsibilities. He had, for instance, permitted a Mass in his cathedral for Dignity, an organization of Catholic homosexuals. He was also criticized for alleged lapses in certain doctrinal matters.

Professor Martin Marty of the University of Chicago, a specialist in Church history, noted at the time: "An efficient process is at work to force a kind of conformity on the American Church."

At the Vatican, a spokesman told a reporter, "If only we had one hundred Cardinal O'Connors in America, we would not be having these troubles."

3

The president of a large publishing house tells me that he and his wife go to Mass every Sunday, their children are in parochial schools, but he is angry at Cardinal O'Connor: "He is among those who are closing the doors of the Church. Pope John XXIII opened them wide, but now the Church is turning inwards again."

At the King David Hotel in Jerusalem, I tell a Harvard professor, whose specialty is American history, that I am writing a book about Cardinal O'Connor and the changing American Church. The professor is astonished.

"O'Connor is so far to the right," the history professor says. "Why would you want to spend time on somebody like that? It's not as if he's at all complicated. You can predict every position he takes."

I ask the professor if he knows that the Cardinal is strongly, passionately prolabor; opposes arming the Contras trying to overthrow the government of Nicaragua; favors sharp reductions in military expenditures; has spent large sums of the New York archdiocese's funds on housing for the poor and the working class; and has renounced a book he himself wrote on the war in Vietnam that was uncritically in favor of American participation in that quagmire.

The history professor says he knows none of these things. His view of the Cardinal, like that of many Americans, is based on newspaper and magazine articles, which tend, says the Cardinal, to portray him as if he were Genghis Khan. And as if he were wholly without a sense of irony—about himself and the parade of confrontations that have marked his time as leader of the archdiocese of New York.

On one subject, O'Connor is entirely without irony: the Pope and the traditional teachings of the Church. In that respect—O'Connor's undeviating loyalty to the Holy See—the Vatican indeed knows exactly whom it can count on among the American bishops when the weather gets rough.

For a sense of the unexpected O'Connor—the one who is not nearly so predictable on matters other than Church doctrine—there is this passage from a June 1986 speech he gave before the Catholic Press Association in Columbus, Ohio:

If a personal reference may be permitted, I don't think I have generally been thought of as the preferred confessor for Americans for Democratic Action or the American Civil Liberties Union. Yet, when in congressional testimony I suggested that some of the monies proposed to build more MX missiles be diverted to building homes for the poor, it became quickly obvious that to a certain number of my erstwhile devotees, I had treacherously become a religious liberal and my right to retain my metropolitan pallium became highly questionable.

Indeed, in the same vein, I know of at least one gentleman who resolved never to darken the door of St. Patrick's Cathedral again because of my constant preachments about the poor, which he saw as political statements.

The greatest volume of negative mail I have ever received, however, came . . . [after] a letter I sent to President Reagan on behalf of the Jewish communities that had appealed to me in respect to [the President's forthcoming visit to] Bitburg [and a cemetery there with the graves of S.S. men]. How you classify that one ideologically is anybody's guess, but I do know that for some I had forfeited not only my political integrity but my baptismal certificate.

The O'Connor who wants to take money away from the military to build housing for the poor is part of that changing American Catholic Church, most represented by the National Conference of Catholic Bishops' pastoral letters condemning the continuing nuclear arms race and the continuing scandal of an American economic system that abandons so many to deprivation and hopelessness.

On the other hand, the O'Connor the Vatican wishes could be cloned is part of the Holy See's increasing impatience with dissent from certain of its teachings, and not just those teachings that have been divinely revealed and therefore are infallible. As a prelate who does not disapprove of the sanctions against Father Curran and Archbishop Hunthausen, O'Connor stands against those in the Church, including some bishops, who fear that the Pope's growing insistence that the American Church purge itself of dissent will weaken its intellectual and indeed spiritual energy.

This sterility is more likely to become an affliction of the hierarchy than the laity, for increasingly, lay Catholics in the United States have disregarded papal pronouncements with which they disagree. Birth control, for instance. But the hierarchy, so visible and so easily monitored by Rome and its Papal Nuncio in the United States, is learning from Rome the perils of dissent—or apparent dissent.

In view of the fact that contemporary Catholics are better educated and generally of a more independent, inquiring mind than many of those in the "immigrant church" of the nineteenth and the beginning of the twentieth centuries, many of them may well lose respect for Church leaders who censor themselves in continual fear of being censored by Rome.

There is also the possibility that some bishops—softly, obliquely—will resist the Pope's determination to bring the leadership of the American Church into line. Should this happen, Cardinal O'Connor will not be among them. Quite the contrary, he is likely to openly, publicly, take to the field against them.

John J. O'Connor, therefore, is a pivotal figure in the American Church. In terms of social issues, he is passionately concerned with the poor and with other victims of injustice. And as the American Church as a whole continues to call attention to those wrongs, it has gained considerable credibility among non-Catholic liberals who recognize that the Church can be an influential ally in Congress and elsewhere in the decades ahead.

But if the American Catholic Church's social conscience is overshadowed by the Holy See's determination that it must be increasingly and visibly subservient to Rome, then the American Church may well come to be regarded by outsiders as a closed institution. It may matter less and less that the Pope, like the American bishops, deplores economic injustice. The image of the Church could revert to that of earlier times—a Church closing its doors. As when, during the controversy about Father Curran, Archbishop James Hickey of Washington said flatly: "There is no right to public dissent in the Church."

If this should be the unswerving obedient spirit of the future American Church, then Cardinal O'Connor may well be revered by some in the next century as having been its quintessential leader, his loyalty to the Holy See overshadowing his record on poverty and other social issues.

O'Connor sees no conflict between his unyielding doctrinal orthodoxy and his work in helping his Church make all kinds of Americans aware of the need for fundamental political, social, and economic changes if there is to be a just society. He does not seem to understand that a Church seen as hostile to nearly all independent theological thinking within will not be trusted as a source of independent thinkers able to deal with the social concerns of the Church.

"With these messages of rigidity from Rome," an American theologian has said, "who will want to enroll in seminaries? Certainly not youngsters with inquiring minds."

Because O'Connor—whichever way the battle for the spirit of the American Church turns out—will be at the core of that struggle, he is a logical, sometimes tumultuous, centerpiece for this exploration of the changing American Church—and the powerful resistance to that change.

But first, an account of how I, a Jewish atheist, came to write this book about the Church and its "Genghis Khan."

2

WHEN I first interviewed Cardinal O'Connor, I made a point of telling him that I am a member of the Proud and Ancient Order of Stiff-Necked Jewish Atheists. (He asked me to repeat that, and wrote it down, presumably for his file of newly discovered sects.) I felt it necessary to declare myself so that he would know, as they say, where I was coming from in writing about him and the Church.

As a boy in largely Catholic Boston, I felt the Church as a ubiquitous if mysterious presence. Ubiquitous in its unquestioned political power. The slightest chill of disapproval from a silken emissary of William Cardinal O'Connell would instantly change more than enough votes in the state legislature or the city council to bury a proposed bill that had at first appeared to be a sure thing.

The Church was also visually ubiquitous. Not in my Jewish ghetto, of course, where a cross, with or without Jesus on it, was not permitted anywhere, under any circumstances. The cross, after all, conjured up pogroms, even to those of us who had only heard of pogroms from parents and grandparents telling of how they had escaped from the ravening disciples of Christ in the Old Country.

Nor was the Church visible in the dwindling territory of the patrician WASPs of Boston—in such of their exclusive enclaves as Louisburg Square. The George Apleys and Henry Cabot Lodges were even more mysterious to me than the Catholics, because at least I went to school with a goodly number of Catholic children, but nary a highborn Protestant.

In much of the rest of Boston, the Church loomed like a fortress, or rather many fortresses. The churches themselves, most of them built big and strong enough to withstand endless sieges by the Visigoths or the Protestants, whoever came first. And the priests were part of the landscape in most of Boston. I would no more have thought of speaking to one of these men, all in black, than I would have of passing the time of day with any of the brawny Irish lads whose souls were presumably in their care.

At the time, in the latter half of the 1930s and early 1940s, Boston was the most anti-Semitic city in the nation, and most of the practitioners of that popular form of group defamation were Catholics. It was far from only verbal. Kids in my neighborhood knew better than to go out at night alone.

And even when we weren't alone, gangs of young churchgoers would descend upon us, loosening our teeth and discoloring our eyes so that we might pay at least partial penance for having killed Christ.

A particular impetus for Jew-hunting was the series of nationally broadcast Sunday afternoon talks of Father Charles E. Coughlin, parish priest of the Shrine of the Little Flower in Royal Oak, Michigan. A man with an uncommonly melodious voice and a head full of cracked obsessions, Father Coughlin came to believe that the Jews were all predatory international bankers and yet at the same time cunning leaders of the international Communist Party, including most of the members of the Politburo. In either Satanic function, Jews were a perpetual threat to the financial and ultimately physical and spiritual well-being of all decent American families.

In addition to his radio broadcasts, which reached 40 million listeners—none more enthusiastic than those in Boston—Coughlin also published a weekly paper, *Social Justice*, which provided such historical treats as the quintessentially anti-Semitic "Protocols of the Elders of Zion." The paper was sold in front of the Catholic churches on Sunday before each Mass.

It was never reported that any Boston priest spoke critically of the undiluted anti-Semitism regularly coming into the city from the Shrine of the Little Flower in Royal Oak, Michigan. Nor was it reported that any of the youngsters in parochial school classes were given any antidotes to Father Coughlin's poison. Nor was it reported in the diocesan newspaper, *The Pilot*, that the poison existed.

As for Cardinal O'Connell and the rampant anti-Semitism in Boston, Anthony Lukas has pointed out in *Common Ground* (New York: Alfred A. Knopf, 1985) that "just as Pope Pius XII failed to condemn Hitler's concentration camps, so when bands of Irish youths ranged Blue Hill Avenue (they called it 'Jew Hill Avenue'), harassing and beating Jews, the Cardinal was conspicuously silent."

Not surprisingly, at the age of fifteen, I considered the

Catholic Church ever present, mysterious, and my enemy. Until the advent of Frances Sweeney. She taught me that there could be a difference between some of the laity and the rest of the Church, as it was at the time. A fiercely devout Catholic, Fran—the editor of a muckraking weekly originally devoted to the merciless exposure of political corruption in Boston—was enraged by the silence of her Church on the increasingly malignant anti-Semitism in the city.

She wrote editorials flaying the Cardinal, his bishops, and his priests, as well as city officials and the establishment press, for acting as if no heads were being broken on the Jewish streets at night while police officials dismissed the spilled blood as "kid stuff." She asked why there was no preaching in the churches, especially the Catholic churches, condemning this wickedness. And she sent out volunteer high school and college students, myself among them, to report undercover on where the money was coming from to print and circulate all those anti-Semitic screeds.

Fran was so persistent that she eventually fell under the baleful eye of the Cardinal, who summoned her to his awesome presence and threatened, indirectly, to cast her out of the Church if she continued to be a public scandal by criticizing the Church. She was greatly shaken, for she could not conceive of a resonant life outside the Church. But Fran told the Cardinal that it was anti-Semitism that was a public scandal, and she would not be silent about it or about those who remained silent as it spread.

I began to change my mind about Catholics, some Catholics. And Frances Sweeney began to change my mind about myself. One day, when all her volunteer reporters, most of us Jewish, were assembled, Fran gave each of us a set of questions to answer. She wouldn't tell us why. A week later, she threw the papers on a table in disgust and said that the questions had been a test, a test of our attitudes toward groups other than our own. The results, she icily announced, revealed that we—especially the liberal Jews among us—were among the most prejudiced people who had ever taken these tests. And we were most ignorant, most prejudiced, when it came to Catholics.

I did not forget the humiliation of that morning. I also did not forget Father Coughlin, the silent Cardinal O'Connell, and the Irish thugs who swaggered into my neighborhood in the name of their Savior. I used to wonder whether, during confession, they had to cite their assaults on us as being among their sins. I doubted it. Chastened as I was by Fran's tests, I nonetheless imagined the priests hearing confession as having well-thumbed copies of *Social Justice* alongside them.

But at Boston Latin School, where I spent six years, I did come to know Catholic boys with whom I felt comfortable and even liked. And through jazz, my obsession in those years and ever after, I got to know a couple of jazz priests. (There were labor priests, so why not jazz priests?) They played recordings on the radio, showed up at Sunday jam sessions, and wrote articles about the ineluctable relationships between God and the jazz spirit.

I once became so bold as to invite one of the jazz priests home to dinner. My mother, when told, was in a state of consternation.

"What do those people eat?" she asked me.

I didn't know, but suggested fish.

During the 1960s, covering and participating in the civil rights and antiwar movements, I learned more about non-parochial Catholics who spoke truth to power. Particularly in the turbulent context of the broadsides, demonstrations, and civil disobedience against the war in Vietnam. Priests such as Daniel and Philip Berigan and nuns such as Elizabeth McAlister, who seemed to be continually arrested for trying to block the war machine.

Some bishops were also out front in antiwar protests, but not many. Most either prayed for the President and his war or were silent. Indeed, Francis Cardinal Spellman of New York, visiting American troops in Vietnam during Christmas in 1965, proclaimed: "My country, may it always be right. Right or wrong, my country."

The Berigans and McAlister (who is now Mrs. Philip Berigan, back among the laity with her husband) are still going to prison for gumming up the war works. But now, two decades later, a good many bishops and archbishops would agree with their goals, if not necessarily with their means. And there are a number of priests who themselves have committed civil disobedience.

Not Cardinal O'Connor, but he, too—who led American soldiers in the Sorrowful Mysteries in a mud-soaked hole in Vietnam as they were about to go into combat—has sufficiently changed within himself so that he is able to say, publicly, when he thinks his country is wrong, as in its arming of the Contras trying to overthrow the Nicaraguan government and its ceaseless stockpiling of nuclear weapons.

The former Sister McAlister, when she was in prison in 1984 for having damaged the cones of nuclear missiles, wrote a letter that appeared in the *National Catholic Reporter.* She called "into unity all who struggle against the probability of nuclear annihilation . . . all who struggle against the oppression of colonial seizures, who struggle against capital punishment, who struggle in behalf of life, for the born and the unborn . . . We must widen the frame."

That is a statement by a Catholic with which I thoroughly agree. Including the opposition to abortion. I didn't get to that last point for a long time, but I arrived there, as I have told Cardinal O'Connor, without God. There is nothing contradictory in a Jewish atheist civil libertarian adhering to a consistent ethic of life. A "seamless garment," as some in the Catholic Church call it.

Yet there are other teachings of the Church that I find as opaque as I did the Church as a whole when I was a boy. The secondary position of women, for example. In that respect, though, there are ties between the religion in which I was raised and Catholicism. In the Orthodox Jewish *shul* I attended, women were not allowed to sit with the men. They were in the balcony, second-class worshipers. And then, as now, there were no women rabbis among the Orthodox, no women cantors.

What made no sense to me in my own *shul* makes no sense to me in the Catholic Church. And more and more women in that Church are rising in fierce disputation on this issue. Some bishops are in sympathy with the demand that the priesthood no longer be restricted to males, but those bishops are much less likely to broadcast these views in a time when the Vatican is casting a cold eye on anyone in the hierarchy who questions official teaching. As for Cardinal O'Connor, he is loyal to the Pope in this, as in all such matters. And, as O'Connor says accurately, so long as this Pope is alive, no woman will be a priest.

The next Pope may be another matter. The Church, like the Earth, does move. But the Church, O'Connor included, underestimates the strength and determination of Catholic feminism. Just as it evades the consequences of the steady decline in the number of priests. A letter in the November 30, 1986, *National Catholic Reporter* from Sharon Daniels, Cortland, New York, noted with alarm:

... where is our Church today? It may still be growing, but the needs of laypeople have not been met because of the severe shortage of priests. Small parishes are closing and others are so large that they overwhelm the priests who remain.

How can bishops answer our needs? Perhaps by offering priests the option to marry. After all, we're accepting married clergy from other faiths, why not extend the same privilege to our own hardworking priests? ...

The future of the faith worldwide depends on facing the challenge of a dwindling priesthood. For centuries, other Christian communities have flourished with a married clergy. There is no persuasive reason to continue the Catholic discipline of celibacy, given the gravity of our current problems.

But under this Pope, the discipline of celibacy in the priesthood will remain. Yet, if priests could marry, and if women could become priests, there would be no shortage of vocations, and the future of the faith would be more secure.

Nonetheless, the Church in this regard will go on as before. For some time to come, at least. The Church can be very, very stubborn. Sometimes necessarily so in order to survive. At other times, the stubbornness is more of custom than necessity.

Either way, as theologian Rosemary Radford Reuther has observed, "being a Roman Catholic in the United States has never been easy."

3

AS MY INTEREST in the conflicts and changes in the American Catholic Church grew over the years, I discovered a strain of American history that had been unknown to those of us discovering America in the public schools of Boston. There, and in many other places, American history is taught primarily as if it essentially started in New England and Virginia.

Yet, long before the Puritans and other seekers from England, there were Spanish Catholics—both conquistadors and missionaries—ranging through Florida, New Mexico, Arizona, Colorado, and even as far north as what is now called Kansas.

The Spanish explorers and military men on the American frontier were of the view that the native Americans, somewhat like Jews, had no souls and therefore no rights. A few priests thought otherwise, and in the sixteenth century, one of them, Bartolomé de Las Casas, became the first human rights advocate in the New Land. Well, sort of.

As Martin E. Marty explains in his *An Invitation to*

American Catholic History (Chicago: Thomas More Press, 1986): "[Las Casas] supported the idea of importing blacks to replace the Indian serfs. . . . The priest soon repented of his proposal, but it was fateful and unfortunate, to say the least, for Africans. This is not to say that black slaves were in America because of Las Casas. It is to say that some defenders of Negro slavery salved their consciences or pointed to others' inconsistencies by citing Las Casas."

Not for the first time a priest had found that good intentions needed thinking through.

Meanwhile, as more Catholics came to the New World— some to save souls, others trying to keep their own intact— native anti-Catholicism began to flourish. Even though many of those natives had themselves not been in the country all that much longer than the dreaded Catholics.

Said Mark Twain in *Innocents Abroad*: "I have been educated to enmity toward everything that is Catholic." That education in enmity went back to colonial days. In New York, a law was passed in 1700 that gave all Catholic priests until November 1 to get out of town. Anyone defying that deadline would be "deemed and accounted an incendiary and disturber of the public peace and safety and an enemy to the true Christian religion."

The sentence for those who defied this law: life imprisonment. If the priest escaped and was recaptured, he would be dispatched forthwith to the arms of Satan. After all, in a Thanksgiving Day sermon in Boston, the Pope was described as "the Grand Vicar of Satan." (An earlier version of the Fugitive Priest Law had been enacted in Massachusetts in 1647.)

During much of the eighteenth century, Monsignor Florence D. Cohalan notes in his *Popular History of the Archdiocese of New York* (U.S. Catholic Historical Society, 1983), Catholics there could stay, but were by law "forbidden to vote, hold office, bear arms or serve on juries."

In Boston, meanwhile, Sam Adams, the radical revolutionary, was working hard toward the day of American emancipation. He ignited the Stamp Tax riots and formed the Boston Committee of Correspondence, which was to help shape the Declaration of Independence. And Sam Adams was to be one of the signers of that Declaration.

But there was more than independence from George III on Sam Adams's mind. He brooded about a monarch he considered even more evil, for this monarch had designs of dominion over the whole world. In the *Boston Gazette* (April 7, 1768), the firebrand of the American Revolution warned the freedom fighters that "much more is to be dreaded from the growth of Popery in America than from the Stamp Act."

Indeed, there was such brooding about Rome in the colonies, Martin Marty notes, "that the mere report of a woman wearing a cross was enough to inspire suspicion of a papist takeover in a town."

Into and throughout the nineteenth century, Catholic immigrants continued to be welcomed into the American family as if they carried rather loathsome contagious diseases. In 1840, a classified advertisement—one of many such—appeared in the *New York Evening Post*: "Wanted: a cook or chambermaid. She must be American, Scotch, Swiss or African—no Irish."

In Boston, all through the nineteenth century and into the beginnings of this one as well, the Yankees were more direct in their help-wanted ads: "Only Protestants need apply."

Catholics I went to school with at Boston Latin told me of signs their parents and grandparents had seen at lodging houses: "No dogs or Irish."

This bigotry was bred all through American society. George Bancroft, the most renowned nineteenth-century historian of the republic, said of the Catholic priesthood that "no band of conspirators was ever more closely welded together."

And just as Jews were to be bedeviled by the malignly invented Protocols of the Elders of Zion, so American Catholics were branded with a fake "Jesuit Oath," said to have originated in the seventeenth century. Urgent news of it was circulated widely in rural America, and a partial text was included in James Hennesey's *American Catholics* (New York: Oxford University Press, 1981): "I will, when opportunity presents, make and wage relentless war, secretly and openly, against all heretics, Protestants and Masons, as I am directed to do, to extirpate them from the face of the whole earth; and that I will spare neither age, sex, or condition, and that I will hang, burn, waste, boil, flay, strangle and bury alive these infamous heretics; rip up the stomachs and wombs of their women, and crush their infants' heads against the walls in order to annihilate their execrable race . . ."

There might be times when it was not prudent for those bound by the Jesuit Oath to rip up stomachs and bash infants' heads against the walls. Under these circumstances, it was said, the Knights of Columbus—entrusted with the carrying out of the oath—had to promise to "secretly use the poison cup, the strangulation cord, the steel of the poniard, or the leaden bullet." The choice by which murder was to be done in each case was to depend on the orders received from the Pope or the superior general of the Jesuits.

This quite vivid example of group defamation was being circulated as late as the second decade of this century. There are likely to have been Catholics in these years who were reminded by the Jesuit Oath of what Abraham Lincoln said in 1855 about the aggressive Know Nothing Party, which was dedicated to casting Catholics from the body politic. Said Lincoln: "As a nation, we began by declaring that all men are created equal. We now practically read it: 'All men are created equal except Negroes.' When the Know-Nothings obtain control, it will read: 'All men are created equal except Negroes, foreigners and Catholics.'"

By the 1920s, Catholics were of great interest to the five-million-strong Ku Klux Klan, which showed such abundant hatred of Catholics, let alone blacks, in the South, the Middle Atlantic states, and the Midwest that some families remain infected to this very day.

A sense of the deep looniness that accompanied nightmares about Catholics at the time is provided by James Hennesey, professor of the history of Christianity at Boston College, who notes that during the 1920s, "Alabama passed a convent inspection bill [and] Governor Sidney J. Catts of Florida announced that the Pope was planning to invade Florida and transfer the Vatican there" (*American Catholics,* p. 25).

In 1928, the American tradition of seeing Catholics as sinister international conspirators continued with the defeat of Al Smith in the presidential election. "For his co-religionists," Hennesey writes in *American Catholics*, his loss was "one more reminder, and on the highest level of political sensibility, that they and their church were an object of mistrust and suspicion to an uncomfortably large number of their fellow citizens."

The days were long gone when Catholic schools, churches, and seminaries had been burned down by "nativist" mobs—as happened in Boston and Philadelphia in the 1830s and 1840s. And hardly anyone remembered the Order of the Star-Spangled Banner that, more than a century ago, was devoted to keeping Catholics out of public office. Catholics did not expect their churches to be torched in 1928, but they knew that outside these churches a good many Americans still believed that Catholics and their children did not have quite the right stuff for America.

4

IT IS a story Tip O'Neill likes to tell. President John Fitzgerald Kennedy—who had finally proved that a Catholic could lead the nation—had been asked to speak before the Catholic Youth Organization. And would he also fit some time into his tight schedule to speak to two other gatherings that day: members of the hierarchy and a gathering of priests and nuns?

The President declined to address members of the hierarchy. Tip O'Neill recalls JFK saying: "We've checked out the bishops and the cardinals, and most of them were with Nixon. But the priests and the nuns, those who work in the vineyard, they were with me all the way. Their votes, their prayers, everything else. Let me see the nuns and the priests."

Chuckling, Tip would conclude: "And the President left the archbishops high and dry."

The story illustrates a common perception, among both Catholics and non-Catholics, that for many years the hierarchy was almost invariably on the side of the establishment—political, economic, or military. Actually, however, America's Catholic bishops have been somewhat more varied in their priorities—even before the social activism of the past twenty years.

Consider James Cardinal Gibbons of Baltimore, who, in 1886, publicly supported transit workers who were striking against a seventeen-hour working day. (He was criticized by the *New York Times* for meddling in non-Church affairs.) The next year, Gibbons, in Rome to receive his red hat, spoke of the "heartless avarice" of capitalism while successfully defending the Knights of Labor against a possible Papal condemnation. (The Knights of Labor, the second national union in this country, organized in 1869, encompassed skilled and unskilled workers, small businessmen, farmers, and housewives. More than half were Catholic. An industrial union, the Knights had reached a membership of 700,000 by the early 1880s.)

Over time, Catholic prelates and priests became deeply involved in other struggles of the unorganized and disenfranchised. For instance, a more recent Church leader in Baltimore, Laurence Cardinal Shehan was, in 1962, far ahead of President John Kennedy on civil rights—ordering the desegregation of all the Catholic schools in the archdiocese. He marched with blacks to Washington, fought insistently for open housing, and afterward went on to say about the Vietnam War that it was "a scandal the Christian conscience can no longer endure."

On the other hand, it is also true that many bishops, archbishops, and cardinals, until recently, spent their lives as if they were continually posing for a sketch by George Grosz.

A notable illustration of that cast of mind and tilt of miter was Francis Cardinal Spellman of New York. In the late 1940s, in a quite remarkable act of courage, fueled by desperation, the grave diggers who worked for the New York archdiocese went on strike. These members of United Cemetery Workers, Local 293, had been earning $59 for a six-day, forty-eight-hour week. When the negotiator for the archdiocese gave the grave diggers a final offer of $1 more a week and no reduction in hours, the workers stopped digging graves and set up a picket line.

Two months into the strike, Cardinal Spellman ordered a large contingent of seminarians from St. Joseph's Seminary at Dunwoodie in Yonkers to go to Calvary Cemetery in Queens and start digging graves. The Cardinal, once having been handed a spade, was himself the first to dig.

Paul O'Dwyer, whose brother, William, was mayor of New York City at the time, remembers that day well. "It was in winter, and the frost was down about three and a half feet in the ground. The *Daily News* had a picture of the Cardinal, who was a little man, with his little foot up on the spade. And Bill said to Mike Quill, the head of the Transport Workers' Union, who was in the Mayor's office that day, 'What do you think of that picture, Mike?' Mike looked at the picture, the hard ground and the small Cardinal, and he said to the Mayor, 'The poor bastard is not going to go down very far.' "

Cardinal Spellman eventually gave the grave diggers a modest raise, but he succeeded in greatly weakening the union, whose members were Catholic. As John Cooney notes in *The American Pope* (New York: Times Books, 1984), a biography of Cardinal Spellman, they opened each of their meetings with the beginning of the Workers Prayer of the Association of Catholic Trade Unionists: "Lord Jesus, Carpenter of Nazareth, you were a worker as I am."

With regard to Cardinal Spellman's use of the seminarians to greatly weaken the strike, some of the grave diggers whose places were taken by the scabs were the fathers of those strikebreakers. "You see," Paul O'Dwyer says, "the Cardinal made it a test of discipline."

Cardinal Spellman was an admirer of Senator Joseph McCarthy, as were a number of other Catholic bishops of the time. In April 1954, McCarthy spoke at the annual communion breakfast of the Police Holy Name Society in New York. By his presence and his remarks, Spellman made clear his staunch support of the Senator.

Yet—as an index that generalizations about Catholic prelates were misleading even in those intimidating years—five days after Spellman endorsed McCarthy, Bishop Bernard Sheil of Chicago verbally assaulted the Senator from Wisconsin at a convention of the UAW-CIO. ("A monstrous perversion of morality . . . and calculated deceit.") I had heard of Bishop Sheil from Frances Sweeney, the dauntless Catholic editor in Boston who had educated me about the diversity of Catholics. Sheil was a particular source of long-distance strength to her. They agreed on who the enemies of decency actually were.

Sheil, a founder of the Catholic Youth Organization in 1930, was a man of passionate determination that justice be done. For the workers. For the poor. For anyone being exploited and diminished by the cold and the mighty. Paul O'Dwyer, another Catholic with the same lifelong priorities, remembers Sheil coming to a big meeting of a prominent patriotic organization. The meeting was segregated. So Bishop Sheil sat with the blacks.

One of Bishop Sheil's admirers was a young priest in Philadelphia, Father John J. O'Connor, who in time became a cardinal.

But again, there were indeed plenty of the bishops and cardinals who, as John F. Kennedy said, were with the Nixons of this land. George Meany used to tell of how one of them, with unwitting help from Communists, defeated a bill that tried to exalt the welfare of children over the sanctity of private property.

In 1937, Meany, as head of the New York State Federation of Labor, was trying to get the state legislature to ratify the Child Labor Amendment to the New York State Constitution. Meany recalled: "The Catholic bishop of Albany came in his ecclesiastical robes and he was bitterly opposed to the Amendment. And so he testified at the hearing. We lost it right at that hearing because the galleries were full of the Commies and the [other] radical groups and they just booed and booed and booed [the bishop]—which was exactly what the opponents of the Amendment wanted." The radicals wanted the child labor amendment but could not restrain their hatred of Popery.

In social matters, except for a minority of the bishops and cardinals—such as Sheil and Shehan—the impression given by many in the hierarchy was that they were much more comfortable with society's decision makers than with those affected by their decisions. And in their own ecclesiastical corporations, they autocratically made all the decisions worth making, including the ones concerning the small wages and long hours of their employees.

These were the princes of the Church who had become so mighty that they never looked down. Among their stiff-necked number were: John Cardinal Cody of Chicago, Patrick Cardinal O'Boyle of Washington, Francis Cardinal McIntyre of Los Angeles, William Cardinal O'Connell of Boston, and Francis Cardinal Spellman of New York. To them, any approach to substantive change in the society was greatly suspect.

But there came a change in the Church, both the American Church and the Catholic Church as a whole. One way to gauge it is to look at the changing place of a small, independent Catholic magazine, *Commonweal*. When there was a darkness over the land and its name was Joseph McCarthy, the *Brooklyn Tablet*, the official paper of that diocese, proclaimed: "The editors of *Commonweal* are not fit to be called Catholics." Among the more egregious sins of the magazine was its total lack of respect for Senator McCarthy—unlike the great majority of the official Catholic press.

This public lashing of *Commonweal* so pleased the editors of the *Catholic News*, as the New York diocesan paper was called then, that they reprinted the denunciation on their front page in a box. It may be they saw the box as a coffin both for the magazine and for those who, in those days, were contemptuously called *"Commonweal* Catholics."

Commonweal is no longer that isolated. There is always the possibility of another Joe McCarthy, but if one were to arise, *Commonweal* would no longer be among a very small minority of Catholic journals to smite him. And, moreover, the magazine would be joined by many of the laity, priests, bishops, and even some cardinals.

What, then, has happened to bring *Commonweal* more into the mainstream—though hardly right in the middle— of Catholic thinking on many other matters besides McCarthyism? Why are there more *Commonweal* Catholics in the hierarchy as well as among the laity?

James O'Gara, managing editor and then editor of the magazine for thirty-two years, wrote on his retirement in 1984: "There is no doubt that the climate of opinion in the Church has changed drastically since the 1962–65 Vatican Council. That Council brought many things to pass that *Commonweal* has been arguing for since 1924, from the Mass in English to greater lay participation, and an enlarged conception of the church as a church of service rather than a church of privilege."

That Vatican Council (Vatican II) had come about because the need for change in the Church had been restlessly manifest in Europe, America, and elsewhere. One particularly vivid signpost had been the worker-priest movement in France that the Vatican eventually quashed in the 1950s. As Eugene Kennedy—a former priest who is now a professor of psychology at Loyola University in Chicago—says in *The Now and Future Church* (Garden City, N.Y.: Doubleday, 1984): "The monarchical framework of the Church could no longer house the energies building throughout the Catholic world. Vatican II expressed and released but did not cause them."

One of the products of Vatican II—an indication that the Church was becoming less solipsistic—was *Nostra Aetate.* This document told Catholics that the Church disapproved and indeed repudiated anti-Semitism. Furthermore, at long last, Jews, the dead as well as the living, were officially cleared of guilt in the killing of Jesus Christ.

Of all that happened at Vatican II, one of the most fundamental changes was in the perception of how authority ought to be exercised in the Church. In *A Concise History of the Catholic Church* (Garden City, N.Y.: Doubleday, 1977), Thomas Bokenkotter notes:

Until the arrival of Pope John and the Second Vatican Council, the typical Catholic took the authoritarian structure of the Church as a dictate of divine revelation. They thought of the Pope as a kind of superhuman potentate whose every word was a command invested with supernatural authority; even the bishop they regarded with awe. In this state of affairs, few Catholics questioned the autocratic procedures customary in the Church, though to outsiders they often appeared medieval. The bishop, for instance, was seldom challenged in his claim to rule his diocese as a personal fief, and the same held good for the pastor in running his parish. . . .

In the light of the new understanding of the Church projected by the Council, however, many Catholics found these authoritarian structures intolerable . . . and began to agitate for democratic reforms.

There has, however, been considerable resistance to
Vatican II. The critics, including some prelates, do not say
they object to the essence of Vatican II—the opening of the
Church to the world. That principle is too firmly grounded
in current Catholic thinking to be directly questioned. The
objectors claim instead that much of the "new direction of
the Church" is actually a distortion of Vatican II. The present Pope so feels, and therefore is pulling in the reins—
particularly in America, where some priests and bishops,
the Pope believes, have become so democratically minded
that they are insufficiently obedient to the teaching authority of the Holy See. The charge is that they have misinterpreted Vatican II's openness to change as an invitation to
dissent. The Pope's supporters remind one and all that the
Church is not a democracy.

When dealing with what he considers to be a slackness
of discipline, and therefore of faith, the Pope can take puni-
tive measures against priests, bishops, and cardinals. But it
is impossible for him to whip all the laity into line. He can't
very well excommunicate civilian dissenters en masse. And
year by year, the laity is indeed becoming selective in its
adherence to the teachings of the Church.

The Church in America is no longer the "pray, pay, and
obey" Immigrant Church for the Irish, Italians, and other
Catholics of European descent. (It is still, of course, the
Immigrant Church for many of the growing numbers of
Spanish-speaking Catholics, but a good many of them do
not regard Catholicism as necessarily requiring regular ties
to the institutional Church.)

For those Catholics whose parents, grandparents, and
great-grandparents regarded the Church as their fortress
against an alien and hostile society, such protection is no
longer necessary. They have made their way into that society, exercising influence and power in many fields.
Nor—although anti-Catholicism has hardly been eradi-
cated (especially among liberals)—do Catholics any longer
fear whatever bigotry is directed against them. And with

regard to the Church, they decide for themselves what to believe.

As Eugene Kennedy emphasizes in *The Now and Future Church*, "a more independent, deeper intellectual class" of American Catholics has emerged, and its members are "no longer ready to accept what Church leaders [teach] without examining it thoughtfully. . . . There [has been] a sharp diminution of guilt over disagreeing with certain positions, such as the teaching on birth control, and a progressive blurring of the differences between Catholics and other groups on a wide range of moral and political issues."

It is particularly on questions of sexual morality that the Holy See—no matter how many priests and bishops it punishes for wrongful thought—is powerless to compel all or sometimes most of the 54 million American Catholics to stay within all Church teachings. *New York Times* reporter Elaine Sciolino noted on November 4, 1984 (and later surveys have shown similar patterns): "An estimated one-quarter of the 1.5 million American women who have an abortion in a given year are Catholic. More than 90 percent of sexually active Catholic women have used methods of contraception that have not been approved by the Church, according to a 1982 study by the National Center for Health Statistics. There are an estimated 8 million divorced Catholics, and the vast majority of those who have remarried have done so outside the Church.

Moreover, she writes that "surveys by the National Opinion Research Center (affiliated with the University of Chicago) between 1982 and 1984 indicate that 72 percent of Catholic women would consider abortion under certain circumstances; nearly half of American Catholics do not consider premarital sex wrong at all; 32 percent say that sexual activity between members of the same sex is not categorically wrong, and only 10 percent believe abortion should be illegal under all circumstances."

Also illuminating is a finding of a 1986 study by Dean Hoge, a sociologist at the Catholic University of America: 47 percent of the American Catholics surveyed supported the

ordination of women as priests. These respondents consisted, in large part, of younger and better-educated Catholics. And more men than women supported the idea of
women as priests.

These surveys and the more recent ones may give a somewhat misleading sense of the fissures within the American
Catholic Church. They surely exist, and are growing, but
there has yet to be a volcanic division. And the binding
reason for going to Church remains the same for all sides.

In any case, the Church is indeed changing, and many in
it—who would not agree among themselves as to where the
changes should lead—do feel, in the words of Archbishop
Rembert Weakland of Milwaukee: "We are living at a time
in which we must re-imagine the Catholic Church."

To what extent, however, is re-imagination possible? To
try to find out, I decided to explore the life and ideas of a
prelate who exemplifies both the "left" and the "right" of
the American Church. On the one hand, he is an intense
believer in expanding the active social mission of the
Church. And on the other hand, on matters of doctrine, he
is a fiercely loyal subject of Rome.

John Cardinal O'Connor has vigorously disagreed with
Ronald Reagan and the Pentagon on issues of both war and
the needs of the poor, but he utterly refuses to concede any
fault, any mistake, on the part of John Paul II. Including the
Pope's chastisement of certain American bishops, priests,
and nuns.

Cardinal O'Connor has blasted those responsible for
housing in New York City, charging them with warehous-
ing low-income people in places that are "not fit for pigs."
But, in a decidedly unliberal move, he upheld an edict by
his Vicar General that appears to bar from all parishes in
the archdiocese any speaker who differs from the official
teachings of the Catholic Church.

Which of the Cardinal's many dimensions, most of them
considerably more complex than the press has indicated,
will help determine the future of the Catholic Church in
America? O'Connor is the most visible and, to say the least,

the most controversial prince of this Church in this republic. Is he its future, its past, or a potentially explosive fusion of both?

⚔

5

WAITING one August afternoon in 1984 for John J. O'Connor, the then Archbishop of New York, in a small room near his office at the Catholic Center, the headquarters of the archdiocese, on First Avenue and Fifty-fifth Street, I heard his voice in the corridor. Usually, he speaks softly and reflectively, but on this occasion his voice was loud and unyielding. "Over my dead body," he was saying to an assistant, "will any person be fired because he or she belongs to a union and is exercising the right of collective bargaining." The Archbishop—who in April of the next year was named a cardinal by Pope John Paul II, the sixth Archbishop of New York to be so named—was angry that afternoon over management tactics during a strike against thirty-one New York City hospitals and nursing homes by District 1199, a union representing health-care workers. The League of Voluntary Hospitals and Homes, bargaining for the hospitals, had told its members to threaten the strikers with being permanently replaced if they did not come back to work. O'Connor, furious at the directive, ordered four archdiocesan hospitals affiliated with the league to have nothing to do with what he called a "union-busting" maneuver. And in the corridor he was making sure his instructions were clear.

The Archbishop was still frowning when he came into

the room where I was waiting, but he quickly broke into a smile. He smiles easily, and has an easy air of authority, having served in the Navy for twenty-seven years, eventually becoming Chief of Chaplains and achieving the rank of rear admiral. Sturdy, with large ears and a generous nose, he wears glasses, and on the lapel of his black clerical suit there is always the emblem of the pro-life movement—a rosette, whose stem spells out the word *life*.

"My father was a union man," the Archbishop said, sitting down in a chair next to mine, "so the right to belong to a union is in every fiber of my being. I would not be here in this job now if it hadn't been for the influence of my father. He had a very, very strong sense of justice. And a very, very strong sense of the dignity of the individual person."

From a chain around the Archbishop's neck hung a pectoral cross that had been given to him by his predecessor, Terence Cardinal Cooke, who had also been actively opposed to abortion, but more quietly than O'Connor. Five months before our conversation that afternoon, O'Connor's way of speaking about abortion had propelled him into a fierce controversy in New York.

When he was about to leave his post as Bishop of Scranton—in which he had served only eight months—O'Connor had appeared on a New York Sunday-noon television program, "News 4 orum." A number of subjects were touched on during the interview: the homeless; the diminishing number of vocations for the priesthood; the assertion by White House Counselor Edwin Meese that some who go to soup kitchens are not in real need (denied by O'Connor); and his father ("If in his judgment, which wasn't always charitable, [a] multimillionaire had made his or her money on the backs of the poor or [by] exploiting the coal miners or the railroad workers, or whatever, then he didn't care what museums [he] founded"). One section of the interview proved inflammatory, however. After saying that neither he nor the Church condemns any woman who has an abortion "out of confusion and desperation," O'Connor compared "the killing of four thousand babies a day in the United

States, unborn babies," to the Holocaust. He told of standing in Dachau: "I . . . put my hand in the semicircular red brick ovens and felt on the floor of the oven the intermingled ashes of Jew and Christian, rabbi, minister, priest, lay person. . . . And I thought, Good Lord, human beings actually did this to human beings." It was the next sentence that brought upon the incoming Archbishop the anger of many of the city's residents: "Now, Hitler tried to solve a problem, the Jewish question. So kill them, shove them into ovens, burn them. Well, we claim that unborn babies are a problem, so kill them. To me, it is really precisely the same."

O'Connor also said during the television interview, with a dark humor in which he often indulges, "I suspect I'll be going into New York as Our Lord went into Jerusalem on Palm Sunday, and there were a lot of hosannas and cheers and warm welcomes. But I try to remember what happened a few days later, you know." On March 13, two days after the program, the *Times*, in an editorial, "Hitler and Abortion," told the Bishop he might not be ready for New York. O'Connor's linking of abortion to the Holocaust had "highly offensive implications," the *Times* said. One of them was that "Hitler had a problem called the 'Jewish question,' and that only his remedy was evil." Another offensive implication was that women who make the "usually painful choice of an abortion" are "practicing Nazi genocide, the organized, calculating and malevolent mass murder of millions." The editorial ended by recommending that Bishop O'Connor adopt "a change of tone" if "he means to instruct the community at large."

For weeks before the television interview, a sense of cheerful anticipation had been building in New York at the coming of—according to all reports from Scranton—an unpretentious, gregarious, hardworking, witty bishop whose ministry was marked by a special ability to see and to listen to people as individuals. The essence of the Scrantonians' assessment of the Bishop appeared as part of an extensive analysis of O'Connor the following year in the *National Catholic Reporter*, a publication that is considerably less orthodox than O'Connor in Church matters and has at times been sharply critical of him: "Even a year after O'Connor's departure, to talk to Scrantonians is to sense [that] he gave many of them something he personally did not know he was handing out: dignity. He did it when he rejoiced with them in the opening of their latest pride and joy, their new Hilton. He would go from visiting a sick priest to a Labor Day festival without breaking his stride. He'd push into crowds of students at Scranton University, straight from the podium, wearing a 'Scranton U' hat, to talk with them about their futures. Scranton found his vitality infectious. . . . And Scrantonians repaid him in kind. When the word came through he was to leave . . . they named the 300 block on their main street after him: Archbishop John J. O'Connor Plaza."

When he did leave, there was a farewell Mass in the University of Scranton gymnasium. Thousands of people attended, by no means all of them Catholic. As one observer said, they spoke of him not with platitudes but with examples: how he had helped the handicapped; how, for the first time in the diocese, the teachers' union in the parochial schools had someone in management who was prolabor and set in motion a substantial upgrading of their salaries. The mayor of Scranton, James B. McNulty, said of the departing Bishop, "We're the out-of-towners who really enjoyed the previews. Now a hit show moves on to Broadway."

John J. O'Connor's New York opening, however, was marred by the connection he had made between the Holocaust and abortion. The Bishop of Scranton, not yet installed in New York, had felt deeply hurt by the *Times* editorial. The day it appeared, Ari Goldman, a reporter for the *Times*, called him in Scranton. Goldman felt that since the editorial had been so harsh, it would be fair to ask O'Connor for his reaction. The Bishop said he was outraged that the editorial indicated he had implied that Jews *were* a problem in Germany and that only Hitler's "remedy" had been evil. O'Connor pointed out that the editorial had not mentioned what he said on the television program about the impact on him of his visit to Dachau. He did not retreat from his linkage of abortion to the Holocaust. "The abortion mentality that has swept the country, that has simply declared the unborn to be nonhuman—this is what I compare to the Holocaust," he told Goldman. It does not differ in essence, he added, "from that mentality that legalized putting Jews to death in Nazi Germany."

The day after O'Connor's interview with Goldman appeared, the *Times* said in a brief editorial, "Of Analogy and Abortion," that the Bishop's remarks from Scranton were less inflammatory than what he had said on television in New York, and the newspaper expressed the hope that each side in the debate over abortion would "respect the humanity and piety of the other. It is in that spirit that we welcome Bishop O'Connor to New York, a gloriously contentious, tolerant, and democratic community."

The new Archbishop had never experienced a welcome quite like this one. "I'm still surprised at the furor my analogy created," he told me that summer. "I had used it in a synagogue in Scranton and received a standing ovation. Afterward, old Jewish people, with tears streaming down their faces, told me they had been in the Holocaust, and agreed with me that if we appear to be callous to life in one context we're going to be callous to it in another." (Years later, O'Connor told me that it was his visit to Dachau that generated his intense antiabortion feelings.)

O'Connor went on with a smile, "As for the New York *Times*, I had lunch there with the editors not long after their welcoming editorials. Everything under the sun was discussed—but not abortion. I'm still somewhat outraged by the first editorial but a little bit amused by the second. The impression I got from the second one was that I could now come to town, because the New York *Times* says it's all right."

The Archbishop grinned. "Actually, I thought, Goodness, if every time the New York *Times* doesn't agree with me I take the *Times* to be the voice of New York and want to turn tail and run, I'll never be able to contribute anything to this job and to this city. So"—he smiled again—"I decided to open in New York anyway. And the *Times* was very gracious in its coverage of the installation."

6

ON MARCH 19, 1984, John J. O'Connor was installed as the eighth Archbishop of New York, his archdiocese encompassing the boroughs of Manhattan, the Bronx, and Staten Island, and, to the north, the counties of Westchester, Rockland, Putnam, Orange, Sullivan, Ulster, and Dutchess. With 1.8 million Catholics, it is the fourth-largest archdiocese in the United States (after Los Angeles, Chicago, and Boston), and it includes 411 parishes, 265 parochial elementary schools, 62 archdiocesan and parochial high schools (with a total student body of slightly over 120,000), and 13 colleges and universities. There are more than 200 affiliated social-service agencies and programs in the archdiocese, and, excluding such facilities as hospitals and nursing homes, it has more than $800 million worth of real estate that is tax exempt. Living in the archdiocese are about 2,500 priests and about 5,000 nuns.

Present in St. Patrick's Cathedral on the day John J. O'Connor became Archbishop were five cardinals, eighteen archbishops, more than a hundred bishops, over a thousand priests, an abundance of political dignitaries, and choirs of voices and of brass. Archbishop Pio Laghi, the Apostolic Pro-Nuncio—that is, the Pope's personal representative to the United States—read a letter from the Pope on the occasion of O'Connor's assuming his new position in the hierarchy. "You do not work and toil alone," the letter said. "You are supported by the successor of Peter, the Bishop of Rome. . . . This is the day of new beginning." Archbishop Laghi then gave O'Connor a crosier—a staff in the form of a shepherd's crook—to symbolize the Archbishop's charge to be caretaker of his flock.

From the graceful stone pulpit in the cathedral, the Archbishop, who had looked somber while the papal representative spoke, began his response on a joyful, mischievous note. He showed the audience a New York Mets cap that had been presented to him as a sign of his belonging in the city, and he brought to the pulpit ten-year-old John J. O'Connor, an altar boy from the Bronx, who had written him a warm letter of welcome, saying, "I want to be just like you when I grow up." The senior O'Connor gently placed his miter on the boy's head and over his ears, and the youngster beamed.

The Archbishop read a few letters from other New York elementary school children, one of which said, "Bishop O'Connor. That name I was surprised to hear. Until now I did not know who you were. I'm very curious about your life because I've never heard of you before." O'Connor laughed. "Try that on your ego!" he told the crowd.

Later, he grew serious, recalling that he was being installed on the feast day of his patron saint—Joseph, the husband of Mary. (Joseph is O'Connor's middle name.) "I see him as a personal model, because he was a man so often confused and perplexed," the Archbishop said. "He was engaged to a woman who became pregnant without his involvement, and was expected to believe that this was an act of God. He was foster father to a boy who could wander away from home, cause agonizing grief to both parents, then chide them for looking for him. How often Joseph seems simply not to know what to do except to trust in God." The Archbishop also mentioned his happiness that "the New York *Times* has welcomed me to New York," and his ceaseless astonishment at the city of New York itself, where there is "life at its calmest, life at its most turbulent, life in all its exciting splendor."

In the weeks and months that followed, O'Connor's first priority was to learn as much as he could, as quickly as he could, about the archdiocese. But as he began the day, his initial prayer was always the same—and it still is. "I ask God to keep me from preventing anybody from doing any good," he told me. "I make that prayer because somebody might be about to do something good, but because of my arrogance, my vanity, my stupidity, or my misunderstanding, I might in some way prevent it. In my position, you can indeed impede an awful lot of good, and that possibility terrifies me." O'Connor spent much of his first ten months as Archbishop of New York on the road—traveling throughout the archdiocese. He visited 100 of the 411 parishes, moving by car, helicopter, and ferryboat. In April, he went to the detention center on Rikers Island and celebrated Mass behind barred doors for 150 inmates. "You are not junk," he told them. "You are not pieces of something to throw away. You are sacred images of God." In the city, he celebrated Mass at St. Patrick's Cathedral weekday mornings at eight; heard confessions on Saturdays; held staff meetings; met with committees; counseled members of his flock with personal and family problems; visited the sick; walked the streets of Harlem, the Lower East Side, and the Bronx to look into housing conditions; and performed marriages.

One day, during a meeting of the Priests' Council of the archdiocese, mixed marriages were being discussed. The question of whether a Jewish-Catholic couple ought to be permitted, if they chose, to seek a dispensation from the rule that the wedding be held in a Catholic setting, since some couples might prefer neutral terrain—a country club or a catering hall. The Archbishop, known for his orthodoxy in Church matters, entered the discussion. He said he did not see why, if the parish priest felt that the alternative site was appropriate, a dispensation should not be sought from the archdiocesan chancery. O'Connor added, according to the archdiocesan weekly, *Catholic New York*, "What I cringed about as a young priest" was the required setting for mixed marriages. He had witnessed weddings "in a beat-up, seedy rectory," he recalled, "and I had a pastor who wanted it to be as seedy as possible," and he added, "You couldn't even put on a surplice." The heavy air of disapproval, he said, made the rites "practically revolting."

The Archbishop became a regular columnist for *Catholic New York* after coming to New York, and one week he revealed to the paper's readers, numbering a 130,000, that in another matter as well his devotion to tradition was not absolute: "I am not one of those secretly nostalgic for the Mass in Latin. I believe English can be spoken and prayed as reverently as any language on earth." And concerning another change in the practice of worship he wrote, "I love facing God's People at Mass—never did like having my back to them all through those years."

These, he noted, were changes brought about in the 1960s by the Second Vatican Council, which had also emphasized "the horrors of war and exploitation of the poor." The Archbishop made it plain, however, that in certain fundamentals of what he called "the old-time religion" his orthodoxy remains unswerving: "Nowhere does the [Second Vatican] council tell us . . . that as long as we resist war, help the poor, abhor racism and sexism and all such exploitation and disguises for violence, we don't have to worry about such old-fashioned sins as adultery or fornication or lying or stealing or infidelity or disloyalty or missing Mass on Sundays. And . . . we still teach what we have always taught about heaven and purgatory and hell. I like to spend a goodly portion of Lent meditating hopefully on the first, doing enough penance to try to avoid a lengthy sojourn in the second, and praying quite vociferously for deliverance from the third!"

And the Archbishop still taught, without deviation, that abortion was wrong. He no longer mentioned the Holocaust in that connection, however. "I must confess I have deliberately avoided that analogy," he told me ten months after he became Archbishop. "Obviously, I did not have a feeling for the sensitivities involved. People were offended in good faith. Many people were offended. I do think there were others who used the occasion as a vehicle to attack me because of their passionate conviction that I and the Church are completely wrong about abortion. But since there were those who were genuinely offended, I decided not to use the analogy anymore."

7

FROM THE BEGINNING of his work in New York, O'Connor has made a point of meeting regularly with groups of priests and nuns. In the first two months, for instance, he held what he calls a "talking session" and a "listening session" with each of five large groups of women religious, in different parts of the archdiocese. In the talking sessions, the Archbishop told the women that he planned to enable them to gain more respect by emphasizing to priests that they should treat the sisters as equals and involve them more in the making of decisions. To one of the groups he said, "You are just as much the Church as we are."

In his meetings with the women, he told me, he had to deal with some anger at male dominance in the Church. "There are some women religious who will not be happy until women are ordained priests," he said resignedly, "and they construe everything that this Pope does, or that the bishops do, as an injustice, because they consider the inability of women to become priests the basic injustice. So they think it hypocritical if we talk about the poor or if we talk about racial inequality, even if we talk about the need for peace, because in their minds the Church at its core is perpetuating a fundamental violence of discrimination."

I asked him if there was any possibility that the position of the Church on women as priests might change.

"I feel certain that in our lifetime there will be no change," O'Connor said. "There are theological obstacles, and these, in my judgment, have nothing to do with male chauvinism. The priesthood of Christ is rooted in the history of the Old Testament, going back to the earliest days of priesthood in Israel; and, of course, we believe that Catholicism is, as it were, the fruit of Israel. Women were not allowed to be priests in Israel. Nor are they now in Israel, or among Orthodox Jews anywhere. Christ, for a further example, selected twelve apostles, and the apostles were men."

As the months went by, an increasing number of women in the Church were protesting what they referred to as their inferior status. The Chicago-based National Coalition of American Nuns, which claims a membership of 2,000 of a total of 114,000 Catholic women religious in the United States, pointed out in its January 1986 newsletter that it had first called for the ordination of women in 1970. Sixteen years later, it noted, "Catholic women in unprecedented numbers are enrolled in seminaries and schools of theology." The newsletter continued,

This causes joy and strengthens our courage because women were thus admitted to graduate theology schools less than fifty years ago. . . . Now, close to fifty years later, we see that women have achieved excellence in their theology and Scripture studies in many seminaries. They have attained academic scholarship and have been an example to the men enrolled in the same studies. Upon earning a master's degree, however, the men go on to ordination and the women, barred from Orders because of sex, have to search for modest positions in parishes which oftentimes do not want them and most of the time are unable, they say, to pay even subsistence salary.

We women of the Catholic community do not seek jurisdiction over the male-church power estate. In asking for ordination, we seek only to preach, to administer the sacraments, and to teach the Gospel to the poor. We remind our churchmen that many of the faithful are not hearing the Good News because there are not enough ordained ministers. There are those [without priests], for example, in nursing homes, refugee camps, prisons, hospitals for the physically and mentally ill, public housing developments. . . .

The acute dissatisfaction of the National Coalition of American Nuns is widely shared, I found in reading Catholic publications and talking to Catholic women, lay as well as religious. In a conversation with O'Connor after he became a cardinal, I asked him again about this deepening division in the Church. It was late afternoon, and he was visibly tired. He had a bad cold, but had refused to cancel any of his appointments in a tight schedule that had started early in the morning. With his director of communications, Father (now Monsignor) Peter Finn, and another priest, he sat sipping tea in the small room used for interviews at the Catholic Center.

"It's a very difficult question," the Cardinal replied. "Very difficult. And it keeps coming up. I had three hours with, I think, forty-two women religious this morning, representing ten different communities. And I had a group like that two weeks ago. There'll be two more next week. We talk about many things, but some of the women have this strong feeling about ordination. And some"—he smiled— "have a strong feeling that I should go back to Scranton."

I said that some of the resentment on the part of women I had met arose not only in connection with ordination but also from such lesser but wounding forms of exclusion as the refusal of bishops to allow girls to serve at the altar at Mass, Vespers, and other forms of worship. Even Joseph Cardinal Bernardin of Chicago, considered one of the more liberal members of the American hierarchy, had said that the tradition of forbidding girls to serve at Mass in his archdiocese would be observed.

"I don't see that as by any means a crucial problem," the Cardinal said with some irritation.

"There are women who see the banning of an altar girl as a symbol," I said.

"I recognize that," the Cardinal replied. "Currently, the discipline of the Church is that you can't have girls at the altar—*acolytes* is the correct term—and so long as that is the discipline, I won't do it here. But I would be willing to have altar girls as soon as the discipline is changed, and my suspicion is that it will be. But if that happens we ought not to exaggerate its meaning. If it's looked at as a step toward ordination, then we're just fooling ourselves."

The Cardinal started to cough, and Father Finn suggested that he might want to rest, since he was to deliver a lecture on Thomas Merton that evening at Columbia University.

The Cardinal waved the idea away, and turned back to me. "This gets complex," he said. He paused, looked past me, fingered the cross he was wearing, sipped some more tea, and sighed. "Could Christ have appeared on earth as a woman? Indeed, I have heard the argument that Christ will return as a woman. Could He have come as a woman? I don't know why He couldn't have. We do speak of God the Father and God the Son and God the Holy Spirit. God is all three and yet each is distinct. Yet, as we say this, we know that it is a very profound mystery, which we don't begin to understand." He was silent again. "It is conceivable," he resumed, "that the relationship could be between Mother, Daughter, and a feminine Holy Spirit, if you will, as a trinity. It is conceivable. But what we do say is that the Holy Spirit is the personified love between the Father and the Son. Each is equal to the other. The Father does not precede the Son, nor does the Son precede the Holy Spirit. They are distinct but not separate. The Son comes from the Father, and the Holy Spirit proceeds from both. Beyond this point, we do not *understand* the Trinity. We take it on faith."

"But you do raise the possibility that Christ could have come not as the Son but as the Daughter," I said.

"Christ always referred to his *Father* in heaven. And Christ always spoke of Himself as the Son. Why would He have done that if there was any possibility that He could have been a woman and that God could have been either His Father or His Mother? This is where you run into a theological problem. You can't just wave a magic wand and say it wasn't so."

Yet since the Church does change, I said, was it entirely inconceivable that a future Pope might decide that the barring of women from the priesthood, having been based less on theological than on historical grounds, would no longer be Church doctrine?

There was a long pause. Father Finn and the other priest in the room leaned forward. "How can I answer that and be quite honest?" the Cardinal said hoarsely. "This Pope will never change that decision. But a future Pope *could* announce that he is going to do something totally unexpected. But would such a thing, depending on what it is, be accepted by the Church? Might he even be deposed?" The Cardinal looked at me. "The Pope is bound in certain areas by divinely revealed teachings; that is, doctrines concerning faith and morals which have been defined by Popes in the past with the divine assistance of the Holy Spirit. Such teachings cannot be changed, because they are always true. They are infallible teachings. No successor Pope can do anything about them. For example, a Pope cannot say there are four persons in the Trinity. As for theological tradition, the Pope is pretty well bound by that. But is he bound by that in the same way he is by infallible, divinely revealed teaching? By definition he is not. Could he pronounce differently if he was convinced that his new position was theologically sound? I'd have to say yes."

"Could a Pope pronounce differently even if he didn't think his new position was all that sound?"

The Cardinal rubbed his nose. "I guess he could. A Pope could yield to political pressures. Popes have done so in the past." He looked at his hands, pressed his fingertips together, and said slowly and carefully, "What are we really talking about? I suppose we're talking about this: To my knowledge, it has never been infallibly declared that women cannot be ordained to the priesthood. There has never been a formal, ex-cathedra pronouncement by the Pope that it is infallible teaching that only men can be priests."

"So it is conceivable that sometime in the future women may be ordained?"

The Cardinal nodded, cleared his throat, and said, "Yes, it is conceivable. But, I remind you, not in the lifetime of this Pope."

8

A FEW DAYS LATER, I talked about the pressures for the ordination of women with Eugene Kennedy, who is a professor of psychology at Loyola University, in Chicago, a former priest, and a chronicler of the changing American Catholic Church. Kennedy told me that in the course of interviewing various bishops for the second of these he learned that when some of them had visited the Pope, not long before, the Pope had given them explicit instructions concerning their nominations of auxiliary bishops. "The Pope told them that they were not to submit the name of anyone associated in any way with any movement for the ordination of women," Kennedy said.

Not only women but a number of priests, too, have pointed out that the Pope's intransigence on this matter will worsen an already serious problem in the Church—a decline in vocations for the priesthood. Reverend Edmond P. O'Brien, of Holy Cross Church in Brooklyn, said at a conference called to discuss the problem, toward the end of O'Connor's first year as leader of the New York archdiocese, that the Catholic Church should learn from the Episcopal Church, which had been ordaining women for ten years. "They've got people lined up to be priests," Father O'Brien said.

In May 1986, the *Official Catholic Directory* reported that the number of Catholic priests in America had declined during the previous year by 135. That left 57,183, but the figure included semiretired priests. There have been projections that by the year 2000 there would be only 17,000 active priests in the United States. Commenting a few years ago on similarly bleak findings of other researchers, *America*, a Jesuit weekly, noted, "For many, the obvious solution to the vocation crisis will come only when the patriarchal church revises its restriction of the priesthood to male celibates. This is a position that must be seriously evaluated in the years to come, and it will be."

Cardinal O'Connor is deeply concerned about the problem. In September 1985, he told a meeting of the Priests' Council of the archdiocese, "In 1965 there were forty-nine thousand seminarians in the country. In 1985, there are only eleven thousand. That is a tremendous, drastic, and radical loss."

I asked the Cardinal how this loss had come about, and what he thought should be done to reverse it.

"During the past twenty years or so, it became very unpopular to be a priest or a nun," he said. "The Church was part of the establishment, and, starting in the early nineteen-sixties, any and all parts of the establishment were under fire. Vietnam intensified that attitude. We had the flower children and the yippies, the counter-culture and the so-called greening of America. All of it hostile to the establishment. A great number of Catholic priests and sisters left their ministries in those years. And many who stayed developed a near-passion for advanced degrees in secular disciplines. They became much more happily identified as clinical psychologists, for instance, than as priests or sisters. They didn't feel comfortable, they didn't feel secure, about being just priests or sisters. Simultaneously, many of those who were also teachers in Catholic schools were giving all sorts of signals to the kids, from the grade schools to the colleges. The kids got the message that they could do a lot more good in the world in ways other than becoming priests or sisters."

The Cardinal went on, mordantly, "There was another kind of signal. One day, Sister Mary Jones doesn't show up to teach her regular class in religion. She's run off and married Father Smith, who was teaching algebra in the next classroom. Worsening the situation was a critical strategic blunder that the Catholic Church made twenty years ago. We took all the challenge, all the hardship, all the sense of sacrifice out of becoming a priest or a sister or a brother. When I was a kid, there was an abundance of vocations, and, believe me, it was a hard gospel that was being preached. When you went into the seminary, the faculty let you know, without any ambiguity, where you stood. Their attitude was 'You don't really deserve to be here, and we're going to do our best to prove you don't belong here and to get rid of you. But if you stick it out, then maybe, maybe we'll give some consideration to ordaining you for the priesthood.' The discipline was stern and tough. Not all of it was good, because not all of it was internalized. But enough of it was. And you sure got the idea that if you wanted to be a sister or a brother or a priest, you were literally going to have to lay down your life. Not just in some romantic sense of that term—like during an overseas mission—but in the daily drudgery of being a priest. In the realities of living in a rectory with people that you might not be temperamentally harmonious with. The reality of going out on sick calls at three in the morning, and tramping hospital wards, and going in and slugging it out in a classroom day after day, whether it was teaching chemistry or geography, or whatever. And you learned that the so-called curate or associate in a parish got something like forty bucks a month."

The Cardinal smiled warmly at his memories of bleakness. "There was a shining star. Tough as it was in the production phase, and tough as it was going to be in the execution phase, you were going to become a *priest* or a *religious.* But then, twenty, twenty-two years ago, along with the rest of society, we started offering the world on a silver platter to those who were thinking of going into the priesthood. First, let me tell you more about what it was like twenty years before that, when I was young. The Maryknoll Missioners put out a black-and-white movie called *The Miracle of Blue Cloud County.* I even remember the name of the priest—Mark Tennien. I didn't know whether he really existed, but that's the name he had in the movie. They showed Father Mark Tennien going off to China and living with the peasants there. Initially, he was rebuffed, rejected. That was the cross he was bearing, and he was carrying it joyfully. That movie fired me up. Boy, I wanted to be Mark Tennien! But twenty years later what kind of films were we showing? A seminary with a beautiful swimming pool in it. I mean that literally—that's what we were showing. The dominant emphasis in our films of the sixties was 'What's in It for You If You Come into the Religious Life, If You Decide to Be a Priest?' "

The Cardinal believes that the compelling spirit of Father Tennien can return. "I am naive enough to believe that the average kid today still has deep within him the desire to sacrifice. I believe we all do. We all want to give of ourselves. We all want to be better than we are. I even think some of the kids who roam our streets vandalizing, marauding, doing far worse things, have the desire to give of themselves, and if you could get to that desire you could change them."

9

THE CARDINAL'S CONVICTION that there is some degree of selflessness within everyone is rooted in his own history, from boyhood on. The fourth child of Thomas and Dorothy Gomple O'Connor, he was born on January 15, 1920, in southwest Philadelphia, a working-class neighborhood of Irish, Italian, and East European families. His older sister, Mrs. Dorothy Hamilton, has told the *National Catholic Reporter*, "We never had all that much, but he always seemed to be looking for anyone who needed help." She added that her brother would run errands for neighbors but would refuse any pay. As a child, O'Connor showed considerable interest in helping retarded children, and when he was ten he tried to defend a retarded girl who was being taunted on the street by a gang of boys. O'Connor went after one of the boys and, he recalls ruefully, was knocked to the ground. He was small for his age. His nickname on the streets was Shadow; to his family he was Jack.

O'Connor's father, born in Philadelphia, was a skilled painter specializing in gold-leafing—very precise painting of the delicately ornamented ceilings of churches and auditoriums. While O'Connor was still Bishop of Scranton, he recalled, in *Newsday*, watching his father at his specialty. "Did you ever see a gold-leafer at work? He'd have this book of leaves, and he'd have a brush of extraordinarily fine feathers, and he had a full head of gray hair. And it was almost like lightning. He would tip the brush to his hair, and you could hardly see it. The static electricity would pick up his hair and pick the leaf off the book. . . . It's a lost art now; he was almost one of a kind by his day."

Thomas O'Connor was a man of strong and frequently

expressed opinions, many of them concerning the rights of labor as these were forcefully promulgated by Popes Leo XIII and Pius XI, whose writings he knew well. His wife was a woman of extraordinary gentleness, as her son emphasizes whenever he speaks of her. While he was still a boy, she lost her sight, and her husband stayed home to care for the children. A year later, her sight returned. "She attributed her cure to St. Rita of Cascia, and afterward she made a novena at St. Rita's Shrine every year, having to take two trolleys and a bus to get there," O'Connor recalls.

His mother's temporary blindness, O'Connor believes, greatly intensified his interest in the disabled—an interest he has continued to pursue, particularly with regard to retarded children. Almost everywhere he has been assigned, he has set up classes for retarded and other disabled children. O'Connor has said from time to time that he would have been content to spend his life working with the retarded. On the other hand, he has come to enjoy each new stage of his rise in the Church. When he was named Archbishop of New York, he said, "I love being a priest, and being a bishop ain't bad, either."

Growing up Catholic appeared to create no particular tensions in O'Connor as a boy. Quite the opposite: In a column in *Catholic New York* about his family life, he told of the warmth of the shared faith. "Good Friday was especially solemn for us. . . . It wasn't quite so much what we did as how we *felt*. . . . We knew that something dreadful had happened some 1,900 years ago, but we didn't feel sad so much as . . . *solemn.* I guess we didn't feel sad because we knew it had all turned out fine or there wouldn't have been any Easter Sunday." For Lent, his mother always gave up sweets. "I have known some big sacrificers in my day," the Cardinal wrote, "but when it came to going off sweets, my mother made John the Baptist look like a glutton for eating wild honey with his locusts in the desert. . . . Holy Saturday was kind of a day of waiting. Easter was already in the air, and the fact that my mother was counting the hours before she could descend on a cream puff somehow did not really distract her from her deep personal sense of the Resurrection. . . .

"We were a ham-and-cabbage Easter Sunday family, with Colman's hot English mustard for the ham, and soft-boiled potatoes that were really soft and white. My mother would cook it all and dutifully eat her share before plunging into the dessert she had been sacrificing for forty days. Her joy was marvelous, and we shared it as a very real part of Easter itself." The Cardinal couldn't resist doing some preaching on the subject of his childhood: "I'm glad I was reared the way I was. Nobody ever told us we were being psychologically twisted and spiritually deformed by my mother's and father's old-fashioned ways of observing Lent. Perhaps if they had been more sophisticated I might be more liberated, and not believe a fraction of what I believe today, which is amazingly like what they taught me to believe when I was hardly a half-dozen years old. I suppose I'll always gravitate toward fish on Friday and the Stations of the Cross, and have a rosary in my pocket. And I will always feel awed by the Pope and even by my own auxiliary bishops."

O'Connor started his education in public elementary school and went on to junior high school. When he was thirteen, his parents enrolled him in West Catholic High School for Boys, and it was there, because of the teaching of the Christian Brothers, that he began to feel he might have a vocation for the priesthood. (Members of the Brothers of the Christian Schools, which was organized in seventeenth-century France to meet the needs of the children of the Catholic poor who were being denied an education, take vows of poverty, chastity, and obedience, and of service to the poor through education, and work as teachers.)

When O'Connor decided he did indeed have a vocation and told his parents, his father was disappointed, having expected him to help keep the art of gold-leafing alive. But in 1936 John O'Connor, with four hundred dollars from his parents for the tuition, went to learn to be a priest at St.

Charles Borromeo Seminary, in the Overbrook section of Philadelphia. The discipline was strict and constant, and no student was encouraged to believe he would survive. Nine years later, a month before his twenty-sixth birthday, O'Connor was ordained a priest of the Philadelphia archdiocese. Over the next seven years, he taught at Catholic high schools, becoming a guidance counselor; taught at a night school for adults; conducted two Catholic radio programs; worked in the psychiatric wards of hospitals; and taught the mentally retarded. At the same time, he was an assistant in a parish, celebrating morning Masses and, on weekends, counseling engaged couples and prospective converts. When John Cardinal O'Hara of Philadelphia started to plan a center for retarded children, he enlisted O'Connor in the project. The priest felt he now knew what he was going to be doing for the rest of his life, and he was pleased at the prospect.

10

WHEN the Korean War began, Francis Cardinal Spellman, of New York, the military vicar of the American Catholic Church, asked for more chaplains, and in 1952 O'Connor, with no great enthusiasm, entered the Navy, because there was a need. He came in as a lieutenant junior grade, and after assignments in Philadelphia, at the Naval Hospital and the naval base, he was transferred to the Destroyer Force, Atlantic Fleet. By 1955, O'Connor was a full lieutenant and was working as an assistant for moral leadership to the chief of chaplains, in Washington. After five years there, he moved on to a guided-missile cruiser, *Canberra*, for his first extended sea duty. In 1962, he was assigned to Monterey, California, as chaplain at the Naval Postgraduate School. There he lobbied successfully with diocesan authorities for the setting up of a program for the education of the handicapped.

In 1964, O'Connor was sent to the 3rd Marine Division in Okinawa, which was scheduled for combat duty in Vietnam. When the division moved on to Vietnam, O'Connor went along as assistant division chaplain. For the better part of a year, he celebrated Mass every day, sometimes under fire; comforted the wounded; counseled Marines having breakdowns; wrote to the families of the dead; and, on occasion, ventured into field positions where, until he arrived, there had been no Catholic chaplain. One such trip was described years later in the *National Catholic Reporter* by a Marine officer:

It was kind of funny. Father had been out to the 9th Marines, one of our divisions, and his driver evidently missed the turn. They had gone too far, the people were no longer waving to them. They realized they had made a mistake. There was no place to turn around, so they just turned the jeep a little bit when a sniper opened up. They must have been at extreme range, the bullets weren't quite reaching them.

The driver froze in his seat. Father had to go around, lift the kid out of his seat, turn the jeep around and drive back. We were eating lunch when he got back. Marines don't give much sympathy, and he was pretty rattled by then. We said, "O God, Father. We're over here trying to pacify the people and you're out there antagonizing them."

O'Connor wrote a book, *A Chaplain Looks at Vietnam*, (Cleveland: World Publishing Co.) that was published in 1968. On the jacket he is identified as "Chaplain, United States Navy/Serving with the Marines." The text is a justification, moral and legal, for American intervention in Vietnam. The alternative, he wrote, would be "a Communist take-over . . . the frightful power of the unconfronted

e frequent use of the Lacouture quotation, thereby
·ing out the view of some of his admirers and detractors
 while he is capable of admitting past error, or igno-
:e that led to error, he simultaneously holds as much of
previous ground as he can.

'or his service in Vietnam, the chaplain received the
ion of Merit. In recommending him for the award,
·is Walt, commanding general of the 3rd Marine Divi-
, wrote, "It is my opinion that no single individual in
 command contributed more to the morale of the indi-
ial Marine here in Vietnam than Father O'Connor, who
it the majority of his time in the field with the men."

)n returning to the United States, O'Connor was as-
ied to the Marine Corps Recruit Depot, at Parris Island,
th Carolina, and then to the Marine Corps School, at
intico, Virginia. In Virginia, although he was entitled to
:ers' quarters on base, he chose instead to live off the
ε, so that people could come to see him without fear that
r military colleagues would speculate about why they
ited to see the chaplain.

;oon after he arrived, O'Connor started to search for re-
led children on the base, having decided to set up a
ifraternity of Christian Doctrine class for them. He was
ially told that there were no retarded children there. He
it ahead anyway, and Tom Mattimoe, a Marine lieuten-
colonel at the time, now retired, told the *National Cath-
· Reporter* in 1985 of the day the classes for retarded
ldren began: "I couldn't believe it. Honest to God, there
·e people coming out of the walls. People just didn't talk
ut it, I guess. I had friends who turned up with children
) were retarded, and I'm talking about friends with sev-
een-year-olds. He just brought them all out. It was a very
ching thing. They'd always been totally ignored any
ce I'd ever been to before. No one presumed they were
und."

While at Quantico, O'Connor received permission to
ly for a Ph.D. in political science at Georgetown Univer-

'war of liberation.' " Toward the end of the
chaplain, sounding very much like Pre
Johnson and Richard Nixon, prayerfully
statement by John Foster Dulles at the 1954
ence, which had failed to negotiate a lastin
France and the revolutionaries in Vietna
ways easy to achieve—by surrender. Your (
not propose to buy peace at that price. We d
the American people want peace at that]
that is our national will, and so long as tha
by a capacity for effective action, our Nat
future with that calm confidence which is
who, in a troubled world, hold fast to that

O'Connor came to have severe reserv;
book. "That's a bad book, you know," he tol
first year as Archbishop of New York. "It w
view of what was going on. I regret having]
did not, he feels, take sufficient account of
mous cost in lives, resources, and the bruta
of the American troops. Nor was he aware
many decisions concerning the conduct (
taken for political rather than military re

The Cardinal still believes, however, tl
writing about the war while it was going
often deliberately, in favor of the North
Vietcong forces. He is quite gratified tha
journalists have since admitted their partis
book, *In Defense of Life* (Boston: Daughters
O'Connor took particular note of a change
French journalist Jean Lacouture, whose w
etnam were often quoted by antiwar force
States during the 1960s and early 1970s: '
Milan's *Il Giornale Nuovo*, Lacouture sta
simulated defects of the North Vietnames
information because he believed that the ca
Vietnamese 'was good and just enough so t
expose their errors [or] expose the Stalini
[North] Vietnamese regime in 1972.' " Th

sity, and while on the way to the doctorate he wrote a mono-graph, "The Professional Officer and the Human Person." (He also has master's degrees in advanced ethics and clini-cal psychology.) In 1970, he went to sea again, assigned to the Cruiser-Destroyer Force, Atlantic Fleet, out of Newport, Rhode Island. Two years later, he was appointed the first Catholic senior chaplain at the United States Naval Acad-emy, in Annapolis, and in 1975 he became Navy chief of chaplains in Washington, with the rank of rear admiral. In that position, he traveled more widely than he ever had before—to Antarctica, the Persian Gulf, the Indian Ocean, and the Far East, among other places.

II

ADMIRAL O'CONNOR had had enough of the military service. He wanted to go home to Pennsylvania. "One after-noon in March 1979, still in my Navy uniform, I had just come from lunch with John J. Krol, the Cardinal Arch-bishop of Philadelphia," Cardinal O'Connor recalls. "I was exhilarated, because of the conversation we had had. I'd told him, 'Look, I've done everything I've been asked to do, and I've tried to do all of it faithfully. And I'll do anything you tell me now, but I will be so grateful if you will let me come home. Not in an administrative or an organization job but just in a quiet little suburban parish. I'll go as an assist-ant for a year or two years, however long it takes to break in again.' And Cardinal Krol had said yes."

O'Connor went back to Washington, "absolutely eu-

phoric." Two weeks later, on Holy Thursday, he was called
to New York by Terence Cardinal Cooke, whom he had met
a number of times during Cooke's military travels as secretary to Cardinal Spellman.

"I had no idea why Cardinal Cooke wanted to see me,"
O'Connor says. "I was waiting in a little office at 452 Madison Avenue, and when he came in I stood up. He said, 'John,
you'd better sit down. The Holy Father wants to make you
a bishop.' I guess I should be ashamed to say I burst into
tears. They weren't tears of joy. I wasn't going to be able to
go home. I had gone into military service only because of
Korea. I never had any desire to enter the military. It
seemed the right thing to do. But at the time I was working
with retarded children, which I loved. And I was teaching,
which I loved. Once I got into the military, the Church kept
asking me to stay. So, twenty-seven years later, I had been
so grateful to be returning to what I thought was going to be
an ordinary life. I asked Cardinal Cooke why the Holy Father wanted to make me a bishop. He said, 'He wants you
to serve in the military vicariate.' " The vicariate is a diocese, but it covers the world, for it serves Catholic members
of the armed forces and their families wherever they are
stationed. The head of the vicariate also supervises all
Catholic chaplains. Cardinal Cooke was then in charge of
that office, as his predecessor, Cardinal Spellman, had been.
(Today the vicariate, renamed the Archdiocese for the Military Services, operates out of Silver Spring, Maryland.)

" 'You do what the Holy Father wants you to do,' Cardinal
Cooke said. Six weeks later, I was in Rome being ordained
by the Pope; and on June 1, 1979, after twenty-seven years in
uniform, I retired from the military service." He was now
auxiliary bishop to Cardinal Cooke. Because of all the years
he had spent in the military, O'Connor was not well known
in what might be called the domestic Church. In a couple
of years, however, his name was quite familiar—and controversial—among his fellow bishops, because of his participation in the drafting of a pastoral letter by a bishops'
committee on what the Second Vatican Council had called

"a moment of supreme crisis" in the human race's "advance toward maturity." The question before the committee was what the position of the American Church should be concerning the possession and use of nuclear arms.

A pastoral letter is a teaching document, a communication to the faithful, and anyone else interested, by a bishop or a group of bishops. The subjects vary from matters of faith and morals to civil rights, health care, and farm policy. In the United States, the first pastoral letter was circulated on May 28, 1792, two and a half years after Pope Pius VI established the first Catholic diocese in America, the Diocese of Baltimore. In that initial letter, the Bishop of Baltimore, John Carroll, wrote about, among other things, the "Necessity of Vocations to the Priesthood." He hoped and prayed that "zealous and able pastors" could be found who were "accustomed to our climate and acquainted with the tempers, manners, and government of the people, to whom they are to dispense the ministry of salvation." And, as bishops have from time to time in all nations, Carroll reported that he was saddened and angered by lax attendance at Sunday Mass: "Every inconvenience is not sufficient to exempt you from the obligation of attending at Mass on Sundays and other days prescribed by the Church. The obstacle must be grievous and weighty, amounting almost to an impossibility, moral or physical."

One hundred and eighty-nine years and many pastoral letters later, the National Conference of Catholic Bishops was faced with a formidable challenge—the writing of a pastoral letter on how to achieve peace in an age of nuclear weapons. In January 1981, Archbishop John Roach, of St. Paul–Minneapolis, then president of the conference, decided that a committee should be formed to draft a statement on the problem, which would be debated at one or more meetings of all the bishops. Roach appointed as head of the committee Archbishop Joseph Bernardin, of Cincinnati, who later became Archbishop of Chicago, and later still was elevated to the College of Cardinals. Bernardin is greatly respected by his colleagues for his remarkable ability to orchestrate widely different views toward a concensus without any of the participants' feeling they have been steamrollered by the majority. In addition to possessing seemingly endless patience, Bernardin speaks with great care. A Jesuit academician told me, "O'Connor often shoots from the hip, without a safety net, but Bernardin wouldn't even say grace without a text—and the most recently revised text at that."

Bernardin selected as members of the committee Bishop Daniel Reilly, of Norwich, Connecticut; Auxiliary Bishop George Fulcher, of Columbus, Ohio; and two polar opposites—Auxiliary Bishop Thomas Gumbleton, of Detroit, and Auxiliary Bishop John J. O'Connor, of the military vicariate. Gumbleton was then and still is president of the American branch of Pax Christi, a Catholic organization one of whose priorities is the theology and practice of nonviolence; he is a pacifist. O'Connor had been in the military most of his adult life, and was still involved with the armed forces through his assignment to the military vicariate.

"I was billed as the Genghis Khan of the committee," O'Connor told me, with a rather pleased laugh. "The resident barbarian. The token militarist. All of us on the committee did have different experiential backgrounds, but, fortunately, we had Cardinal Bernardin and his great ability to ferret out harmonies where there might have seemed to be only dissonances. He kept bringing things together. It was difficult, for all of us. The two and a half years I served on that committee were fascinating, agonizing. The deliberations were often anguished. What we were doing was so important that we had to be absolutely honest with each other. And that would have been impossible without conflict, tension, misunderstanding, intense debate."

In a number of public statements during those two and a half years, Cardinal Bernardin tried to explain why the bishops were involving themselves in a question that one might have thought was up to the President and Congress to decide. Were they not directly engaging themselves in political matters? Bernardin noted that the issue of nuclear weapons is not only political but also profoundly moral and religious—and such matters are the very business of bishops. It is their responsibility to keep the dialogue open in the Church and in society on ways to reduce the danger of nuclear war.

"In the committee, our mandate was to try to do a complete reevaluation of war and the things of war," O'Connor told me. "We might then be able to contribute to a reduction in the possibility of war. We adopted as an absolute the teaching of Pope John Paul II that peace with justice is possible. That's what a whole lot of people have missed about the pastoral letter. We were all agreed that peace with justice is possible."

There was much disagreement, however, on how to arrive at peace with justice. Jim Castelli's book *The Bishops and the Bomb* (New York: Doubleday-Image, 1983), based in part on the files of the committee, provides considerable detail on its debates and on the disagreements over successive drafts of the pastoral letter at the meetings of the National Conference of Catholic Bishops. It also provides a sense of the continuing debate in parishes around the country:

In Portsmouth, Virginia, 277 members of the three-hundred-family Holy Angels Church signed an open letter to Congress urging "the unilateral destruction of our nuclear arsenal." The parish was no doubt influenced by the rhetoric of Bishop Walter Sullivan, who gave a speech in at least eight places in the Richmond diocese arguing that if it's immoral to use nuclear weapons, it's immoral to possess them, and therefore "it's immoral to produce them or be associated with them."

Sullivan's rhetoric prompted a letter from Bishop O'Connor to the Norfolk *Ledger-Star* challenging his conclusions. "I know of nothing in official church teaching that suggests that our military people are engaged in immoral activities in carrying out their responsibilities," he said, arguing that "it could be immoral" for a government to disarm unilaterally if it left the nation vulnerable. The Richmond Priests' Senate responded with a resolution backing Sullivan.

12

IN THE FOUR YEARS since the bishops' committee ended its deliberations on nuclear arms, there has been an impression, particularly among liberal Catholics, that O'Connor was indeed the unswerving Genghis Khan of the group, and in Jim Castelli's *The Bishops and the Bomb* he is portrayed much of the time as the unofficial representative of the Reagan Administration on the committee. (For one thing, O'Connor consulted privately with Secretary of Defense Caspar Weinberger between sessions of the committee.) Yet Castelli also notes that the position of the bishop from the military vicariate was sometimes unpredictable. One of the experts who came to talk to the five bishops was Harold Brown, who had been Secretary of Defense in the Carter Administration. After Brown described the destruction that can be caused by various missile systems, O'Connor asked, "Aren't we really talking about rationalizing insanity?" There was silence. Then Brown said, "Yes."

It was O'Connor who wrote the first draft of a section addressed to Catholics who work on the manufacture of nuclear weapons: "We cannot at this time require Catholics who manufacture nuclear weapons, sincerely believing they are enhancing a deterrent capability and reducing the likelihood of war, to leave such employment. Should we become convinced that even the temporary possession of such weapons may no longer be morally tolerated, we would logically be required to consider immoral any involvement in their manufacture. All Catholics in weapons industries should evaluate their activities on a continuing basis, forming their consciences in accordance with the general principles enunciated in this pastoral letter."

The final version of this section, as it was worked out by

the committee, recognizes "the possibility of diverse concrete judgments being made in this complex area," and goes on, "Those who in conscience decide that they should no longer be associated with defense activities should find support in the Catholic community. Those who remain in these industries or earn a profit from the weapons industry should find in the Church guidance and support for the ongoing evaluation of their work."

If O'Connor was not Genghis Khan throughout the deliberations, however, he was resolutely resistant to any language that might be taken to mean condemnation of any defensive use of nuclear weapons. He noted in a section of a draft he wrote, "The danger of escalation and the uncontrollability that goes with it clearly makes offensive nuclear warfare immoral, but it is not at all clear that such danger outlaws a nuclear defense against nuclear aggression. Or if it does that, it would outlaw an effective defense with conventional weapons as well, since this would provoke a continuation of the nuclear attack, the danger of escalation, etc. The only alternative would be obligatory surrender. Besides being highly questionable, this would make papal . . . insistence on the right to self-defense meaningless."

The majority of the committee rejected a majority of O'Connor's proposals and changes, but he won a significant one-word change in language in the third draft of the pastoral letter. He objected strenuously to a call in the second draft for a "halt" to the testing, production, and deployment of new nuclear weapons systems. That would be a freeze. O'Connor insisted that *halt* be changed to *curb*, because the stronger language would rule out the possible development of safer, smaller, and more reliable nuclear weapons, which could be used, if it became absolutely necessary, in self-defense without creating uncontrollable devastation. After all, the Second Vatican Council had declared, "As long as the danger of war persists and there is no international authority with the necessary competence and power, governments cannot be denied the right of lawful self-defense, once all peace efforts have failed."

In committee, O'Connor prevailed on that point because Cardinal Bernardin and the other bishops wanted to present a consensus report to the National Conference of Catholic Bishops. *Curb* seemed to be O'Connor's sticking point: if *halt* was not changed to *curb*, he might well file a dissenting report.

The third draft of the pastoral letter contained a statement of a nation's right to self-defense, which "includes defense by armed force if necessary as a last resort." Using nuclear weapons against civilians, however, was condemned. And, in a sentence written by Bishop O'Connor, the draft stated, "It would be a perverted political policy or moral casuistry which tried to justify using a weapon which 'indirectly' or 'unintentionally' killed a million innocent people because they happened to live near a 'militarily significant target.'"

The five bishops stated in their third draft, "We abhor the concept of initiating nuclear war on however restricted a scale," and "resist" the deployment of possible first-strike weapons. The second draft had used *oppose* instead of *resist*. The substitution of the somewhat weaker word represented another of O'Connor's few victories in committee.

Press coverage of the third draft focused on his more substantive victory—the change from *halt* to *curb*. The Reagan Administration, which had been apprehensive about the pastoral letter and had made available a number of its officials to consult with the drafting committee, now declared itself considerably less apprehensive. A headline in the *Times* on April 7, 1983, said: "ADMINISTRATION HAILS NEW DRAFT OF ARMS LETTER—SAYS BISHOPS 'IMPROVED' THE NUCLEAR STATEMENT." Some prominent conservative Catholic laymen also celebrated the "improvement." Representative Henry Hyde, of Illinois, sent a letter to his colleagues in the House in opposition to a nuclear-freeze resolution, pointing to such newspaper headlines as the Baltimore *Sun*'s "BISHOPS BACK OFF FREEZE IDEA," and claiming that "the Roman Catholic Bishops have refused to endorse the nuclear-arms freeze."

The drafting committee met again, to consider additional amendments. They were aware that a growing number of bishops around the country were uneasy at the press's interpretation of the shift from *halt* to *curb*. At last, during this committee meeting, Cardinal Bernardin said, "I've been defending *curb* for three weeks now, and I don't know about you, but I'm ready to go back to *halt*." The change was so moved, and the vote was four to one, with O'Connor dissenting.

When all the bishops assembled in Chicago on Sunday, May 1, the *curb*-versus-*halt* question was debated on the afternoon of the second day. Immediately after O'Connor spoke for his position, he was undercut by one of the most respected of the bishops, the conservative, often autocratic, John Cardinal Krol, of Philadelphia. With characteristic crispness, Krol said that since the Church's hope and intention were the eventual elimination of all nuclear weapons—not just a reduction in their number—*halt* was clearly the more accurate reflection of the Church's position. There was no official tally of the subsequent vote on whether *curb* or *halt* would prevail, but O'Connor was defeated by a margin of at least ten to one.

Later in the debate, an amendment proposed by John Quinn, Archbishop of San Francisco, was passed, registering another setback for O'Connor: "We judge that resort to nuclear weapons to counter a conventional attack is morally unjustifiable." Not only is offensive nuclear warfare immoral but so is the use of nuclear weapons in self-defense against a conventional attack, no matter how overwhelming the enemy's forces.

What may have been both the most provocative comment and the one most relevant to a conference of bishops had been offered during the debate on the second draft of the letter, in November 1982, by Raymond Hunthausen, Archbishop of Seattle: "We acknowledge in the draft that peace is a gift from God. How then can we accept a strategy which makes nuclear weapons 'the absolute basis' for our security? That's idolatry."

When the time came for the final vote to be taken, it was clear that a number of the bishops not only opposed any use of nuclear weapons but also had serious doubt that it was possible to morally justify the possession of them. The bishops were not ready, however, to call for an end to the concept and practice of nuclear deterrence. Instead, the pastoral letter, "The Challenge of Peace: God's Promise and Our Response," as it was approved by a vote of 238 to 9, went no further than "a strictly conditioned moral acceptance of nuclear deterrence." The bishops immediately added, "We cannot consider it adequate as a long-term basis for peace."

While nuclear deterrence was being grudgingly accepted, the final version of the letter opposed under any circumstances the use of any kind of weapon against predominantly civilian targets. It also stated, "We do not perceive any situation in which the deliberate initiation of nuclear war, on however restricted a scale, can be morally justified. [We] support . . . immediate, bilateral, verifiable agreements to halt the testing, production, and deployment of new nuclear weapons systems. . . . In the words of our Holy Father, we need a 'moral about-face.' The whole world must summon the moral courage and technical means to say no to nuclear conflict; no to weapons of mass destruction; no to an arms race which robs the poor and the vulnerable; and no to the moral danger of a nuclear age which places before humankind indefensible choices of constant terror or surrender. Peacemaking is not an optional commitment. It is a requirement of our faith. We are called to be peacemakers, not by some movement of the moment, but by our Lord Jesus. The content and context of our peacemaking is set not by some political agenda or ideological program but by the teaching of His Church."

"The Challenge of Peace: God's Promise and Our Response" received more attention than any other pastoral letter in the history of the American Catholic Church. The statement was a direct criticism of the United States government's position on nuclear arms. The London *Tablet*, a weekly Catholic magazine, observed of the bishops, "They have confronted the biggest issue of the times, withstood political and ideological pressures of the most intense kind and forthrightly specified how Catholics should approach the issues of nuclear war and work for a peace which is more than a balance of terror."

13

THERE WAS an additional significance in the American bishops' having approved a document that put them at odds not only with the Administration but also with a majority of the American people, who strongly believed in the deterrent value and the necessity of nuclear arms. It is generally a belief that does not include such of the bishops' strict conditions as an end to the production of new nuclear-weapons systems. In a speech at the University of Chicago in November 1984, John O'Connor, who by then had become the Archbishop of New York, talked of the historic dimensions of the pastoral letter on war and peace. He noted that Gerald P. Fogarty, a Jesuit historian at the University of Virginia, saw the letter "as ushering in a new era" in American Catholicism. O'Connor was referring to an article by Fogarty, "Public Patriotism and Private Politics: The Tradition of American Catholicism," in the quarterly *U.S. Catholic Historian.*

The pastoral letter on nuclear arms "marked a departure from past practice of support for government policy and of silence on political issues, except those which pertained to education or family life," Fogarty had written, continuing, "Why the pastoral became so newsworthy has to be seen in part within the context of the long history of Catholics having to prove they could be loyal Americans. On the one hand, so great was the suspicion of Catholics that they had to show their patriotism by participating in the nation's wars. On the other hand, in times of peace, the bishops and clergy tended to keep religion a private matter and not to speak out on issues which had become political. . . . In many ways, the bishops' pastoral of 1983 was at least as important an event in the history of American Catholicism as the election of Kennedy. Not only were Catholics politically accepted, but they were also integrating their religious faith and concern with their responsibility for the total welfare of the nation and the world." As a contrast to the criticism of national defense policies by the bishops in 1983, Fogarty cited Francis Cardinal Spellman's visit to American troops in Vietnam during Christmas in 1965. Spellman, paraphrasing the resounding words of Stephen Decatur, had proclaimed, "My country, may it always be right. Right or wrong, my country."

Archbishop O'Connor, in his speech at the University of Chicago and in later conversations, said that working on the pastoral letter had been of historic significance to him personally. He had learned a great deal. He had been forced to think hard about Church teachings in relation to nuclear arms, about Church involvement in politics, and about his own capacities for change. Of the Church and American politics, O'Connor said in the Chicago speech that many of the bishops' recommendations in the pastoral letter "are explicitly based on the Gospels and on Church teaching." He went on:

In other words, they are "religious." Was the entry into the political arena difficult? Quite; indeed, quite painful. Could [the bishops], should they, have remained mute? In my judgment, and apparently in the judgment of the overwhelming majority of bishops, to do so would have been inordinately irresponsible.

Recently, the famous Church historian, Monsignor John Tracy Ellis, quoted the pope he calls one of the most otherworldly (read, least "political") of modern pontiffs, Pope Pius X: "We are forced to deal with politics because the Pontifex Maximus, invested by God with this highest of offices, does not have the right to divorce politics from the realm of faith and morals." It seems to me that if the pastoral letter on war and peace may be used as a criterion, the bishops of the United States, *mutatis mutandis*, appear convinced that they do not have the right to divorce politics from the realm of faith and morals. . . .

The bishops speak because they cannot remain silent: the evil and danger of nuclear proliferation and the lurking possibility of nuclear war involve our nation in decisions that transcend the military and political. Fundamental *moral* choices are at stake and these choices must be informed by rational moral discourse, given the numbing awareness that "we are the first generation since Genesis with the power virtually to destroy God's creation."

O'Connor told his audience that another five-man committee of bishops was working on a pastoral letter on Catholic social teaching and the United States economy. It was already evident that the letter's focus would be on economic justice. O'Connor predicted, "The bishops will once again be enjoined to stay in their churches and negotiate with the angels, leaving the daily issues of life and death, such as starvation in Ethiopia, abortion, nuclear war, and the arms race, to those presumably better equipped to manage such matters, and at least secular enough to be 'objective' about them. I cannot imagine the bishops or their coreligionists of other persuasions doing so, whatever the criticism."

For all his dissents in the committee and his objections during the debates when all the bishops were present, O'Connor had voted for the final document, and he went on to endorse the pastoral letter vigorously. For two and a half years, he had been exposed to a much wider range of people than he had known during his many years in the service. The committee had heard experts in foreign policy, defense policy, and political science. The Secretary of Defense had met with the committee, and so had members of the State Department and the National Security Council; but also bearing witness before the five bishops were practitioners of nonviolent resistance, including a mother of six who was under a two-year suspended sentence for an antinuclear action.

"We read articles from journals almost as they were coming off the press," O'Connor told me. "We were in contact with bishops in various parts of the world, with the Holy See, and, above all, with one another. We prayed together, we talked together, and tempers—usually mine—would flare. We did finally achieve a balanced document. The way we were able to do it was through the device of the three categories of moral authority. By the time we were working on the third draft, we had come to agree on using those categories.

"First, there is natural law, or universal moral principles that are written in the hearts of human beings everywhere. People are bound in conscience to adhere to that which is inherent in natural morality, whether the Catholic Church has spoken or not. For example, judgments at Nuremberg were based not on written law but on universal moral principles. Then there is the formal teaching of the Catholic Church over the course of the centuries. What did the Second Vatican Council teach? What do bodies of bishops teach? These are considered official Catholic Church teaching. Third, there is a broad area that we call prudential moral judgment. And from Day One my problem in the committee was that I could never have supported a document that implied in any way that what we eventually came to recognize as a prudential moral judgment was either formal Church teaching or inherent in universal moral law."

I asked the Cardinal for a specific example of prudential moral judgment, as opposed to a judgment that would be binding on Catholics.

He replied, "The universal moral law and the Church both teach that you may never, under any circumstances, attack innocent human beings, noncombatants. That is of a totally different order from saying, 'After studying this to the best of our ability and admitting we are not military strategists or tacticians, we do not feel that troops should be stationed five miles from anybody else's border.' That's a prudential moral judgment, and dissent from it by Catholics is entirely legitimate. Those judgments are not binding in conscience, but Catholics should give them serious attention. No first use of nuclear weapons is another example of a prudential moral judgment. It is not official Catholic teaching. It is the moral judgment of the majority of the American bishops, and no Catholic may dismiss it lightly. Once the differentiation between these three categories was applied to our letter, I was able to support it."

O'Connor still, however, had certain reservations, he said. In May 1983, at the final meeting of all the bishops to discuss and vote on the third draft, O'Connor proposed a number of changes in the document. He was voted down on most of them, but he planned to give a speech on several he thought especially critical. It was to have been, he told me, an impassioned speech. But just before he was to speak, Archbishop Pio Laghi, the Pope's representative to the Church in America, came up to him, put an arm around his shoulders, and said, "I want to tell you that the Holy Father loves you very much."

"That's very gratifying," O'Connor said, "but I'm about to make this intervention—"

"The Holy Father has appointed you the Bishop of Scranton."

"I was absolutely stunned," O'Connor recalls. "Everything went out of my head. I mean that literally. I got up, and when I spoke I was a blithering idiot. All I could think of was: I'm finally going to be a pastor. It was a slightly bigger parish than I'd anticipated, but my roots were in Pennsylvania, I knew Scranton, and I was overjoyed. But my speech about the changes I wanted to see in the pastoral was awful."

14

O'CONNOR was installed as Bishop of Scranton on June 29, 1983. In September, he sent a letter, "First Impressions and Initial Observations," to all the priests in the diocese. The letter reveals a great deal about him—his priorities, his way of handling his authority, his definition of the priesthood, including his own.

His first priority, the Bishop of Scranton made very clear, was opposing abortion. In language that later involved him in extended controversy as Archbishop of New York, he wrote, "I will give no support, by word or action, that could in any way be construed in favor of any politician, of any political party, who professes either a specific pro-abortion position, or takes refuge in a so-called 'pro-choice' position. I categorically reject the evasion: 'I am personally opposed to abortion, but this is a pluralistic society, and I must respect the rights of those who disagree with me.'"

O'Connor also wrote, "It is absolutely essential that we assure a just wage for our teachers. I do not pretend to know at this time where the money is to come from, but I have very strong feelings on this matter." Until O'Connor came to the diocese, organizers for the union representing teachers in the Catholic schools had been coldly resisted by principals and pastors. In his September letter, Bishop O'Connor said, "I want to make it very clear that every teacher in every Catholic school must be completely free, without harassment or pressure of any sort, to join any one of the appropriate teachers' associations. . . . It would be gravely irresponsible for anyone to exercise harassment or exert pressure making it difficult for a teacher to join such an association. At the same time, I will categorically resist any pressure on any teacher to join any association or to be forced to pay dues or otherwise contribute to any association to which he or she does not belong."

O'Connor's concern for the schools in the diocese ranged from finances to the content of the courses (how Catholic were they?), and encompassed "small things that can reveal big things such as the behavior of our Catholic-school students," he wrote. "It may seem trivial or old-fashioned to some, but I hope that our school system is such that if a sister or a priest walks into a classroom, the entire class stands in greeting. I hope that our school system is such that if a sister or priest passes on the sidewalk outside a Catholic school when students are leaving classes, they greet him or her respectfully. Are these things really trivial?"

His years of military service as a naval chaplain were reflected in this passage: "There can be no such thing as 'I will not accept that assignment.' Nor may any pastor arbitrarily say: 'I will not accept that assistant.' The priest who will not accept any assignment could find himself without any assignment. The pastor who will not accept an assistant could find himself without any assistant." While he would try hard to accommodate any priest with a legitimate complaint about an assignment, "we must not baby ourselves in this regard," the Bishop wrote. "We were ordained for the people."

Wherever O'Connor has been assigned, he has considered preaching a special responsibility. He told the priests of Scranton that he expected the same commitment from them. "I consider preaching our most important responsibility next to the offering of the Eucharistic Sacrifice itself," he wrote. "People plead for bread; we may not give them stones. Our preaching must be clear, it must be scripturally oriented, it must be intelligible and meaningful for the people, and it must be delivered plainly and audibly. The pulpit is not the place for theological speculation. Our people are crying for fundamentals." Furthermore, preaching must be "long enough to be instructive," he continued. "We must remember that, for the most part, our people receive *no* religious instruction except what they receive at Mass on Sunday. Too often, we let the schedule of Masses and parking problems determine the length of sermons. . . . Many of [our people] watch television by the hour. Why must we rush them out of Mass as though forty-five minutes were a sacred restriction? Can they really believe that *we* believe the Liturgy of the Word, or the Mass itself, is the most important action we can possibly perform—the very heart and soul of our faith—if we rush it?"

The new Bishop also had something to say about the kind of music that was being heard in the churches of the diocese: "Some of it is abominable." He was disturbed by the tendency of some cantors, or song-leaders, "to select responsorial psalm modes that border on the operatic, virtually unsingable by the people, and seeming to contribute little but a display of the cantor's vocal abilities," he wrote, "And while we are grateful to see that most 'folk-music' groups are appropriately attired for the sanctuary, we still note attire, here and there, which is more fitting for outdoor barbecues."

One of the first assignments O'Connor gave himself in Scranton was to make four half-hour videotapes in which he explained the newly published pastoral letter on war and peace, which called for a halt to the testing, production, and deployment of new nuclear weapons systems. "These went out over a regional television station, and they were made available to all our schools," he told me when I talked with him some ten months later. "That shows that I did indeed support the document. In clear conscience. I did insist, in Scranton and, later, in New York, that the pastoral letter be taught in its entirety, because all of us have an understandable tendency to lean heavily on those parts of a document with which we thoroughly agree. I've also insisted that the pastoral letter be taught with a very clear sense of the three categories it includes: universal moral principles, official Church teaching, and prudential moral judgments."

O'Connor's letter to the priests of Scranton also mentioned a historic appointment—that of Mary Ellen Keating as diocesan director of communications. She was the first lay woman named to so high a position in that diocese.

O'Connor adhered to his pledge in the letter that teachers should receive a just wage. He did, however, make one promise in the letter that he did not fulfill. He said he would meet "individually with three priests, every Tuesday and Thursday, in my office," adding, "At this rate, it will take almost two years to see every priest, but I hope you agree that's better than never!" The Bishop could not fulfill that promise, because he was in Scranton only eight months. "I was very happy in Scranton," O'Connor told me. "Those are good, simple people." But one Monday morning the phone rang, and it was the Papal Nuncio, Archbishop Pio Laghi. "We were kidding around for about ten minutes, just laughing, wisecracking, talking about the weather, and he says, 'By the way, the Holy Father has appointed you Archbishop of New York.'"

There was a long pause. "Come on," O'Connor said. "Are you kidding?"

"I'm not kidding," Laghi assured him.

O'Connor was "traumatized," he recalled. "It was just like the time in Chicago. But to be Archbishop of New York? Cardinal Cooke had died. In fact, the last public event he had attended was my installation in Scranton. I had, of course, heard the subsequent speculation about all those big honcho bishops who were in line to be Cardinal Cooke's successor. Their names were in the papers all the time. But I really wasn't paying much attention, because I was so happy where I was."

I asked O'Connor why he felt he had been chosen over the "big honcho bishops."

He smiled, "Of course, we like to believe that the Holy Spirit has something to do with the appointment of bishops," he said. "Gee, if I didn't believe that, I wouldn't be in this business at all."

15

In addition to whatever role the Holy Spirit may have played, there were reports during the selection process that Pope John Paul II had a very definite idea of the kind of man he wanted as the new Archbishop of New York. Monsignor Florence D. Cohalan, a historian of the New York archdiocese and a close observer of the politics of the Church, recalls something he was told by close friends who visited the Vatican while the Pope was making up his mind: that John Paul II had been heard to say, "I want a man just like me in New York."

"The Pope had seen O'Connor from time to time, and he remembered him," Cohalan told me. "There are not many lions or eagles around these days. Many of the bishops are like second- or third-level civil servants. Social workers, actually. They wouldn't think of rocking a boat. They wouldn't know how to rock a boat if they wanted to. But O'Connor is strong. He's the kind of man who can say no and make it stick. That's one of the most beautiful words in the English language—*no*. The Pope saw that O'Connor was a man who could say no, and yes, too, and give reasons for both."

O'Connor recalled that he had also heard that the Pope was saying he wanted an Archbishop of New York like himself. "But no one in authority, and certainly not the Pope, has confirmed that that's what he said," O'Connor noted.

When I asked him in what ways the Pope might have felt that the two were similar, O'Connor did not hesitate.

"Obviously, I am perceived as being theologically very orthodox. And I am. There's no question about that. And the Holy Father is theologically very orthodox." O'Connor laughed. "That's what he gets paid to be."

Not surprisingly, O'Connor has been an unyielding public supporter of the Pope during the divisions within the American Church in recent years. The most widely publicized were caused by the Vatican's disciplining of Father Charles Curran, a professor of moral theology at Catholic University in Washington, until he was stripped of his right to teach there in the summer of 1986, and, also, the Holy See's humiliation of Archbishop Raymond Hunthausen, of Seattle, who was relieved of much of his authority in September of the same year.

Curran, in his writing and teaching, had maintained that the Church's opposition to birth control, abortion, long-term homosexual relationships, and remarriage after divorce should be less rigid. Hunthausen was charged with, among other things, allowing contraceptive sterilizations in Catholic hospitals in his archdiocese, permitting non-Catholics to receive communion at Mass while also allowing Catholics to receive communion at Protestant services, and giving permission for a Catholic homosexual group, Dignity, to celebrate Mass at Seattle's Saint James Cathedral.

"They are Catholics," the Archbishop said. "How could I deny them a church?"

Many theologians and members of the laity were volubly displeased with the actions taken against Curran and Hunthausen. Even some prelates—notably Archbishop Rembert Weakland, of Milwaukee, and Bishop Thomas Gumbleton, of Detroit—publicly criticized the actions of the Vatican. And Bishop James Malone, of Youngstown, Ohio, the outgoing president of the National Conference of Catholic Bishops, told his colleagues last November at the annual meeting of the conference that "no one who reads the newspapers of the past three years can be ignorant of a growing and dangerous disaffection of elements of the Church in the United States from the Holy See."

Throughout this often bitter debate, John Cardinal O'Connor has persistently supported the Vatican's actions and downplayed the divisions in the American Church, thereby greatly underestimating the depth of the dissension. "All of us," he says, "take those things far too seriously. After all, we have a huge body of bishops in the United States, and disagreements are very natural in so large a group, especially when it includes every conceivable temperament, background, experience level, and section of the country. Also, there are always tensions between Rome and the Church in other countries. There are always tensions between every headquarters and activities in the field. As the Archbishop of this huge diocese of New York, I would be shocked if every priest, every nun, every lay person agreed with everything I do. In fact, I think they'd be crazy if they did. There'd be something wrong with them, because I do some dumb things.

"So you're always going to have these tensions, but I do not see them in the Church of the United States at this stage as nearly so volatile as some people think."

As for what he would call the stereotype of this Pope's trying to crush dissent, O'Connor says that "rather than blocking our progress, Pope John Paul II is trying to pull us into the future by reminding us of the truth, which is timeless."

O'Connor does concede that if there are enough cries of alarm about the state of the American Church the Church can be damaged. "It can go through a lot of unnecessary turmoil simply by this constant insistence that the problems are very profound and that there is tremendous tension. But the Church will not crash. The Church is not the stock market. Peter is not the chairman of the board; he is the rock on which Christ has built his Church and not even the gates of hell will prevail against it."

The Vatican is well aware of the Cardinal's support during its time of troubles with the American Church. Last September, the *New York Times* quoted an unnamed senior Vatican official: "The problem with O'Connor is that there is only one of him. The situation in the United States would be different if there were two hundred like him." And the Catholic historian Monsignor John Tracy Ellis told me,

"The Pope is very fond of O'Connor. Of course he is. Don't you think they're two of a kind?"

O'Connor is not displeased when resemblances between him and John Paul II are suggested. He did it himself when we were discussing the reasons that might have gone into his having been chosen Archbishop of New York.

"People say," O'Connor told me, "that the Pope is very much of a linguist. I fool around a bit with languages. He's world-class at languages. I can survive in maybe Italian, French, German, Spanish. I used to work at Chinese and Lithuanian and Polish, but that was just off-on-the-side stuff. I like to preach. I preach every Sunday. I preach every morning. I write all of my own stuff. That is, I write notes—I don't use a text when I preach. The Pope likes to preach. He preaches every Wednesday in St. Peter's Square, and I'm given to understand he writes his own stuff. He travels extensively as Pope. I have traveled extensively through the years." O'Connor made a tent of his fingers. "I think everybody knows I feel a sense of fierce loyalty to the Pope. This sense of loyalty is something I was brought up with. Now, it's obvious that the Pope was personally involved in the selection of the Archbishop of New York, and that he would have clearly specified what characteristics he was looking for."

"Why is it obvious?" I asked.

"Because of the significance of the archdiocese of New York. Since he became Pope, he's been involved in the selection process for any major diocese that has been open. And he knew me. That is, when I first met him in Rome, on the day in 1979 when he ordained me bishop of the military vicariate, he seemed to know about me. I met him again during an *ad limina* visit to Rome. *Ad limina* means 'to the thresholds.' Every residential bishop throughout the world is supposed to make a visit to the Holy Father every five years to report on the condition of his diocese. I made my first visit, however, two years after I was ordained. All the bishops in the New York region were going, and Cardinal Cooke was very insistent that I go, too. On that visit, we all had lunch with the Holy Father. There were about a dozen of us. By accident or design, I was seated across the table from him, and he directed the conversation, the questioning, to me. He mostly wanted to know about the pastoral letter on war and peace. The committee was still working on it, and the Holy Father wanted to know what impact the pastoral letter would have on the Church and on the people. I gave him an essentially positive report. I did get to feel very embarrassed, because during an hour's lunch he spent forty minutes directing questions at me. The next day, after a session in which he spoke to us about the sacrament of penance and reconciliation, each of us went up to the Holy Father to shake hands. When I came up, he said, 'That was a very interesting discussion we had yesterday. I would like you to tell Cardinal Casaroli'—Agostino Casaroli, the Vatican Secretary of State—'what you told me.' I canceled some other things for that evening and saw the Secretary of State, and I think I gave him, as I had the Holy Father, confidence in how we were going about writing the letter. I said there were things in it that wouldn't have been there if I had been writing the draft, but that any other committee member would have said that, too. I told him it would come out a reasonably balanced document.

"Now, did that conversation with the Pope in Rome have anything to do with my appointment as Bishop of Scranton? I can only speculate. I'll tell you how the process works when a diocese is open. A minimum of three names must be presented, and they must have been cleared throughout the region. When it came to Scranton, for instance, Cardinal Krol, of Philadelphia, and all the other bishops of Pennsylvania would have had to review the names. If they approved the names, the papal nuncio would present the list to the Pope. I guess when the Holy Father saw the names I was still fresh in his mind, so that's how I got to Scranton.

"Getting to New York, however, was a different ball game. I had not been back to Rome since that lunch, and nobody heard my name mentioned during any of the discussions, anywhere, about the next Archbishop of New York. Indeed—and this is going to sound pietistic—I would not have recommended me to be Archbishop of New York. I would have questioned whether I had the experience for the immensity, the complexity, of this job. I had lived four years in New York as Cardinal Cooke's auxiliary bishop in the military vicariate, but I was out of the city seventy-five percent of the time. I sat with the bishops of the New York province in their meetings, but I didn't know anything about the administration of this archdiocese."

Two months after O'Connor became Archbishop of New York, he was in Rome, and he received an invitation to lunch from the Pope. As O'Connor came into the room, John Paul II greeted him with a broad smile. "Welcome," he said. "Welcome to the Archbishop of the Capital of the World!"

16

NOT LONG AFTER John O'Connor became the eighth Archbishop of New York, in March 1984, he set off a furious controversy in the city and throughout the country. At issue was whether O'Connor had violated—or, at best, blurred—the separation of church and state by supposedly telling Catholic voters whom to oppose at the polls. A corollary charge was that, contrary to the precepts of the National Conference of Catholic Bishops, he had attacked one candidate, Geraldine Ferraro, by name.

The warfare began when O'Connor said during a television press conference on WPIX, in New York, on June 24,

1984, "I do not see how a Catholic in good conscience can vote for an individual expressing himself or herself as favoring abortion." O'Connor had spoken in a similar vein in Scranton; and on February 1, 1984, the day after his appointment as Archbishop of New York was announced, he had said on Cable News Network, "If a candidate for political office were going to support, to nurture abortion, then as a citizen, I would say that regardless of his or her other qualifications, I could not in conscience vote for that individual for political office." While in February O'Connor had referred only to what he himself would do in the voting booth, by June he seemed to be suggesting a course of political action for all Catholics.

The Governor of New York, Mario Cuomo, challenged the Archbishop little more than a month later. In a front-page interview in the *New York Times*, Cuomo said, "Now you have the Archbishop of New York saying that no Catholic can vote for [Mayor] Ed Koch, no Catholic can vote for [City Comptroller] Jay Goldin, for [then City Council President] Carol Bellamy, nor for [Senator] Pat Moynihan or Mario Cuomo—anybody who disagrees with him on abortion. . . . The Archbishop says, 'You, Mario, are a Catholic who agrees with me that abortion is an evil' . . . The Archbishop says, 'OK, now I want you to insist that everybody believe what we believe.' "

In late June, during an interview in *Newsday*, Cuomo had darkly predicted what might happen to American democracy if the Archbishop's political philosophy, as the Governor defined it, were to prevail: "So I'm a Catholic governor. I'm going to make you all Catholics—no birth control, you have to go to church on Sunday, no abortion. . . . What happens when an atheist wins? Then what do I do? Then they're going to start drawing and quartering me."

The Archbishop, having never before been confronted by so forceful and imaginative a polemicist, was somewhat taken aback. He told the *Brooklyn Tablet*, a Catholic weekly, that he had never made "a statement to the Governor or anyone else such as 'OK, now I want you to insist that everybody believe what we believe.' " On television, and in meetings with reporters, O'Connor kept asking what the reaction would have been if he had said that he did not see how a Catholic could in conscience vote for an individual explicitly expressing himself or herself as favoring racism. He doubted very much whether he would have been attacked for threatening the separation of church and state. Abortion is also a matter of human rights, he said, and it is not an exclusively Catholic concern. Those opposing abortion include Protestants, Jews, and people without any religious faith. Yet if a Catholic bishop speaks against abortion in an election year, O'Connor claimed, he is accused of trying to impose the will of the Catholic Church on the body politic.

A number of editorial writers and columnists had nevertheless been convinced that the Archbishop was not only gravely breaching the separation of church and state but also harming Catholics. In a lead editorial on September 15, the *New York Times* warned, "It might as well be said bluntly: . . . the . . . effort to impose a religious test on the performance of Catholic politicians threatens the hard-won understanding that finally brought America to elect a Catholic President a generation ago." The syndicated columnist Carl Rowan also expressed concern that if such Catholic bishops as John O'Connor did not restrain themselves they would lead Americans into "another period of religious bigotry." Rowan used as a standard of proper clerical behavior a statement by John F. Kennedy: "I believe in an America where the separation of church and state is absolute."

Of all that happened during the 1984 presidential campaign, O'Connor told me one night, he had been most shocked and dismayed by the repeated prophecy that if anti-Catholicism were to rise again in the nation he and such other bishops as Bernard Law, of Boston, who were focusing on abortion would be responsible. "What I was doing, have always done, and will continue to do is present the official teaching of the Church as clearly as I can," he said. "Anyone interested in the teaching of the Church can then decide whether what a candidate says accords with this teaching. Surely I have a right to make clear the teaching of the Church."

The alarmed critics of the Archbishop appeared to question how much of a right he actually did have, as a cleric, to get involved in political issues, especially during a campaign.

Archbishop John Roach, of St. Paul–Minneapolis, in his 1981 presidential address to the National Conference of Catholic Bishops, had tried to clarify the ground rules of the debate from a Catholic perspective: "On the one hand, Catholic theology can and should support and defend the separation of church and state, the principle that religious organizations should expect neither favoritism nor discrimination because they are religious. On the other hand, we should not accept or allow the separation of church and state to be used to separate the church from society."

The Establishment Clause of the First Amendment prohibits the *state's* favoring or discriminating against a religion, but it is not intended to restrict the views of any private organizations or individuals, secular or religious. Speaking before the American Bar Association during the 1984 campaign, when Archbishop O'Connor seemed to some to be on the ballot, Cardinal Bernardin said, "The purpose of the separation of church and state in American society is not to exclude the voice of religion from public debate but to provide a context of religious freedom where the insights of each religious tradition can be set forth and tested." Bernardin also tried to dispel "the mistaken notion that morality is limited only to personal matters."

17

AS THE PRESIDENTIAL CAMPAIGN continued, the Archbishop of New York became even more controversial, for in September he charged that the Democratic vice-presidential candidate, Geraldine Ferraro, had "said some things about abortion relevant to Catholic teachings which are not true." O'Connor was speaking of a two-year-old letter that Ferraro had signed, along with two other Catholic members of Congress, inviting their Catholic colleagues to a breakfast briefing called by Catholics for a Free Choice, an organization that supports a woman's right to have a legal abortion if she so chooses. O'Connor said he had only recently become aware of the letter. The sentence he objected to said that the briefing "will show us that the Catholic position on abortion is not monolithic and that there can be a range of personal and political responses to the issue."

In her book, *Ferraro: My Story* (New York: Bantam, 1985), Geraldine Ferraro wrote, "Did the letter say the Catholic Church's teachings were not monolithic? No. The letter said the Catholic *position* was not monolithic. There are prominent Catholic leaders and theologians who do not agree with the Vatican, along with some nuns, brothers, and priests."

It was O'Connor's view, however, that the phrase "the Catholic position on abortion is not monolithic" could easily be interpreted to mean that the *official* Catholic position on abortion is not monolithic. He believed he had to make it clear that to imply in any way that there had been a change in official Catholic teaching on the issue was to convey an untruth. "I have to speak out when a position of the Church is being misrepresented," he said. "It's one thing to say you're not going to follow the teaching of the Church. But it's quite another thing to change the teaching of the Church, to tell that to others, and fool yourself."

Ferraro answered O'Connor four days after his public criticism of her, in a speech in Scranton. "When I take my oath of office, I accept the charge of serving all the people of every faith, not just some of the people of my own faith," she said. "I also swear to uphold the Constitution of the United States, which guarantees freedom of religion. These are my public duties. And in carrying them out I cannot and I will not, seek to impose my own religious views on others. If ever my conscience or my religious views prevented me from carrying out those duties to the best of my ability, then I would resign my office before I'd betray the public trust."

The Archbishop of New York made no further references to Geraldine Ferraro by name, and she continued to emphasize, as she later did in her book, that while she supported the right of a woman to have an abortion "personally, I have always been against abortion." Her supporters applauded her ability to distinguish between her private views and her responsibilities as a public official, but Charles Krauthammer, writing in *The New Republic* that September, made a point that O'Connor had also stressed in private conversation: "When Geraldine Ferraro . . . says she's 'personally opposed' to abortion, she means this: I wouldn't have one myself and I wouldn't want my children to have one, but I won't go around telling people whether to have one or not. Unfortunately, Ferraro is confusing belief with practice. If a person says, 'I refuse to own slaves, but I won't go around telling others what to do,' it is correct to say that he does not practice slavery, but can one really say he is opposed to it?"

By early September, another archbishop had been accused of advising the populace on how to vote. In a statement that was also signed by seventeen other New England bishops, Archbishop Bernard Law, of Boston, declared abortion to be "the critical issue of the moment," and he counseled voters to judge candidates by their positions on abortion. The controversy over whether the Catholic

Church, as represented by Archbishops O'Connor and Law, had overstepped itself became so intense that on October 13 Bishop James W. Malone, of Youngstown, Ohio, the president of the United States Catholic Conference—an organization of the Catholic hierarchy with different functions from the National Conference of Catholic Bishops but with the same membership—issued an official statement.

Malone said, "We do not take positions for or against particular parties or individual candidates. Bishops are teachers in the Catholic Church, entrusted with the responsibility of communicating the content of Catholic moral teaching and illustrating its relevance to social and political issues. . . . Having stated our positions, we encourage members of our own Church and all citizens to examine the positions of candidates on issues and decide who will best contribute to the common good of society." Bishop Malone said that "we are not a one-issue Church," but that "in speaking of human dignity and the sanctity of life, we give special emphasis to two issues today." He explained, "They are the prevention of nuclear war and the protection of unborn human life. . . . In debating such matters, there is much room for dialogue about what constitutes effective, workable responses; but the debate should not be about whether a response in the political order is needed."

Malone's statement—particularly his emphasis on the point that the bishops do not support or oppose particular parties or candidates—proved somewhat reassuring to a number of the critics of O'Connor and Law, but there were liberal Catholics who continued to blame what they called the "single-issue" bishops for creating a distorted view of the hierarchy as a whole. On October 26, the *National Catholic Reporter* said in an editorial that O'Connor's initial assertion that Catholics could not in good conscience vote for a candidate supporting abortion and his subsequent attack on Geraldine Ferraro had led the Administrative Board of the United States Catholic Conference to ask Bishop Malone to straighten out the misapprehension that the Church was engaging in partisan politics.

Also leading to Malone's clarifying statement, according to some sources in the hierarchy, had been Archbishop Law's insistence that abortion was "the critical issue" in a campaign in which the Democratic candidates for President and Vice-President supported the right to an abortion and the incumbent President did not. Adding to the disquiet were the appearances at Reagan campaign rallies of Cardinal John Krol, of Philadelphia, and Bishops Edward Head, of Buffalo, and Peter Gerety, of Newark. O'Connor made no such appearances.

"It may be unintentional," said the *National Catholic Reporter*, "but O'Connor, Law, and a few other bishops are undermining the authority of the U.S. bishops and of their national conference. The rest of the bishops, attempting to maintain their fraternal spirit, appear unable or unwilling to disagree publicly with the mavericks. And so all the bishops, against their stated will, appear to be partisans in the political arena. And people rightly object."

During the campaign, and after, O'Connor did not indicate that he had the slightest regret about anything he had said. In December, he pointed out that he did not believe, and never had believed, that bishops should make partisan statements, but he felt as strongly as ever that they should address questions of public policy. "Are we to preach morality in a vacuum?" As for his having singled out Geraldine Ferraro, O'Connor noted, "I merely attempted to state Church teaching. If I am remembered as the bishop who broke ranks by naming a candidate with regard to a moral issue, that's not important. What is important is whether I helped to clarify the nature of abortion and the fact that as Catholics we are all bound by the same moral teachings in private and public life."

18

IN CONVERSATIONS during the next few months, O'Connor often referred to the charge that he had implicitly endorsed Ronald Reagan by criticizing Geraldine Ferraro and otherwise focusing on abortion as a political issue. O'Connor was amused by it. "During those same months I was talking about hunger, homelessness, the ill-housed, racism, and the horrors of nuclear war," he said. "These were all issues identified with criticism of the President, but nobody accused me of implicitly endorsing Walter Mondale on those occasions. But controversy, from whatever direction, doesn't surprise me. The Church will always be in tension with the world." He mentioned, with a grin, an incident of internal tension. "I've been told that a long-time financial supporter of St. Patrick's Cathedral has taken to attending Mass somewhere else, because, as he put it, 'the Archbishop is always preaching about the poor.'" The Archbishop said he didn't think it likely that he would stop preaching about the poor.

Nor did he stop criticizing certain actions and policies of the Reagan Administration. He opposed the American mining of the waters off Nicaragua, and he visited that country, with four other bishops, in late February of 1985, as chairman of the Bishops' Committee on Social Development and World Peace. During the trip, and after, O'Connor, while he criticized the Sandinista government for its interference with religious and political freedom, strongly opposed American military support for the counterrevolutionary forces. In written testimony presented before a subcommittee of the House Committee on Foreign Affairs in April of that year, he said, "Direct military aid to any force attempting to overthrow a government with which we are not at war and with which we maintain diplomatic relations is illegal and, in our judgment, immoral, and therefore cannot merit our support."

The previous month, O'Connor had appeared before the House Subcommittee on Housing and Community Development to testify in favor of a bill authorizing $22 billion for new low- and moderate-income housing. The Reagan Administration had eliminated nearly all funds for new housing from its 1986 budget. O'Connor told the subcommittee members, "I honestly don't believe [the housing crisis] is a matter of budget. It's a matter of attitude and leadership."

Among those asking questions of the Archbishop was Representative Mary Rose Oakar of Ohio. During the presidential campaign, she had attacked O'Connor on the House floor for his "single-issue" criticism of Geraldine Ferraro, while pointing out that she herself had voted against abortion. Now Oakar asked the Archbishop his views on the morality of increased military spending while the numbers of the poor were increasing.

"If I were a member of Congress," O'Connor answered, there would be "no question about the moral thing to do." Given the present crisis, he said, "it's wrong" to increase military spending but not housing allocations.

On March 15, Bishop Malone, writing on behalf of the 285 Catholic bishops in the United States, sent a letter to each member of Congress urging that no funds be allocated for the production of MX missiles. Malone pointed out that the bishops, in their 1983 pastoral letter on war and peace, had specifically cited the MX missile as a weapon they had grave reservations about, because it possesses "a capability that threatens to make the other side's retaliatory forces vulnerable." Such weapons, the pastoral letter had said, are potentially destabilizing, because they appear to be useful primarily in a first strike; also, this very expensive weapon is "likely to be vulnerable to attack."

In addition, Malone noted that a year after the pastoral letter, Cardinal Bernardin and Archbishop O'Connor had appeared before the House Foreign Affairs Committee to emphasize the need for Congress to examine whether each new proposed weapons system is absolutely essential to deterrence. By that criterion and on the basis of its cost, Malone wrote, the MX should not be produced. Instead, he said, the funds should go—and he cited O'Connor's testimony before the House Subcommittee on Housing and Community Development—to address "the fact of hunger in our midst, the homeless who walk our streets, the lack of access to adequate health care even for middle-class households."

The day before Malone sent his letter to Congress, Archbishop O'Connor wrote to Representative Henry Gonzalez of Texas, the chairman of the subcommittee before which he had appeared earlier that month. The letter began with a statement that O'Connor had made during his testimony: "I spent some twenty-seven years of my life in the uniform of this country that I love . . . serving those who were trying to protect the human person here and all over the world. I respect the effort of the government to provide the defense that we need and deserve. But I must plead in conscience—personally and as a bishop and as a representative of the U.S. Catholic Conference. I want to go on record with a plea that every dollar budgeted for weapons systems be scrutinized with excruciating care, not only in terms of the morality of any intended use of such systems, but in terms of the urgent needs of some thirty-five million people in our society [and] hundreds of millions throughout the world, who are homeless, who are ill-housed, who are desperate for a restoration of the dignity, the sense of worth and sacredness that can come only with proper housing." In the rest of the letter to Representative Gonzalez, O'Connor, the man who said he had been regarded as the spiritual heir of Genghis Khan when he served on the bishops' committee that drafted the pastoral letter on war and peace, now attacked the MX missile.

19

LOCALLY, meanwhile, the Archbishop, who was regularly telling New Yorkers how much he loved them and how much he needed their love in return, became involved in another bitter controversy. On April 25, 1980, the Mayor had issued Executive Order No. 50, which prohibited all those entering into contracts with the city from discriminating in employment on the basis of "sexual orientation or affectional preference." An addition to previous prohibitions against discrimination on the basis of race, color, sex, handicap, or marital status, this new order was designed to protect homosexuals and bisexuals.

The executive order went into effect on January 21, 1982, but enforcement provisions were not added until the summer of 1983, when Terence Cardinal Cooke, O'Connor's predecessor, was critically ill. The Salvation Army and Agudath Israel, an Orthodox Jewish organization, refused to comply with the order, on the ground that it violated their moral and religious principles. Their contracts with the city included the provision of such social services as day-care facilities, counseling services, and senior-citizen centers. The Archbishop announced that the archdiocese would also resist the executive order, and all three organizations brought suit challenging the Mayor's authority to issue the order—since under the state constitution regulations of that kind are within the province of a legislative body.

The archdiocese had contracts with the city for social services that, together with matching state and federal funds, amounted to more than $100 million a year. They involved funds to help with the operation of the Catholic Home Bureau, Catholic Charities Counseling Services, the Kennedy Child Study Center, and Under 21/Covenant

House. In private conversation, the Archbishop had been saying for some time that if he was ultimately faced with having to comply with Executive Order 50 or do without city funds, he would forgo the money.

On December 13, 1984, O'Connor accepted an invitation by the Mayor to join a press conference. The Mayor was to announce that he was going to ask for a moratorium on converting single-room-occupancy buildings into high-rent housing, and he wanted O'Connor there because it was an idea that O'Connor had been vigorously advocating as a way of at least not reducing current low-income housing. At the press conference, the Archbishop was asked about Executive Order 50. "We will not sell our souls for city contracts," he said, and he told the reporters that if the courts decided against the archdiocese he would somehow find the money to continue the child-care programs without city assistance.

The Mayor, startled, said, "That's impossible."

The Archbishop, who, by faith and practice, believes that nothing is impossible, smiled at the Mayor and went on, "We have said repeatedly that we have no problem whatsoever in employing people admitting to or not admitting to homosexual inclinations. If an individual avows engagement in homosexual activity, then we want to be able to say whether or not we will employ that person in this particular job, and we feel this is a perfectly appropriate thing for any agency. You know, we have five thousand seven hundred youngsters in the child-care agencies, and they are the ones currently at issue." He explained that it would be wholly alien to Catholic teaching to employ in a child-care agency someone who openly advocated homosexuality.

In a long statement printed in *Catholic New York* on January 17, 1985, O'Connor presented his full case against Executive Order 50. One element of the order "seems to have gone completely unnoticed by the public (and I have noted no reference to it in the media)," he wrote, and the article continued:

The Bureau of Labor Services Regulations issued for the enforcement of Executive Order 50 *actually mandate that agencies such as ours "actively recruit" members of all protected groups for all positions . . .*

While Catholic agencies certainly have an obligation to help all peoples and to contribute to the good of the overall community, by the very fact that they are Catholic they must carry out their mission in accordance with Church teaching. The minimum requirement the Church must impose on its employees or prospective employees is that they function within the strictures of Church teaching, whether or not they personally accept such teaching, and that they do not disrupt the Church's mission. Who can make this judgment about an employee or a prospective employee except the Church, or the Church agency, involved? It is the judgment of the Archdiocese of New York that to yield this prerogative would constitute an exceedingly dangerous precedent and invite unacceptable governmental intrusion into and excessive entaglement with the Church's conducting of its own internal affairs.

The Archbishop made it clear that he entirely supported the barring of discrimination on the basis of race, creed, color, national origin, sex, age, handicap, or marital status. But homosexuality, he said, presented a particular problem in terms of Church teaching:

Homosexual inclination, in our theology, is not morally wrong. Homosexual behavior is. We bear no malice toward homosexually active persons. We abhor their being harassed or persecuted in any way. At the same time, we do not believe that homosexual behavior should be declared lawful or that such behavior should be elevated to a protected category.

We do not believe that religious agencies should be required to employ those engaging in or advocating homosexual behavior. We are willing to consider on a case-by-case basis the employment of individuals who have engaged in or may at some future time engage in homosexual behavior. We approach those who have engaged in or may engage in what the Church considers illicit heterosexual behavior the same way. . . . We believe, however, that only a religious agency itself can properly determine the requirements of any particular job within that agency, and whether or not a particular individual meets or is reasonably likely to meet such requirements.

While the Archbishop of New York was maintaining that his opposition to Executive Order 50 was based on Catholic teaching, the diocese of Brooklyn, which includes Queens and which had some $40 million in child-care contracts with the city, not only did not join in the lawsuit but said that it had no problems with meeting the requirements of the executive order.

Auxiliary Bishop Joseph M. Sullivan, the vicar of human services for the Brooklyn diocese, said that signing the agreement did not mean that the diocese implicitly or explicitly approved of homosexual behavior. The diocese would continue to employ people on the basis of their competence for specific jobs and their moral character at work. "If a person did something off the job, in their own home, in their own neighborhood, which was not in conformity with Catholic teaching, I suspect they would be like the rest of us sinners," Bishop Sullivan told a reporter for the *New York Times*. "That's on any issue, whether they got drunk or gambled or committed adultery. I don't believe it's the responsibility or the right of the employer to go monitor what employees do in their own family or neighborhood situations. If there were a flagrant scandal, that might become a problem, but that's the exception." Or, Sullivan continued, if it became clear that an employee of the Brooklyn diocese was "holding out a homosexual life-style to children," the Church would have the right to fire him, even under Executive Order 50. Bishop Sullivan also said that despite Brooklyn's differences with the archdiocese of New York on this matter "it is very important, in the public perception, that we are a united Church." But he apparently could not resist adding that if a diocese were to fire all [its] employees who violated Church teachings "probably a hundred percent would get caught in the net."

Even less diplomatic was Monsignor Howard Basler, the director of social action for Catholic Charities in the Brooklyn diocese. He said in the *Brooklyn Tablet* that he saw no need for the lawsuit aimed at expunging Executive Order 50 because recognizing the right of homosexuals not to be discriminated against in employment "in no way compromises Catholic practice or belief."

Despite the split between the two dioceses—a rare occurrence in any part of the country—O'Connor did not waver in his insistence that he would not abide by Executive Order 50. He was vehemently criticized by spokesmen for homosexual organizations and by many liberals, and was also urged by the *New York Times*, in an editorial, to seek some form of accommodation to "Mayor Koch's humane order." The *New York Times* added, "Hiring a homosexual neither promotes nor condones homosexuality. All it does is deny the right of a public agent to deny citizens the right to work because of private life-style."

20

IN JUNE 1984, as the controversy became more heated, the Archbishop celebrated an evening Mass at Our Lady of the Rosary Church, at Battery Park in lower Manhattan. He had come to make a pastoral visit to members of Courage, an organization of homosexuals that is sponsored by the archdiocese and whose members are pledged to lead celibate lives. O'Connor told some fifty people in attendance that while he intended to enlarge the Church's ministry to homosexuals he could not be a party to Executive Order 50. "We would rather close our child-care agencies than violate

Church teachings," he said. He also noted that somewhat over a year earlier, before he became Bishop of Scranton, he had knelt in the back of that very church during a Mass in which members of Courage had participated. "You didn't know I was there," he said, "and I didn't know I'd be back." On this night in June, the Archbishop, before he left, was presented with a T-shirt that said, in bold letters, COURAGE.

In September, he agreed to meet at the New York Catholic Center on First Avenue with a delegation from the Coalition for Lesbian and Gay Rights. When they came into the building, "the guard at the desk to their left, who knew who they were, said, 'This way, ladies—or whatever,'" according to an account in the *National Catholic Reporter*. "As they went up in the elevator, another person who also obviously knew who they were whispered, 'Good luck.'" At the meeting, no minds were changed concerning Executive Order 50. Two weeks later, Karen Doherty, one of the participants and a member of the Conference for Catholic Lesbians, wrote a letter to the Archbishop that said, in part:

We were glad for the opportunity to speak to you in person. It was very important for us that you see us as we are, very ordinary, everyday people. You impressed me as being a very straightforward, sensitive, and capable man. What I particularly appreciated was the fact that I did not feel talked down to or held at a distance because I am a lesbian woman.

I am saddened, as I know the others are, that we cannot today reach a meeting of our hearts and minds on the issue of homosexuality. Perhaps some day.

I wish you health and happiness in your future years with us in New York. I wanted you to know that, while we strongly disagree, I have a great deal of personal respect for you and the fact that you are willing to stand up for what you believe.

Three weeks later, the Archbishop answered:

DEAR KAREN:
Your letter . . . was extraordinarily kind and touched me deeply. I am indeed grateful. It is my sincere hope and prayer that

through the years ahead I will be able to serve you in some way that you will consider helpful. My convictions about church teachings are very deep. I do not anticipate a change in such teachings, and neither do I see it precluding our loving one another as sisters and brothers in Christ.

Please believe that I will give deeply sincere consideration to any recommendations that can help us in that regard in accordance with the tenets of the church which I am certain we both love.

You and your associates are very much in my masses and my prayers, and I ask that you keep me in yours as well.

Faithfully in Christ,
JOHN J. O'CONNOR

The battle of Executive Order 50 was won by the archdiocese, the Salvation Army, and Agudath Israel when the Court of Appeals, New York's highest court, ruled six to one on June 28, 1985, that "no matter how well-intentioned his actions may be, the Mayor may not unlawfully infringe upon the legislative powers reserved to the City Council." The court struck down the section of Executive Order 50 that had added "sexual orientation or affectional preference" to previous city, state, and federal antibias laws, saying that under the separation of powers the executive branch cannot make such an addition. In September, the Mayor decided not to appeal the decision, saying that the city's case was weak and would probably lose in the United States Supreme Court.

The Mayor remained determined, however, to bring homosexuals under the protection of antidiscrimination measures. He expressed renewed support for the so-called gay-rights bill that had first been introduced in the New York City Council in 1971 and had been brought back every year since but had never passed. The Mayor and other supporters of the bill thought that it might finally be passed by the City Council in 1986, because it included a religious exemption. No religious organizations would be required to use other than religious criteria for hiring employees. Also, the bill disavowed affirmative-action hiring on the basis of sexual orientation. And the bill provided that it could not be interpreted to make legal any behavior that would violate the state penal code.

To allay any further fears, the bill explicitly stated, "It is not the function of this civil-rights statute to promote a particular group or community; its purpose is rather to ensure that individuals who live in our society will have the opportunity to pursue their own beliefs and conduct their lives as they see fit within the limits of the law."

The bill, which is informally known as Intro. 2, prohibits discrimination in housing, employment, and public accommodations because of "sexual orientation," which is defined as "heterosexuality, homosexuality, or bisexuality."

In a series of editorials, the *New York Times* urged the City Council to pass the bill. One of these editorials included a reference aimed directly at the Archbishop. It recalled that Pope John Paul II, in his 1981 encyclical "On Human Work," had said, "Work bears a particular mark of man and of humanity, the mark of a person operating within a community of persons." Accordingly, the *Times* said, "New York City . . . has to demand that homosexuals be deemed part of humanity and community."

In a subsequent editorial, the *New York Times* asserted, "This is not a bill 'validating' homosexuality, as some opponents fear and some homosexuals would prefer. It is a civil rights bill, affirming protections that belong to all citizens and reinforcing the right of some not to have the revelation of their homosexuality devalue citizenship." A coalition of religious leaders, including Paul Moore, Jr., the Episcopal Bishop of New York, and the Reverend Robert Polk, the executive director of the Council of Churches of the City of New York, also expressed approval of the bill.

O'Connor was no less opposed to this bill than he had been to Executive Order 50, and this time he persuaded the diocese of Brooklyn to join him in opposition. On February 6, O'Connor and Bishop Francis J. Mugavero, of Brooklyn, issued a joint statement in which they claimed that the gay-rights bill was "exceedingly dangerous to our society," explaining, "We believe it is clear that what the bill primarily and ultimately seeks to achieve is the legal approval of homosexual conduct and activity, something that the Catholic Church, and indeed other religious faiths, consider to be morally wrong. Our concern in this regard is heightened by the realization that it is a common perception of the public that whatever is declared legal, by that very fact, becomes morally right."

The statement also emphasized a point that O'Connor had been making for months, which was that by defining "sexual orientation" as "heterosexuality, homosexuality, or bisexuality" the bill, if it became law, would have the effect of giving the three forms of behavior equal legitimacy. By doing so, the joint statement said, the legislation "would seriously undermine the moral education and values of our youth and the stability of the family in our society."

John P. Hale, who handles some of the legal affairs of the New York archdiocese and who had been in charge of the litigation against Executive Order 50, told me on the day the joint statement was issued, "If this bill is passed, sure, we'd be above the fray, because of the religious exemption. But we look at impending legislation as it affects not only the institutional operations of the Church but also society as a whole. The teaching function of the Church is very much involved in the legislation. This law will teach that the homosexual life-style is OK."

The Mayor continued to maintain that the bill was no more or less than a basic civil-rights measure. "Allowing people the right to a job, to . . . housing, to go to public accommodations is a fundamental right without in any way giving imprimatur to their life-style," he said.

21

ONCE AGAIN, as with abortion, O'Connor was in opposition to most of the city's leading public officials, its most influential newspaper, and the sizable number of liberals in journalism, the arts, and other fields. He also appeared to be getting little support from the city's Catholics. A *Daily News* poll in early February reported that while 56 percent of the Catholics polled did not think there was a need for a gay-rights law, 72 percent felt that religious organizations should neither actively support nor actively oppose such a bill. The poll results were printed on a Sunday, and that morning I asked O'Connor about the poll as he was on his way to the passageway in the back of St. Patrick's Cathedral that leads to his Madison Avenue residence.

"Well, the poll was based on only five hundred and three people, and I'm not so sure that's a very credible sampling," he said. "But, in any case, suppose the sampling were large, and ninety percent felt this way? I would still agree with what Bishop Fulton Sheen once said: 'What the world needs is a voice that is right not when the world is right but when the world is wrong.' Moreover, in this case I think that when the people do understand the ramifications of this issue they'll be grateful we spent months of legal time opposing Executive Order Fifty and months conferring with the Brooklyn diocese so that together we could elucidate the effects of this legislation."

The homosexual-rights bill was passed by the City Council on March 20, 1986, by a vote of twenty-one to fourteen. The Cardinal said he would fight to overturn the legislation.

While the bill was still pending, I asked the Cardinal why the leadership of the Brooklyn diocese had changed its

mind with regard to barring discrimination against homosexuals.

O'Connor said that soon after Executive Order 50 was
dissolved by the Court of Appeals he had told Bishop
Mugavero that Catholics had become confused when the
two bishops took such different positions on that order.
O'Connor had suggested that they try to resolve those differences, and after several months of meetings by staff
members of the two dioceses the joint statement was agreed
on. There had been speculation by supporters of the bill, I
told O'Connor, that he had put considerable pressure on
Bishop Mugavero to align Brooklyn with New York. And a
member of Mugavero's staff told me there had indeed been
pressure from O'Connor.

O'Connor looked pained. "If I were Bishop Mugavero, I
would be exceedingly insulted," he said. "It's his diocese. I
have no authority there. That's Church law. And he has
been a bishop far, far longer than I have. Also, if this theory
were true, why didn't I 'pressure' or 'threaten' Mugavero
during that long, difficult struggle over Executive Order
Fifty? That would have been the time." He paused, then
said, "I still see in the papers the argument that the Church
is taken care of in this bill because of the religious exemption, so why am I involved? Well, aside from the harm to the
society as a whole from this bill, they may say we have an
exemption but they can still harass us."

O'Connor was alluding to two incidents during the long
litigation over Executive Order 50. Many of the city's homeless are sheltered at night by Catholic churches, and the
Church is paid by the city for the heating costs. In the spring
of 1985, certain city officials had refused to reimburse the
Church for those expenses because it had not complied with
Executive Order 50. O'Connor had called the Mayor, and the
ban had been lifted. Then, in May of that year, as O'Connor
recalled with some bitterness, all the preparations had been
made, and the rent paid, for a Yankee Stadium youth rally
and prayer service, at which forty thousand young people
were expected. Shortly before the date of the rally, archdi-

ocesan officials were told they could not use the stadium because the Church was in violation of Executive Order 50. O'Connor let it be known that if the decision was not rescinded he would not only call the Mayor but also inform the newspapers and broadcasting stations that forty thousand Catholic youngsters had been barred from Yankee Stadium. The rally was held.

As we walked through the passageway toward the residence, I asked O'Connor about an exchange a few days earlier between him and Paul Moore, Jr., the Episcopal Bishop of New York. Bishop Moore had charged that the Cardinal had been "morally wrong" in bringing a lawsuit against Executive Order 50 and was now being "immoral" in opposing the antidiscrimination bill in the City Council. "Anything that sets back the rights of an individual is not right," Moore had told the *New York Times.* O'Connor had icily responded in that newspaper, "The Bishop feels the need to make public comments about my sense of morality. I don't feel the same need. I can only assume he's following his conscience."

O'Connor told me he had nothing to add to his statement. Indeed, he seemed quite pleased with it.

A friend of the Cardinal's, listening in, asked him if the repeated attacks during the repeated controversies didn't get to him after a while. (Not many days before, Gloria Steinem, on being asked by *New York* magazine to list the worst things about the city, had cited O'Connor and AIDS.)

"Well, the lashes don't hurt until you take your shirt off and it sticks to your blood," O'Connor said, with a grin. "I'm called the controversial Archbishop of New York whenever I'm introduced," he went on, without a grin. "Yet I am simply saying what the Church teaches. Of course I don't like confrontation. People think of me as combative, aggressive, but if the Holy Father were to call me tomorrow and say, 'You've had your place in the sun, now go write a book or something,' that would be fine. I would be delighted to go home to Scranton."

22

THERE IS no indication that Pope John Paul II is going to transfer John J. O'Connor to relative obscurity or, indeed, is in any way displeased with O'Connor's leadership of the archdiocese. His naming of O'Connor, on April 24, 1985, as one of twenty-eight new cardinals was seen as an obvious sign of his endorsement of O'Connor's work as archbishop. O'Connor himself saw the appointment that way. "In deepest humility," he said at a Fordham University luncheon, "I must confess, it does have a nice ring to it." But, delighted as he was, he noted somewhat mordantly on the day he was named, "I'm from southwest Philadelphia. I played a lot of hardball there, but never the variety I've discovered here."

As before, however, O'Connor's notification of his new position in the Church had been by way of a curveball. On April 19, he had once again received a call from Archbishop Pio Laghi, the Pope's personal representative in the United States. After some banter, Laghi said he knew that O'Connor was due in Rome for the ordination of New York's new auxiliary bishop, Edward Egan. Could he stay a couple of extra days?

"No," O'Connor said. "I have a Mass for the handicapped at the cathedral here the following Sunday."

"That's really a shame," Laghi said, "because there's a consistory scheduled for May twenty-fifth, and your name is on the list of new cardinals."

O'Connor became the sixth Cardinal Archbishop of New York. The line began in 1875, when Archbishop John McCloskey was appointed the first cardinal not only in New York but in America. There followed John Farley, Patrick

Hayes, Francis Spellman, and Terence Cooke. Before going to Rome, O'Connor appeared at the Yankee Stadium rally, "Youth Alive in Christ," that some city officials had tried to ban. As he made his entrance, the huge scoreboard lit up with the message "WE HAVE A CARDINAL!"

While the Cardinal-designate was in Rome and was about to be formally elevated by the Pope, he delivered the homily on the occasion of Edward Egan's celebration of his first Pontifical Mass. O'Connor told Egan that being a bishop involved bearing "overwhelming burdens." Among them was the need to be "a certain trumpet," speaking the truth whether it was "welcome or unwelcome." And sometimes the truth "falls on deaf ears," the Cardinal-designate said to the new Bishop. "Sometimes those who disagree with your articulation of the truth resent you as its messenger."

Two days later, on May 25, Pope John Paul II addressed the twenty-eight new princes of the Church in St. Peter's Square, saying, "Christ renews to these who have been chosen the task which He gave to the apostles as they were about to leave on the first mission of evangelization. They must go out to their brethren 'with the wisdom of serpents and the innocence of doves' and bring to everyone the good news of salvation. They must have no illusions about the way they will be received. They will often be made a sign of contradiction, sometimes even persecution.... Today, we invoke Him with special fervor, that He may come down upon the new cardinals, filling them with His gifts. May each of them be faithful to his own tasks, even to the shedding of blood, according to the ancient formula which finds in the scarlet insignia a precise and expressive reflection."

After the Pope's homily was completed, each new cardinal came to him and knelt. The Pope placed on each head the zucchetto (a red skullcap) and the red biretta (a stiff, square cap with ridges on its upper side). When all twenty-eight had taken office, the total number of cardinals under the age of eighty had risen to a hundred and twenty. (After a cardinal reaches the age of eighty, he can no longer vote, if the occasion arises, for the next Pope.) In addition to voting in papal elections, the cardinals serve as advisers to the Pope, but they have no special powers—only the aura that the prestige of the office provides.

During his week in Rome, the new Cardinal took the ceremonies and the festivities in stride, but he did express shock at the large size of the press contingent from New York City. The phenomenon was also of interest to another new cardinal, Bernard Law, of Boston, who was heard asking one of his aides, "Does New York have as many media as we do?"

Though obviously delighted by his elevation, Cardinal O'Connor kept saying to friends, "All I want to do is get back home and get back to work." In an interview in *Catholic New York* that appeared on his return to the city, he revealed to Anne Buckley, the editor, that he had only recently recovered from a kidney infection, which had been draining his energy for more than a year. "I've been going at half speed since I've been in New York," he told her. "I haven't been able to give my best shot . . . at meetings, preaching, celebrating Masses, public appearances. I've been dragged down with this infection. . . . I haven't felt vigorous in more than a year, and I'm not accustomed to that."

This information, Anne Buckley commented, was rather astonishing "from one who during those fourteen months has traveled the length and breadth of his ten-county archdiocese and visited three continents . . . become a familiar face on TV and a frequent voice in Washington . . . and survived what he called 'an eggbeater' of controversy, all the while positioning a careful plan for the administration of the Church of New York that has involved a round of listening sessions with priests, deacons, and religious." On returning to New York, O'Connor spoke of how reinvigorated he felt, but the difference in force and stamina before and after his elevation to the College of Cardinals has not been easily discernible.

In October 1985, the Cardinal made Catholic Church history in New York by appointing Dolores Bernadette Grier, of Harlem, to be one of four vice-chancellors in the archdiocese. Her specific responsibility is community relations. (Of the others, one supervises priests and the other two are engaged in administrative work.) Ms. Grier, a convert, who had been involved in various community services in the archdiocese for thirty-five years, became the first member of the laity, the first woman, and the first black to serve as a vice-chancellor. The Cardinal made it clear that her work would not be limited to black members of the Church but would encompass all the parishes in the archdiocese.

At lunch one day in the Cardinal's residence, I mentioned Ms. Grier's appointment to Monsignor Patrick J. Sheridan, vicar for religious of the archdiocese. The Monsignor, whose hair is white, and who has the look and speech of the headmaster of an exclusive private school, said, "You realize that in the nineteen-thirties and nineteen-forties such a thing was unheard of. A woman chancellor! A member of the laity as chancellor! But in New York, as throughout the country, lay people have been very actively participating in Church affairs for the past twenty years or so. They've become an important part of the pastoral ministry. They're on the staffs of parishes—and I mean not just in schools. And there's more to come. There's much more to come."

23

THE INVOLVEMENT of greater numbers of lay Catholics in parish and diocesan affairs is one of many results of the Second Vatican Council, which was called by Pope John

XXIII and lasted from October 1962 to December 1965. The Pope, who died before the Council had completed its work, had long believed, he once said, that "the past will never return" and "new situations require new dispositions." Elected Pope in 1958, at the age of seventy-six, John XXIII took only three months to announce his intention of convoking the twenty-first ecumenical (universal) council in the history of the Church. He wanted to renew the Church. It should no longer be a fortress protecting the faithful from the world but must move into the world and serve the world by working for peace and social justice. "I have to open the windows," he said, "so that the Church can speak to the world in the language it can understand."

The opening of the windows changed life inside the Church as well as the Church's relationship with the world. The documents, and the spirit, of Vatican II made it possible for lay Catholics to become more deeply involved with their Church. The priest no longer celebrated Mass with his back to the congregation (as he had done in order to face the altar), and he no longer spoke in Latin but instead said Mass in the language of the worshipers.

Furthermore, Vatican II proclaimed that the Church is the whole people of God, and therefore everyone in it has a vocation to serve. In the phrase of Church historian Thomas Bokenkotter, there is a "common priesthood of the faithful." Not every one of the faithful can celebrate Mass; only an ordained priest can. But those of the faithful who wish to participate in Church affairs can and do get involved in much more of the decision making than could ever have been imagined in previous centuries. They manage the finances of parishes, plan liturgies, work in administrative positions, read the scriptures in church, and otherwise make their presence actively known. Traditionally, the lay Catholic had been expected—and had agreed—to "pray, pay, and obey." That phase of the past will not return.

If bishops and cardinals were to keep up with the new openness of the Church, they, too, had to change. They

mortgages for the building of housing. I am very seriously praying over and considering putting another three million dollars
into such a loan. But this is a drop in the bucket. Nothing serious
will be done until we truly, passionately believe in the worth, the
dignity, the sacredness of every person. . . . These are public-
policy issues but they go far beyond the political. They go into the
depths of the theological. As a church we have no choice but to
concern ourselves with these matters. . . .

Read the latest book by Senator Moynihan, *Family and Nation.* We are told that one-quarter of the children in our country—
one-fourth of the children in our country—are living in poverty,
absolute poverty. We are told that more than half of the babies
that will be born over the next ten years, if the trend continues,
will be born of unmarried teenagers. . . . We must concern ourselves—whether we are accused of imposing our wills on the rest
of society or not—with pending legislation. We must ask ourselves
what kind of society we want to have, what kind of society human
beings deserve. . . . We must involve ourselves in the fashioning
of such a society.

I have seen a poll that says that more than seventy percent of
the Catholics in this archdiocese do not want the Church involving itself in pending laws. . . . What is the Church supposed to
involve itself in? There are some who do not want the Church
involved in the moral issues of war. There are some who don't
want the Church involved in abortion, in housing, in hunger.
Then I must ask: What is the Church? What is the Church of
Christ? What do we mean by the human family? Is the Church
simply a voice that tells you very, very legitimately how grateful
it is for your sacrifices in maintaining your marriages and your
families? Is the Church simply an institution that offers a Mass
every Sunday?

The Cardinal paused. Then, leaning forward, he said,

You are the Church. *You are the Church.* Those who say that they
don't want the Church involved in issues of public policy are
saying they don't want *you* involved. I am not the Church or the
archdiocese of New York. I am its formal official teacher. You are
the Church—and thousands and hundreds of thousands like you.
I want you involved. I believe that Christ wants you involved. I
want you particularly involved, because you have done such a

marvelous job in trying to create your own families, at whatever sacrifice. You have demonstrated so much courage. You have launched into the deep. As Jesus told Simon, 'Put out into deep water and lower your nets for a catch.'

The Cardinal began to quicken his rhythm. "You have looked more profoundly into the meaning of marriage. You have not treated it trivially, superficially, frivolously, concerned only about yourselves. So I want *you* involved. *You* have been given the grace, the tremendous grace, to recognize the importance—the crucial, the critical importance—of your family. I plead with you." He was speaking more slowly. "I plead with you to recognize the importance of the entire human family, and to bring to the human family here in the archdiocese of New York those gifts, those charisms, that tremendous goodness that has brought you here today."

24

As THE CARDINAL tries to bring the archdiocese of New York into the world, he is, by mission and temperament, far from the remote, autocratic American cardinals of generations past. He is as familiar to most New Yorkers as the anchors on the television news programs they watch. Not only does he himself appear on the news but his Sunday-morning homilies are rebroadcast Sunday evenings on radio station WMCA.

The Cardinal is habitually informal, whether he is answering questions on the street from a passerby or at his dinner table at the residence. His sense—it could be called a driven sense—of the Church in service to the entire community leads him to lobby for more and better low-income housing throughout the city, and that interest brings him to neighborhoods not accustomed to seeing a prince of the Church. Because he is a vivid presence in New York, some of whose residents may wish he had remained on the high seas, many people write to him—as many as five hundred on some days. The letters that can be taken care of by Catholic Charities or by other offices of the archdiocese do not reach him, but all the personal letters do, and he is obsessive about trying to answer each of them eventually. The letter he cherishes most came "from a young woman who had simply heard me say something on television about the right to life of the unborn baby. She wrote to tell me she had literally been on her way to an abortion. And simply because of hearing what I said on television she had decided to let her baby live."

While he is addressed as Boss by some of those who work for him, there is no fear or servility in their relations with him. There is authority in his bearing and his way of speaking, but it is not coercive. This does not mean that he suffers silently when mistakes have been made. However, by contrast with some autocratic cardinals of the not-so-distant past—William O'Connell, of Boston, say, and John Patrick Cody, of Chicago, and James Francis McIntyre, of Los Angeles—O'Connor does not give the sense at any time of being larger than life. He is called Your Eminence, but even in his robes on his throne in St. Patrick's Cathedral he has no mystery about him, nor does he try to cultivate any.

On the third floor of the residence are his quarters. A small refrigerator contains milk and fruit, and there is usually Raisin Bran in a cupboard. The bedroom is largely taken up by a full-size bed, over the head of which is a cheerful, boldly colored painting of Christ on a donkey entering Jerusalem. On a dresser is a pile of red skullcaps.

The Cardinal, having watched the news on television, is usually ready for bed around eleven-thirty, but, being an insomniac, he usually doesn't stay asleep long; he averages about four hours' sleep a night, in fragments. Accordingly, he reads much in the small hours. Interviewing him for a book on the changing American Church, Professor Eugene Kennedy was rather taken by how well informed O'Connor proved to be about both standard and very recent books on theology and Church history. "Some of the books and monographs he talked about have not been published here yet," Kennedy said. "O'Connor had got them from Europe. He'd read a lot of things that I think many other bishops don't even know are in existence."

The Cardinal's considerable library is in his study, off the bedroom. It is the most pleasant room in the residence, with stained-glass windows, a cathedral ceiling, and a long conference table, at which the Cardinal writes notes for speeches, answers mail, and does some of his administrative work. His quarters also include a sitting room and a private chapel, where his morning prayers begin, he says, "before the world wakes up." On the walls of his sitting room and two guest rooms are family photographs and snapshots of various Church figures, including the frequent bearer of surprising tidings, Archbishop Pio Laghi.

O'Connor's days, when he is in the city, are spent mostly at the Catholic Center on First Avenue and Fifty-fifth Street. One afternoon there, I mentioned the late Cardinal Spellman, who had had little tolerance for dissent, often punishing priests who disagreed with him by transferring them to much less attractive positions than they had held. He had also had no use for labor unions, as he had demonstrated in 1949, when he tried to break a strike by the archdiocesan grave diggers by ordering seminarians from St. Joseph's Seminary in Yonkers to dig the graves.

In *The American Pope*, a biography of Cardinal Spellman, which recounts the story of the grave diggers' strike, author John Cooney quotes Monsignor Myles Burke, who taught at St. Joseph's Seminary when Spellman faced down the grave diggers. Burke said, "Very few seminarians wouldn't go, because they were frightened about what would happen if they refused."

I asked the present Cardinal what he would have done if he had been a seminarian at St. Joseph's in 1949 and had been asked to pick up a shovel and help break the grave diggers' strike.

O'Connor thought for some time, and finally said, "I can imagine that I would not have been much of a hero. Because I was a seminarian, my entire life would have depended on the Cardinal. Remember, this was some thirty-five years ago. Much of my schooling would have been paid for by the archdiocese. And the seminary would have been very tightly structured. Also, I would probably have had a tremendous feeling of awe with regard to the Cardinal, and probably a great deal of fear. This does not imply that I think the Cardinal himself was a man to be feared, but I would have feared him as the Cardinal, as the Archbishop of New York. So I would probably have picked up a spade."

Cardinal O'Connor fingered the cross resting on his chest. "Now, as for the present, I can't imagine myself requiring that sort of thing from a seminarian. And, *a fortiori*, I would not do it myself. But, you know, a lot of years have passed and there have been a lot of new understandings in the Church, including a better understanding of the principles of justice."

He paused, frowned, and said, "I should have modified what I just told you about what I would have done as a seminarian back then. Picking up a spade would not have been mere cowardice or self-interest on my part. I just wouldn't have thought to go against the Cardinal. I wouldn't have thought to question the Cardinal. As a young seminarian, I would have taken it for granted that the Cardinal was right. If he said it's right to do something, it's right. But we are in a new age now. The impulse of the Second Vatican Council precipitated so many of the activities in which we in the Church are currently engaged. But you should realize that the whole world, not only the Church, has developed new insights. What was considered a just wage fifty years ago, for instance, would be appalling now. Catholics and their bishops are, after all, part of the society in which they live, and as society keeps developing new insights, so do they."

In a recent book, *The American Catholic Experience* (New York: Doubleday, 1985), Jay P. Dolan, a professor of history at the University of Notre Dame, writes, "As Pope John XXIII said more than twenty years ago, a new day is dawning for Roman Catholicism. Today it is still early morning." I asked if the Cardinal agreed.

"Yes, I think we are still dawning in the world," he replied. "We could be looking at many innovations, some brand-new structures in the Church in the years ahead. But they will be evolutionary. I am passionately committed to the concept that just as a person at the age of forty is essentially the same person he was in the womb—despite all the developments that have taken place in him—so the Church today is essentially as it was nineteen hundred years ago. But at the same time we are maturing, growing, evolving. Consider, for example, that something like sixty percent of all Catholics are now of the Third World. I was in Rome last week and got into conversations with cardinals from Korea, Nigeria, and Uganda. They told me that their seminaries are bursting at the seams." O'Connor smiled. "I believe we're going to see the day when Catholic missionaries from Africa and Asia will be coming to the United States to evangelize here."

The Cardinal believes that, as the Church keeps changing, more of its members will come to realize that they *are* the Church. "As it is now," he said, "when you think about it, how much real power do I have? In Spellman's time, they used to call the Cardinal's residence the Powerhouse. Well, I had a long discussion about power with some of the sisters today. I showed them that whatever power I have is remarkably limited. Remarkably. I have some moral suasion, I hope. But I can't call out any troops. I can't even say to one of those nuns, 'You go there!' I can't reassign a nun, because she works for a religious institution over which I do not have control. I can tell one of our priests that I'm reassigning him, but if he refuses to leave, all I can do—and I wouldn't do it—is turn the matter over to the civil authority. Power is a very nebulous, ambiguous thing. There's an awful lot of absurdity in the concept. So if you're in this job the thing to do is try to be decent, try to believe in people, fight the battles you think have to be fought, and take your lumps."

25

AS SOMEONE who has taken a lot of lumps, the Cardinal gives the impression of being unyielding—stubborn—in his positions. But Eugene Kennedy, who has studied American Catholic bishops, maintains that O'Connor is more flexible than he appears. "He changed a lot of his views on the war in Vietnam, and he has practically repudiated the book he wrote about it. And, for all his dissents while he was a member of the bishops' committee drafting the pastoral letter on war and peace, he came around and supported the majority opinion not only in the final vote but after. Of course, part of that came out of his experience in the Navy, and now in the bishops' conference, that once something is settled you act in harmony with the results."

On a number of issues, however, O'Connor has not changed his views. In January 1986, he issued a pastoral letter to be read at all weekend Masses. The letter called attention to the thirteenth anniversary of the Supreme Court's decision in *Roe* v. *Wade* and described it as "a tragic event in our nation's history . . . a day of national infamy." He added, in a homily during Mass at St. Patrick's Cathedral, "During the time it takes to listen to the pastoral message that I'm reading right now, six innocent human beings have been killed in their mothers' womb." Knowing that there were reporters in the cathedral, the Cardinal went on to say, "In 1984, when I talked strongly on the issues, I was accused of doing so because the national election campaign was in progress. I said then, 'I'll be talking about this in 1985 and 1986 and until the day I die.'"

Nor has O'Connor changed his view that a bishop has the same right to speak about public issues as anyone else. And he is getting more annoyed by what he considers the unfairness of attacks on him for doing just that. He told *Catholic New York*, "I get increasingly distressed that when Catholics express their views as citizens, there is, in some sectors, a claim that we are attempting to impose our views on the rest of society. But when other communities demand legislation that may be in conflict with Church teaching, this seems at times to be considered appropriate. Catholics are not second-class citizens."

Since O'Connor's relentless opposition to the gay-rights bill in the City Council had caused the resentment against him in the homosexual community to grow considerably in the months after his exchange of letters with Karen Doherty in 1984, I called Ms. Doherty to find out if her view of the Cardinal had changed. A businesswoman, she had just come back from a trip out of the country. She was amiable and forthright. "No, I haven't changed my mind about the Cardinal," she said. "I strongly disagree with a number of his positions—obviously including his opposition to the bill in the City Council—but I respect him. I'll tell you something I didn't put in the letter that was printed. O'Connor's predecessor, Cardinal Cooke, would never meet with us. He preferred to ignore the whole issue. But one of his secretaries did meet with us, and he did not have the decency to shake our hands. But O'Connor, at the very beginning of our meeting, made a point of shaking everybody's hand."

She went on to say, "That letter of mine shocked a lot of my gay and lesbian friends, and some of the nuns and priests who support us. The tendency is to say, 'If you're with us you're good, but if you're not you're bad.' But I couldn't have said anything different from what I said in that letter. It would have been a lie. He is a very human person, and he has a lot of integrity. I got the impression that if he was alone in an opinion he'd go to the mat holding that opinion. That's why he's a tremendous adversary. And he has integrity in the way he relates to people. He didn't have to answer my letter. He could have ignored it, the way Cooke would have. It was a risk to write to me, to treat a woman who had identified herself as a lesbian the way you'd treat a human being. I'll always remember that when I first saw him coming into the room he looked grim. He'd never met with a group like ours before. I looked at him, and I cracked a smile. He smiled right back. I said to myself, 'Well, there's a little hope.' I think he has a shot at being the first American Pope, because he so strongly projects the images of leadership. There are bishops toward whom I feel more warmly, or who might feel more warmly toward me than he does, but I don't see any of them with that quality of leadership. He's like a warrior bishop."

The Cardinal tends to see himself in less grand terms. Writing in *Catholic New York*, he noted that he becomes especially aware of the ephemeral stature of a prince of the Church when he visits nursing homes: "I find it a very powerful reminder to . . . see people who were once prestigious, powerful, healthy, and are now helpless, dependent on others to feed them and clean them. You see enough of that and it's hard to take yourself seriously and think of yourself as a figure of historical significance."

If he is remembered, O'Connor said to me, with a sigh, it will probably be for his disagreements with the Mayor rather than for his Mass each morning. In the weekly paper of the archdiocese, he had said, "Every priest would like to be remembered as a priest and all that conveys, rather than as a public figure with all that conveys. I regularly go down to the crypt under St. Patrick's Cathedral, and I look at the tombs of my predecessors, Cardinal Cooke, Cardinal Spellman . . . they're all there. Right in the center is the next marble block with no inscription. That's reserved for me. And all that's important when I move into that crypt is that I have served New York as a good priest."

Early one Sunday afternoon, at the residence, the Cardinal was looking back at his years in the seminary preparing him to be a priest. "I didn't take to the seminary," he told me. "I cordially disliked my early years there. We lived in what was in its day one of the most disciplined and demanding seminaries in the United States. For the first five years, our living circumstances were—well, childish. We lived in dormitories, and the discipline was such that we had no time for ourselves. For the last four years, I lived in a room—a very simple, basic room, but at least a room."

I asked him if he had thought of leaving the seminary at any point during his first five years there. Several priests nearby came closer to hear him answer.

"Oh," the Cardinal said, "maybe five times some days." The priests roared with laughter. "And ten times on other days."

"What kept you from leaving?" I asked.

"I never lost the conviction that I was where I should be. No, that's not true." The Cardinal laughed. "I never thought I was where I should be, but I did know that where I was going was the place I should be going. I thought the goal was worth the sacrifice. I wanted to be a priest, and I was prepared to put up with very severe rigors, emotional and physical."

For all his disappointment every time he thought he was about to return to Pennsylvania as a parish priest, only to be moved higher once more, the Cardinal hardly seems to be suffering as a prince of the Church. Yet a sense of loss does remain. Linda Stevens, a journalist and a friend of his, tells of driving with the Archbishop and Monsignor James McCarthy, one of his secretaries, near Emmaus, in eastern Pennsylvania, one night soon after O'Connor found out from Archbishop Laghi that he was to be a cardinal. "It was a beautiful Pennsylvania country night," she recalls. "The sky was full of stars. It was so peaceful. He was very, very tired. Monsignor McCarthy asked him if he still missed Pennsylvania. 'Every minute,' he said. 'There hasn't been a minute of the last thirty-two years that I haven't missed being in Pennsylvania.'"

On the other hand, O'Connor is aware of how much he has learned about the world and about himself as a result of not having been confined to a single parish. When he first came to New York, a reporter asked, "Cardinal Cooke said he was a simple parish priest—are you a simple parish priest?"

The Archbishop of the Capital of the World, as the Pope addressed him soon after his appointment, smiled, and said, "I'm a priest. How simple I don't know."

26

IN THE MOST CONTROVERSIAL UNDERTAKING of all his years as a priest—a trip to the Middle East at the end of 1986—O'Connor at first appeared to be all too simple, but then revealed himself to be simultaneously spontaneous and subtle.

The prelude to the journey to Jordan and Israel was the Cardinal's three-day stay in Lebanon in June 1986. During a stopover in Rome on his way home, he called for a homeland for the Palestinians, emphasizing that by keeping hundreds of thousands of them in refugee camps, "living in the most wretched circumstances imaginable, we are creating a monster."

At the same time, the Cardinal stressed that he also strongly supported the Jewish people's right to a homeland

and their right "to defend themselves against outside forces."

A number of American Jewish leaders, the Cardinal told me, had been disturbed by his comments after his visit to Lebanon. They thought he did not understand the total context of the Palestinian-refugee problem. He did not understand that the Arab states could have taken them in a long time ago.

In August, Shimon Peres, then Israel's Prime Minister—he shifted to the post of Foreign Minister two months later—invited O'Connor to come to Israel. The following month the Cardinal accepted the invitation, and Jewish leaders, both in America and in Israel, anticipated that the trip might have distinctly positive results. O'Connor, well liked by the Pope, was, after all, the head of the Church in the city with the largest Jewish population of any in the world, and he had shown himself to be genuinely concerned with combating anti-Semitism and freeing Jews from the Soviet Union, and he was continually reminding Christians of the lessons of the Holocaust. Perhaps this staunch friend of the Jews might help Israel in its efforts to win diplomatic recognition from the Vatican or, at least, some upgrading in Israel's diplomatic status there.

On December 24, three days before the Cardinal was to leave for the Middle East, these glowing expectations were almost entirely extinguished. Archbishop Laghi telephoned O'Connor with discordant news. The Cardinal, at the orders of the Vatican Secretariat of State, was to scrap his plans for official meetings in Jerusalem with the President and the Foreign Minister of Israel, as well as with the Mayor of Jerusalem. O'Connor was reminded that Vatican protocol is violated when cardinals make official visits in Jerusalem, a city the Vatican does not recognize as the capital of the Jewish state.

The initial reaction in Israel was hurt and indignation. An Israeli official let it be known that unless the Cardinal visited state officials in their Jerusalem offices "there will be no meetings. No one here wants to feel that they are meeting him on bended knee. But no one wants to embarrass him either. He's been a good friend. We don't believe he was intentionally trying to insult anyone here. He got caught up in Vatican politics."

A number of American Jewish leaders were equally distressed. Rabbi Alexander Schindler, president of the Union of American Hebrew Congregations, noted pointedly that the Vatican had not objected to the Cardinal's official visit to the King of Jordan. O'Connor's trip to the Middle East, added Rabbi Schindler, "now appears tainted, and one wonders whether it would be wise for the Cardinal to make this journey at all under the present circumstances."

O'Connor, however, is temperamentally disinclined to retreat. His office let it be known that the Cardinal had "every expectation and hope of visiting informally with various representatives of the Israeli government."

Lest anyone miss the point, the Vatican noted coolly that "Cardinal O'Connor is traveling on a personal initiative. He is not on a mission for the Vatican."

"I made a mistake," O'Connor told a reporter for the *New York Times.* He said he hoped that his relationship with the Jewish community in New York did not depend on his never making a mistake. Otherwise, "it would be a shallow relationship." Having admitted his error, the Cardinal decided to set a limit to the consequences of that admission. "I want to be a friend to the Jewish community. I want to do everything I can to be supportive, but that doesn't mean I do everything your way. You can't write the script for me."

The trip began in Jordan, where the Cardinal visited Baqaa, a Palestinian refugee center. "I haven't seen any evidence in the world at large," he said, "that there is any sense of urgency about these camps or these refugees. And I'm going to insist on saying, whether people like it or not, that this is a problem we all share."

As usual, when mentioning the stateless Palestinians, the Cardinal added a balancing note: "When I speak of the needs and rights of the Palestinians, I'm concerned about the needs and the rights of the Israelis as well."

Within hours after arriving in Israel, the Cardinal celebrated a New Year's Day Latin Mass at St. Saviour's Church in the Old City of Jerusalem. What he said at the end of the Mass made headlines in Israel, New York, and a good many other places. It was an apology.

"I sat there," he later recalled, "and I saw all the people and all the media, and I decided that this would be a one-time opportunity."

Wearing white vestments and a miter, looking out at hundreds of worshipers, many of them Palestinians, the Cardinal said spontaneously: "It is fitting and it behooves me to say that I deeply regret and certainly apologize for any offenses that might have been perceived as intended by those who govern Israel . . . I failed to be sufficiently thorough in my preparations. I failed to familiarize myself with the protocols normally surrounding a visit by a member of the College of Cardinals. Because of that error on my part, unfortunately, it is quite understandable that the people of Israel and those in the government might well have construed some deliberately intended offense. . . . Whatever compensation can be made during my visit will be made within the restrictions that bind me."

In his homily that day, the Cardinal emphasized that all human beings are "equal in dignity" and endowed with "fundamental and inalienable human rights." And, homeless as many Palestinians are, so, too, were Joseph and Mary. They had to escape to an environment that was hostile to them but were "finally able to return to their homeland."

O'Connor also read from Elie Wiesel's *Night*, in which Wiesel tells of how, as a boy in Buchenwald, he had watched his father die of hunger and illness. At the end, the Cardinal said, Wiesel's father asked him for water, but the boy, in fear of being beaten by the concentration camp police if he did what his father asked, did not bring the water.

Quoting from Wiesel, the Cardinal said, " 'His last word was my name. A summons, to which I did not respond.' " O'Connor then said of Wiesel, "We can sense the pain, the desolation of the innermost secrets of his own heart, the horror of rejection of human dignity." And he went on, "Had the world responded to the cries of the victims of Nazi oppression? Does the world respond now to the cries of the victims of oppression and hunger, the old, the rejected, the unborn children in their mothers' wombs?"

He asked if terrorists would respond to his message "to turn away from the violence of your soul, even if your objectives are just."

The Cardinal closed with a prayer to the Lord of Abraham, Isaac, and Jacob.

His apology having been made, would an Israeli official now see him? Teddy Kollek, the Mayor of Jerusalem, did, and they met in the Mayor's municipal offices. How was that possible, the press asked, since the Cardinal was not allowed to visit officials of the state in their offices?

"Because," the Mayor explained, "the city is not a political entity, it is an administrative entity."

A reporter said he did not understand the distinction.

"Neither do I," the Mayor answered.

In a respite from the diplomatic mine field, the Cardinal visited the Western Wall—the Wailing Wall—in Jerusalem. To many Jews throughout the world, it is the most sacred place of all. When Jerusalem fell in A.D. 70, this wall of the Temple survived. It is the site of fervent, swaying praying—and bar mitzvahs, often accompanied in recent years by the fiery music of Sephardic Jews.

As reported by Patrick Tyler in the *Washington Post*, O'Connor, "flanked by two monsignors, kissed the wall while ultra-Orthodox Jews prayed a few feet away."

It was, the Cardinal said, a very moving experience. "It was very important to me. I've been wanting to do this for many years. This was my first chance. You get the sense of sorrow, of loneliness and loss and suffering of that wall.

"This wall to me is an enormously important symbol of suffering. I prayed for the people of Israel, I prayed for the people of the Middle East, and I prayed, above all, for peace with justice."

After he had prayed at the Wailing Wall, O'Connor said to a Catholic writer living in Israel that he regarded the prayer as an "act of reparation."

Watching O'Connor at the Wall were several tourists. One asked, "Which one is the Cardinal?"

"The one with the red yarmulke," a friend said.

27

THERE WERE times when the Cardinal, on his own, resembled the head of a state. At one point, in the Old City, he was escorted by Catholic prelates in their ceremonial robes, dragomans with staffs, and a uniformed troop of Christian Arab Boy Scouts while armed Israeli troops and police tried to keep back the aggressive TV crews and photographers. Monsignor McCarthy, watching the pomp and furor, likened it to a scene in a Fellini movie.

Still undecided was under what circumstances, if any, the Cardinal could meet with the President and the Foreign Minister of Israel. Compromises were arranged. The President, Chaim Herzog, both works and lives in a presidential mansion. O'Connor talked with him in a room that a member of the President's staff described as Herzog's study. But in that very study the President often conducts official business.

Asked about this as he left the mansion, the Cardinal said that he had made it perfectly clear beforehand that he was not meeting the President in his office, and so far as he was concerned he had not. The Israeli Foreign Ministry did not go out of its way to reassure O'Connor. Instead, it said that the President's mansion is "the highest demonstration of our sovereignty. For us it's similar to your White House."

With somewhat less ambiguity, the Cardinal visited Foreign Minister Shimon Peres at his residence in Jerusalem. But when he left the building a reporter asked O'Connor whether the visit had been with Peres the private citizen or Peres the foreign minister.

By now, O'Connor had had enough. "You'd have to get Solomon to answer that," he said. And looking at the reporter, the Cardinal commanded, *"You* cut the baby."

At home in New York, these exercises in the semantics of buildings were receiving enthusiastic notices among Jewish leaders. "Cardinal O'Connor," said Morris B. Abram, chairman of the Conference of Presidents of Major American Jewish Organizations, "has performed an act of noble ecumenism and high statesmanship." The previously reserved Rabbi Alexander Schindler said, "By visiting the President of Israel in the equivalent of our White House, Cardinal O'Connor made a remarkable concession that is deeply appreciated and that will be long remembered."

During his visit, the Cardinal walked through Yad Vashem, the Holocaust Museum in Jerusalem. He saw large photographs of Jews, reduced to near-skeletons, in their bunks in death camps. He saw piles of corpses dumped into pits. He saw children in the Warsaw ghetto, starving, and women, stripped, soon to be led off to be shot.

When he left the museum, the Cardinal was asked what his feelings were. In a choked voice, he answered, "Anything I would say here is banal. This is totally indescribable. This is the mystery of suffering and we must do anything we can, whatever it is, to preclude this in the future."

After leaving Yad Vashem, the Cardinal met with Zevulun Hammer, Israel's Minister of Religious Affairs, and told him, "It might well be that the Holocaust may be an enormous gift that Judaism has given to the world." Such suffering, O'Connor said, taught the world the "sacredness and dignity of every human person."

The Cardinal did not leave Jerusalem without following

the steps of Jesus bearing the cross along the narrow, winding streets of the Old City. Following close behind were Israeli soldiers with submachine guns.

Later, as his visit was about to end, O'Connor, reflecting on the events of his journey, said to Barbara Whitaker of *Newsday*, "You know, this is a crazy business. You never think of yourself as being in a situation like this. I'm always asking myself, 'Who am I? Why am I here?' You just have to say, 'Here is where God wants me to be,' and you try to do whatever good you can. But it's strange. I'm the least controversial man in the world . . . but I always seem to end up in these situations."

Before he left Israel, the least controversial man in the world visited the occupied territory of the Gaza Strip, which is on the Mediterranean near the Egyptian border. Of the 600,000 people crammed into the narrow space, two-thirds are Palestinian refugees.

As described in the *New York Times*, the Cardinal "rode through a refugee district of mud-covered hovels and shacks of corrugated metal built along an otherwise splendid stretch of beachfront. Barefoot children played on sandy paths and alleys littered with garbage."

Bernard H. G. Mills, director of the United Nations Relief and Welfare Agency in Gaza, told O'Connor that while he and his staff welcomed foreign visitors, "very, very few come. I think this gives the impression to people here that they are forgotten. . . .

"This is a small area with nearly six hundred thousand people crammed in, and no light at the end of the political tunnel. Everyone talks and talks and talks, but there is no truth—nothing to cling to. There is no hope for the future, no hope of finding a job, no political hope, and, of course, the area is under occupation.

"Fear builds fear. We're worried that there will be some minor incident—maybe a woman will be pushed by a soldier and somebody will push the soldier—and before we know it, something will blow. If it happens, I'm afraid a lot of people are going to get killed. And that is not in the interests of the people of Israel, and it is not in the interests of the people of Gaza."

O'Connor, who has visited refugee camps elsewhere in the world, said that the situation in Gaza was "as bad as I have seen." The blame, he emphasized, was hardly Israel's alone. It belonged to the whole of the Middle East.

Before boarding his plane at Ben-Gurion Airport near Tel Aviv, O'Connor focused again on the Palestinians: "They don't have a real identity. They don't have a passport. They don't have a piece of land they can call their own. They can hardly be called a people who have the right of self-determination."

As if that were not burden enough, O'Connor continued, "we have a stereotype in the United States for the Arab and Palestinian. If you use either term, *Arab* or *Palestinian*, many people see 'terrorist.' " Yet, "we are talking about an ancient, noble people with which we have much in common."

28

O'CONNOR'S TRIP to the Middle East had another purpose beside visits to dignitaries and to the forgotten in the refugee camps. Traditionally, the head of the Church in New York is also president of the Catholic Near East Welfare Association, which supports various health, welfare, and nurturing endeavors in that part of the world.

While the Cardinal usually enjoys the fanfare that attends meetings of state, the dissonant chords in that ceremonial music were so pronounced during this trip that he greatly preferred the time he spent—as president of the Catholic Near East Welfare Association—in learning about and encouraging the Church's works of caring and devotion in both Jordan and Israel.

Writing afterward in *Catholic New York* of the Franciscan Sisters of the Divine Maternity and their pre- and post-natal care clinic in Amman—where one doctor sees two hundred patients a day—O'Connor noted: "As with every other activity supported by Catholic Near East, all comers are taken care of regardless of religion.... As with all other sisters one meets in the Holy Land, the Franciscan Sisters live in utter simplicity.

"After a fourteen-hour flight from New York to Amman and a cold, rainy arrival, my own poor unsaintly self would have undoubtedly offered Mass for them, as I did, in their little convent chapel, with considerably more fervor had my teeth not been chattering and my toes numb. Nor had they turned the heat off to impress me. That's the way they live—every day."

The Cardinal had gone to the convent right from the plane. He not only celebrated Mass for the sisters but, devoted to preaching under just about any circumstances, O'Connor also delivered a homily to the five sisters sitting on their folding chairs.

As taken from the notes of Mary Ann Poust, who reported on the Cardinal's journey for *Catholic New York*, this is what he said—and it reveals something of his own priorities of faith and works: "The almost incredible obedience and trust of Joseph and Mary has fascinated me all my life, and I think that has something to do with my becoming a priest. ... The one virtue that transcends all others [is] the virtue of obedience.

"Just in case there are troublesome days for you, if there are days you are frustrated and ask yourself why you're here in this strange land—at least you know you made an impression on one man, one bishop, and that was me."

While in the Middle East, the Cardinal also visited, in Haifa, the Sacred Heart Home for the Severely Handicapped. There, he held hands with fifteen-year-old Monzer. Bedridden, severely retarded, the boy laughed as the Cardinal rubbed his head and made affectionate sounds.

"You are something," the Cardinal said to Monzer. "I'm sorry I have to leave you."

Also at the Sacred Heart Home, O'Connor was greatly impressed by seven-year-old Chady. Writing about the multihandicapped child, he recalled in his column in *Catholic New York* that Chady is "a whiz on a computer, a computer sent him by a non-Catholic New Yorker who's delighted that the Daughters of Charity are taking care of his 'adopted' child."

Chady tried to teach the Cardinal how to work the computer but discovered that O'Connor was, as O'Connor himself said, "hopeless" in these matters.

29

ON SATURDAY, JANUARY 10, as the Cardinal's plane from Israel neared New York, the city's newspapers and television stations received a statement issued by Morris Abram. Listed as endorsing the statement were representatives of fifty-four Jewish groups, nearly every important Jewish organization in the United States.

Acknowledging that the Cardinal had supported "a number of causes to which Jews are devoted" and that he had been bound by Vatican diplomatic policy during his journey—and had, moreover, apologized for the misunderstanding caused by that policy—the Jewish groups were nonetheless displeased. They were displeased by the Vatican because it stubbornly refuses to grant Israel and its capital de jure recognition.

They were also displeased, however, by New York's Cardinal, having been "disquieted and distressed by reports in the press of statements he made during the course of his visit to Israel and Jordan." First, he had kept talking about Palestinians deprived of a homeland. Understandably, said the document, the Cardinal had been "moved by the circumstances of the Arab refugees," but he had not taken into account the responsibility of the Arab world for those refugees.

Second, "we found disturbing and painful his statement that the greatest tragedy in Jewish history 'may be an enormous gift that Judaism has given the world.' "

The statement ended by saying, "Knowing Cardinal O'Connor and respecting his office and person as we do, we look forward to his reflective views now that he is home and to a continuing dialogue with him."

On the next day, after Mass at St. Patrick's Cathedral, the Cardinal reacted to what he had read about the statement. He had not yet seen it in its entirety. Not given to masking his feelings, O'Connor expressed "deep, deep disappointment." The statement, he told reporters, "amounts to a unilateral censure, which I do not appreciate and which makes it difficult for me to move further toward peace." And he added, "Would I make the trip now? I am not at all sure."

Getting angrier as he went on, the Cardinal said, "I didn't follow a script that some people apparently thought I should have followed." On the other hand, he continued, since becoming the Archbishop of New York, by following his own script he had urged President Reagan not to visit the cemetery at Bitburg with its graves of S.S. soldiers; he had shown persistent support of efforts to free Soviet Jews; and he had again and again pointed to the horrors of the Holocaust. But now the Jewish leaders had not even had the courtesy to talk to him about his trip before releasing the statement censuring him.

What most infuriated the Cardinal was the attack on

him for having said that the Holocaust, the greatest tragedy in human history, "may be an enormous gift that Judaism has given to the world."

"If this is considered demeaning to the Holocaust," the Cardinal said, "then it demeans my entire theology, because mine is a theology of suffering."

The leader of a Jewish organization that had not signed the attack on O'Connor told me, "It was so dumb to put in that criticism of what he said about the Holocaust. Why do they think Jesus is on the cross?"

Asked for a reaction to the hostilities between the Jewish leaders and the Cardinal, Israel's press officer in New York, Barukh Binah, swiftly got out of the line of fire. He said that the Israeli government had had no part in drafting the statement. "It was an American response and not the Israeli response at all."

By the next day, the Cardinal had read the entire statement and was no less angry. During an interview on local NBC television, he emphasized again that what had hurt him most was the criticism of his comment on the Holocaust. "When I came out of Yad Vashem, I was heartbroken, as I was heartbroken when I went to Dachau. . . . What I wanted to convey is . . . the nobility with which the Jews accepted the suffering, the tremendous revitalization in Judaism, the fact that maybe we've been saved from great peril since then, like nuclear war, because the world remembers, if only unconsciously. What I said was meant as a tremendous compliment to the Jewish people . . . I can't do much about [building bridges] if I come under this kind of—what I consider to be—extremely unmerited attack. And I've got to say honestly that I feel an apology is in order. . . . This isn't a light thing. Fifty-four agencies have signed this document."

By this stage, several rueful Jewish leaders were saying privately that although the Cardinal had reacted with honest anger and characteristic distaste for euphemism, his response had also been strategically astute. His repeated public invocations of the hurt he had suffered at the hands of the Jewish organizations had drawn attention away from the particular criticisms directed at him in the original statement. The focus now was on whether the Cardinal had been treated unfairly by the timing and tone of the censure. Accordingly, the Jewish groups—not the Cardinal—had been put on the defensive.

Clearly, the Cardinal was very angry. He told the press that this had been "a very demanding journey," the "most difficult" he had ever taken, made "at great personal and professional risk to myself." And he added, "I am not a masochist. I have a huge archdiocese to take care of, and I don't need this kind of thing when, in good faith, I run the risks that I have run with my own Church and with non-Jews to make this trip and to say the things I have said."

The Cardinal received support from a customary antagonist, the *New York Times*, which called the statement by the Jewish groups "overwrought" and a "sorry affair." And the Jerusalem *Post*, in an editorial, said that the Jewish organizations had "criticized the Cardinal in needlessly crude terms."

On Monday, January 19, nine days after the statement by the fifty-four Jewish organizations, eight Jewish leaders met with the Cardinal for nearly three hours at his residence at 452 Madison Avenue. One of those leaders told me soon after, "He was angry. I don't mean he raised his voice, but he was one angry man. What he was saying under the polite language was, 'If you people say you love me so much, what was your rush in releasing that statement? If you were so concerned about what I had to say about a homeland for the Palestinians, why couldn't you wait to find out that I was also saying it had to be a state that would not physically endanger the state of Israel? And when you criticized me for what I said about the Holocaust, did you really not know that the theology of suffering is central to the Catholic faith?'

"On our side, there was a strong desire to get all this behind us. And I think he felt that way, too. He didn't stay mad. He didn't seem to. Who knows how he feels in his heart? But there is no purpose to his staying mad, and there is no political purpose in our staying mad."

The official summary of the meeting, agreed to by both sides, said that it had been cordial and candid and that "both the Cardinal and his guests agreed that there were far more issues on which they held similar views than those on which they differed . . . The Jewish leaders regard the Cardinal's visit [to the Middle East] as a helpful contribution toward greater understanding between the two communities . . . They voiced regret at any misunderstanding that may have been caused by the timing of the statement's release . . . Both the Cardinal and the Jewish representatives, meeting in a spirit of mutual respect and good will, look forward to a continuing dialogue on issues of mutual concern."

This summary of the meeting was an implicit acknowledgment to O'Connor that the Jewish groups had acted too hastily, and not too perceptively. Rabbi Haskel Lookstein, president of the New York Board of Rabbis, told *Jewish World*, an independent weekly newspaper published on Long Island, "I now feel that the timing of the statement was probably a mistake." And as for the Cardinal's comment about the Holocaust, Lookstein said, "We also should have known that the Cardinal would not intentionally have said something [insulting to Jews]. In retrospect, we should have left [that criticism] out of our statement."

The Cardinal said the meeting had encouraged him to work for deeper understanding between Jews and Catholics, including the extraction of "deep-rooted" anti-Semitism from the hearts of some Catholics.

During the warfare between the Cardinal and his critics, he mentioned his puzzlement at having received a telegram from a major Jewish organization that was signed, the Cardinal said, "by a very prestigious rabbi," whose name was on the list of signers of the original statement. The rabbi said that he had absolutely not signed the document. After the peace treaty between the Jewish leaders and the Cardinal, Walter Ruby, a reporter for *Jewish World*, disclosed that not just one but twenty-one of the fifty-four Jewish groups listed as sponsoring the initial attack on the Cardinal "denied having been apprised of or having approved the final draft of the statement before their names were signed to it by the Conference of Presidents of Major American Jewish Organizations. Three other organizations claimed they had supported the preparation of a statement with the understanding that it would be released only after Jewish leaders had met with O'Connor following his return to New York. In fact, the statement was released several hours before the Cardinal arrived."

Not widely reported during the public dispute over the Cardinal's trip was the impression O'Connor had made on some Israelis. Summing up the trip in the Jerusalem *Post*, Haim Shapiro wrote:

O'Connor showed himself as a highly independent person unwilling to be pushed into any mould. This was clear from the outset, when he shocked local Catholic officialdom by delivering a Jewishly oriented homily to an Arab congregation at a mass in Jerusalem and then compounded this by making a public apology to the Israeli government at the end of the Mass. . . .

His independence and spontaneity were also evident when, after a tour of Gaza, he used a press conference at the airport before departing to make an impassioned plea for the Palestinians, even if he did not "blame" Israel for their plight.

But if Israelis were uncomfortable about his statements about the Palestinians, they were probably no more uncomfortable than the Jordanian television interviewer to whom O'Connor said that Israel had the right to exist and to defend its borders.

Back in New York, the Cardinal further displayed his independence—perhaps with an extra thrust of satisfaction—when, a little more than two weeks after the peace conference with the Jewish leaders, he met with seven American Muslim leaders at their request to discuss his trip to the Middle East. "I talked to Jewish leaders," O'Connor said, "and I went to both Jewish and Muslim countries, so I was happy to respond to this group." As for his meeting with Jewish leaders, O'Connor told reporters, "I think it's fair to

say that the Jewish community apologized for any misunderstanding." The Muslims were manifestly pleased with the
press attention that accompanied the meeting, and one of
them, Dr. M. T. Mehdi, said that the meeting with the Cardinal showed that "America is no longer a Jewish and Christian society. It is a Christian, Muslim, and Jewish society."

Asked whether this meeting might renew friction between him and Jewish leaders, O'Connor answered, "I'd be
very disappointed in the representatives of the Jewish community if that happened." As described in the *New York
Times*, another reporter seemed to be trying to renew that
friction by asking the Cardinal why he would meet with
people who do not support Israel's right to exist as a Jewish
state.

"I've met with people who hold all sorts of beliefs," the
Cardinal said.

There were no public comments by Jewish representatives on the meeting between the Cardinal and the Muslim
leaders.

30

WHILE he was returning from Israel, another controversy
was waiting at home for the Cardinal. On January 9, in a
prominently displayed story, the *New York Times* reported
that "the rector of Saint Patrick's Cathedral has refused to
perform a religious marriage ceremony for a man dying of
AIDS who wanted to renew the civil-marriage vows he
made to his wife three years ago."

David Hefner, who had been a homosexual in the past,

married Maria Ribeiro at City Hall in 1984. He was a Protestant and she is a Catholic. Her "dream church," as she puts it, is St. Patrick's Cathedral, and her corollary dream was to have a religious wedding there. In recent months, all her time had been spent caring for her husband. During his four hospitalizations, she had slept on a cot in the same room.

Hefner, wanting to fulfill his wife's dream, went with her in late December 1986 to see the Reverend John Clermont, a priest on the staff of St. Patrick's. They told the priest of their plans, which included, at Mrs. Hefner's request, the playing of "Ava Maria" during the ceremony. They also asked if it would be possible to have a chair or a stool near the altar in case, during the ceremony, Mr. Hefner could no longer stand.

The priest agreed to celebrate the wedding and to make everything comfortable for the Hefners. The wedding was to take place on February 14, Valentine's Day.

Two days after the Hefners' visit to St. Patrick's Cathedral, the priest called to tell them he could not perform the ceremony. Monsignor James F. Rigney, rector of the cathedral, had reversed the priest. His reasoning was that when a life-threatening situation exists, the usual premarriage counseling might have to be longer, and it made more sense to have that take place at the local parish rather than in so large and busy an institution as St. Patrick's. The Monsignor noted, however, that this policy does not extend to those contemplating marriage who are dying of such non-contagious diseases as cancer. Some might have drawn the implication that the rector felt that Hefner, just by being in the cathedral, might be a danger to others there.

David Hefner was greatly saddened by the Monsignor's decision. "If I were a killer, a hired murderer or a thief," he said to Ari Goldman of the *New York Times*, his voice trailing off. "But I'm just a person who happens to have a sickness."

Thomas Stoddard, a civil-liberties attorney who is executive director of the Lambda Legal Defense and Education Fund, a homosexual-rights group, had been a leading antagonist of Cardinal O'Connor during the prolonged battle over whether New York should have a gay-rights bill. Now he told Goldman that the Church's refusal to allow the Hefners to marry in St. Patrick's Cathedral was "nothing less than an expression of institutional distaste and intolerance for those suffering from this terrible modern scourge."

Stoddard saw a direct connection between the rector's decision and an October 30 Vatican letter to the Catholic bishops of all countries that stated that those who support homosexual rights "seriously threaten the lives and well-being of a large number of people."

Monsignor Rigney, in a written statement, explained that "if one party to a marriage is suffering from an illness that may threaten the life of a spouse or child who may later be conceived, compassion must be accompanied by a most serious effort to see that the problem is met in a manner harmonious with church teaching." A serious effort could take a long time and ought to be made where the couple is both better known now "and will continue to be better known."

A bleaker view of the prospects for a Catholic marriage for David and Maria Hefner came from Monsignor William B. Smith, academic dean and professor of moral theology at the archdiocesan St. Joseph's Seminary, in Yonkers. The *Tablet*, the weekly paper of the Brooklyn diocese, interviewed Monsignor Smith, and reported:

AIDS in itself is not an impediment to marriage, Msgr. Smith said. But the impossibility of physically consummating a union—presumably the case for an AIDS patient trying to avoid transmitting the disease to a spouse or child—would be an impediment, he said. If the couple intended to prevent the birth of children, it would be impossible for a priest to witness the marriage, he said. And if they planned to prevent transmission of disease through use of contraceptives, an "intrinsically wrong act," the church could not approve the marriage, he said.

The case seemed to be closed, at least so far as a wedding ceremony in St. Patrick's Cathedral was concerned. And in view of Monsignor Smith's warnings, the Hefners might not be able to be married in any Catholic church.

Then the Cardinal came home. While he was dealing with his censure by the Jewish organizations, O'Connor was also presented with the question of the Hefners' desire for a wedding at St. Patrick's. On Sunday, the day after his return from Israel, he said he would review the case. There would be no problem, he said, if it turned out that their desires met the principles of the Church. Two days later, he came to the conclusion that there was no reason that the Hefners should not be married at the cathedral if they first obtained premarital counseling at their local parish. He added that he would personally welcome them to the cathedral.

A priest secretary to the Cardinal called the Hefners' parish priest with the good news, adding that he should expedite the premarital counseling so that the Hefners could be married at St. Patrick's as soon as possible. Maria Hefner was still counting on a ceremony on Valentine's Day.

In a note on the editorial page, the *New York Times*, by now almost an intimate adversary of the Cardinal, spoke of his "humanity and good sense" in this matter. The note ended, "After the decision to exclude the Hefners was made, a spokesman said the church had not yet devised guidelines to handle such requests. For Cardinal O'Connor, the only guideline needed was decency."

The marriage service took place on Valentine's Day. As the couple walked down the cathedral aisle, the organ played "Ava Maria." The Cardinal, sitting in a pew near the altar, watched the ceremony and then came forward. He welcomed the Hefners to the cathedral, kissed the bride, shook the hand of the groom, and blessed the couple. Afterward, the Cardinal said, "They must be very devoted to each other. I can only pray that, however long they have together, they will be very happy indeed."

A television reporter and his crew approached, and the Cardinal, looking into the camera, said, "There are many who would question my very presence at such a marriage. My response to that is that every human life is sacred. Regardless of what any one of us may have done or may not have done, each of us is made in the image and likeness of God."

Around this time, the Cardinal made another decision that was characteristic of him. In a letter that began "Dear Father," he wrote, "I am looking for ways to make it possible for me to spend more and more 'quality time' with every priest of the archdiocese." To this end, he said that beginning on January 21, 1987, he would be available each Wednesday at his residence, 452 Madison Avenue, following his 8:00 A.M. Mass in the cathedral, "for any priest who can arrange his schedule to come visit with me for twenty minutes or so (certainly longer, if desired).

"No appointments will be required. If you arrive while someone else is there, you will simply be asked to wait. . . . All visits will be completely informal. . . . Many thanks for all that you do and are."

A few days after the beginning of the open house for the archdiocesan priests, I was talking to Monsignor John Tracy Ellis, of Catholic University in Washington, the preeminent historian of the American Church. Although he is more liberal than the Cardinal in matters of theology, the Monsignor admires O'Connor.

"What he has done to let the priests come in just as they please to talk to him, that is unusual," said the Monsignor. "Especially in a large or even a middle-sized archdiocese. The bishops will tell you they can't do it, their schedules are so crowded. But O'Connor decided to do it, come hell or high water, as the expression goes. And for every priest to be able to come to see him without even telephoning! Well, that is a Cardinal who is not aloof."

I asked Monsignor Ellis, one of whose books is a series of appraisals of Catholic bishops he has known, how he thought O'Connor would ultimately be regarded.

"In the very long run, when he's gone to God, it would be my prediction that the appreciation of him will be very high. Because he's an honest man. And he'll be remembered for his forthrightness in looking problems in the face and not running away from them. When the dust has settled, as they say, he's going to come through all right."

On January 15, 1987, the Cardinal was sixty-seven years old. During a meeting with the archdiocese's Priests' Council, he was presented with a cake. Thanking all the council members, the Cardinal was about to report to them about his storied trip to the Middle East. But first, he said, he had something to read to them. A series of prophecies from the day's "Your Stars" column in the New York *Daily News* for those whose birthday fell on January 15: "You experience a quickening of the pace. The question is how quickly you can think and land on your feet. It's not a dull year. . . . You have more time to yourself in February. March opens up a possible executive position—you've earned it. Travel is necessary. May shows personal advancement. Be clear-sighted and decisive. July heightens your love life. Taurus and Cancer find you irresistible. Marry in October."

The Cardinal roared with laughter, as did the priests. It was the best laugh he'd had in quite a while.

31

FOR ALL HIS PASSIONATE BELIEF that the Church must be active in the world—as well as his own need to preach to more than the converted—the Cardinal can be parochial, ingenuous, and sometimes disingenuous in dealing with the world's reactions to him.

A bristling case in point started with a one-paragraph

note to the pastors of all 411 parishes in the archdiocese of New York from the then Vicar General, Bishop Joseph T. O'Keefe. (O'Keefe later became Bishop of the Diocese of Syracuse.) The note was included in a miscellany of items and instructions in an August 18, 1986, letter—one of several such letters sent out to the priests by the Vicar General each year.

The item that was to prove explosive read:

SPEAKERS AT CHURCH-SPONSORED EVENTS

Great care and prudence must be exercised in extending invitations to individuals to speak at parish-sponsored events, e.g., Communion breakfasts, graduations, meetings of parish societies, etc. It is not only inappropriate, it is unacceptable and inconsistent with diocesan policy to invite individuals to speak at such events whose public position is contrary to and in opposition to the clear, unambiguous teaching of the Church. This policy applies, as well, to all Archdiocesan owned or sponsored institutions and organizations.

One of the first to bridle, publicly, at the directive was Patricia Dempsey, president of New York State Catholics for a Free Choice, which vigorously dissents from the Church's policy on abortion. She complained that the archdiocese had now closed the door in her face and in that of her organization. Indeed, "now they've nailed it shut."

Many Catholics and non-Catholics, however, are likely to have understood why the archdiocese would choose to bar speakers dissenting against so intense and basic a concern of the Church as abortion. "It would be like," the Cardinal told me later, "upbraiding a rabbi for refusing to allow a representative of the P.L.O. to speak before his congregation."

But the question of who could speak in the archdiocese soon became slightly more complex. When asked whether the speakers' policy would apply to Governor Mario Cuomo or Geraldine Ferraro (the 1984 Democratic vice-presidential candidate), Bishop O'Keefe said the decision in their cases, and in all cases, would be up to the individual parish priest.

Anyway, said the Vicar General, "I never thought of the Governor when I was drawing up the policy, which resulted from requests for guidelines as to speakers from certain chapters of the Ancient Order of Hibernians."

Meanwhile, enterprising reporters contacted the diocese of Brooklyn, whose spokesman readily asserted that the Church there has no written policy concerning speakers at church events. (Some of the staff of Brooklyn Bishop Francis John Mugavero regard Cardinal O'Connor as rather heavy of hand by contrast with their own bishop's less aggressive style.)

Mario Cuomo at first declined to comment on the Vicar General's directive, but he soon conquered his uncharacteristic resistance to get into an argument.

Declaring that "we lay people have a right to be heard," the Governor told the *New York Times*—which placed his reaction on the front page—that "one of the classic positions against restraint of intellectual activity is to ask: 'How do you define it? How do you implement it?' It's very difficult to see how this would be implemented.

"From what I'm told, it applies to church teaching. But what is Church teaching? When are you teaching infallibly and when aren't you? What people, which people, will decide who agrees with Church teaching? Will you have ecclesiastical courts?"

Monsignor Peter Finn, the archdiocese's director of communications, is usually affable but can also be quite acerbic. He called the Governor's comments "nonsense," noting that a church in Harlem would be unlikely to invite P. W. Botha to its church supper. So, "what's the problem? I think it's very clear as far as the Church is concerned what it means by 'differing with the Church's teachings.'"

The Governor would not let up. The directive, he said, "leaves a lot of questions as to whom it does apply. And when does it apply? What events are they referring to? Is an appearance at a cemetery such an event?

"The Church has the right to make rules for itself. There's no doubt about that. The Church has the right to say, 'If you want to belong, these are the rules.' But depending on what the rule was, one can say whether it was wise or whether it was unwise.

"The Catholic Church," the Governor declared, "is not only the cardinals, the bishops, the priests, and the nuns. The Catholic Church by definition in canon law is the hierarchy, the religious, and lay members. We are the Church, all of us together. . . . The lay people are part of the Church. We have a right in some cases to be heard on the rules."

Vicar General O'Keefe decided to respond to the Governor with large if somewhat damning praise. The Governor is so smart, O'Keefe told the *New York Times*, that "he would confuse young people, and under no circumstances would I invite him to speak to young people at a graduation."

Mario Cuomo urged O'Keefe to read his 1984 speech at Notre Dame in which he said that while, as a Catholic, he was personally against abortion, as a public official he had to uphold the law that supports a right to an abortion and could not impose his personal views on the citizenry as a whole.

The Vicar General responded that he knew of the Governor's speech, calling it "the encyclical by Mario." O'Keefe went on to say that since the Governor appeared to be thinking about running for president in 1988, all this maneuvering by him could indicate that "he might be trying to distance himself from the official teaching of the Church because his Catholicism will be at issue, as it has been in the past."

The Governor, stung, answered: "What I said at Notre Dame, I repeat: I would no more distance myself from my Catholicism than the bishop would."

The Cardinal continued to refuse to comment on the brawl, except to say that he found the Governor's remarks "surprising."

The Vicar General was not done, however, and said that on certain matters, the laity did not have the right to argue. "Nobody," said Bishop O'Keefe, "not myself, or the Cardinal, or the Pope himself, will take a position against the authentic teaching of the Church on abortion."

At that point in the spiraling controversy, the *New York Times* reported in September that "Bishop O'Keefe said he would not allow the Governor to speak before a graduating class at the church that the bishop heads, Saint John the Evangelist, which is part of the Catholic Center at 1011 First Avenue, near 56th Street."

The Governor saw this as further proof that the directive was confused and confusing. For instance, Cuomo said, he opposes capital punishment, as do the Pope and America's Catholic bishops. Does that mean, the Governor asked, that such supporters of capital punishment as the President of the United States can't be invited to speak in a church in the archdiocese of New York?

The Vicar General retorted that obfuscation was being perpetrated by the Governor because he was "talking about capital punishment and abortion as if they were all the same."

By now, the Cardinal felt it necessary to publicly support his beleaguered Vicar General. So, on September 8—four days after the story first broke in the *New York Times*—O'Connor told that newspaper it was "common sense" not to invite speakers who would "attack the Church" to affairs sponsored by the Church. "People get confused," the Cardinal explained, "when someone who's well known for disagreeing with the Church in a substantive manner, not in an insignificant matter, is given a platform."

For instance, "The Church's support, or seeming support, or perceived support, of a speaker who was explicitly in favor of abortion—that would be a scandal, I think. It wouldn't matter who it would be—a political figure or anybody else."

In the same *New York Times* story, Governor Cuomo gave a particularly intriguing display of his skill at broken-field running: "Mr. Cuomo described his latest contretemps with the archdiocese as 'kind of overblown,' but nevertheless seemed to encourage its continuation. Noting that he receives 'hundreds' of letters every time he speaks out on religious issues, the Governor said: 'The whole society is sensitive to this. People are afraid of church-state involvement, and people are right. It's a dangerous business.' "

The Governor also said, however, that the Vicar General's directive was not an improper curtailment of freedom of speech. He made a distinction between a democratic society, in which free speech is a "cherished right," and the Catholic Church, "where there is no presumption of shared authority. The Catholic Church is not a democracy the way [American] society is, and I have no objection to that."

Adding a further and rather darker dimension to the dispute over the Vicar General's ban on dissenters was the news, reported by the *New York Times*, that in June, before the issuance of Bishop O'Keefe's directive, State Assemblyman John C. Dearie of the Bronx, a Catholic, had been banned from speaking at all events sponsored by the parish of which he had been a member since his birth forty-six years before. Dearie had attended the parish's schools before going to Notre Dame, and his two children, three-and-a-half and two at the time, had been baptized in the parish.

In June 1986, however, his parish priest, Monsignor Henry J. Vier, had taken Dearie aside and told him that on orders from "the Cardinal's house," he was henceforth barred from speaking at parish events because of votes he had cast to allow state Medicaid funds to be used for abortions. Dearie had just addressed a communion breakfast at the church he had belonged to all his life.

The assemblyman, who describes himself as "a seriously practicing Catholic," is personally opposed to abortion but felt that since abortion is legal, he, as a public official, ought not to discriminate against poor women who needed Medicaid funds to have abortions.

Through a spokesman, the Cardinal denied that he had given the order to ban John Dearie from speaking at events in his own parish. The spokesman added that the Cardinal was "sorry" if "an overzealous aide" had given such an order. (The order had come from the Reverend Christopher Maloney, a secretary of the Cardinal.) On the other hand, the spokesman did not say it was okay for Dearie to speak in his own parish. That kind of decision, said Monsignor Peter Finn—the spokesman for the Cardinal—was up to each parish pastor. Each pastor need only look to the Vicar General's guidelines, which "speak for themselves."

Assemblyman Dearie was not satisfied with that explanation. "I have no problem with the Cardinal and the bishops," he said, "strongly reinforcing at every opportunity their position on the issue of abortion. That's their job. But there are so many other issues—the homeless, housing, senior citizens—that to simply close the door as a result of one vote . . . To lock the door—in effect, to cut off the communication and the honest evaluation of a legislator trying to make a decision on this very difficult issue, it seems to me in the long and short run is not good policy."

Dearie emphasized that "the positions of the Church are very, very important to me, but if I don't keep an open mind and evaluate my own position, I wouldn't be a very good legislator."

Dearie's two children had been baptized by Monsignor Henry J. Vier, the pastor of his church. Vier said that after being informed by an aide to the Cardinal that Dearie would not be able to speak again at a parish event, "I got up and told the audience that I had instructions from the Cardinal's house to say that the Cardinal did not want any public official to speak before a Catholic gathering if that official favored public funding of abortions.

"I accepted the decision and agreed with it," said the pastor. "It wasn't a pleasant duty. I didn't like the idea of having to do it. But it was required of me."

At this point, the Cardinal was thoroughly exasperated by the furor attendant on the claim that he was barring dissenters from the parishes. "How much further," he asked a *New York Times* reporter, "are the nonsensical allegations going to go on?"

He tied in objectors to his Vicar General's directive with "those who are making an indoor sport out of attacks on the Pope and the Church."

As for Assemblyman Dearie, the Cardinal was especially angry at him. Dearie had said to the *New York Times*—as he tried to figure out why he had been banned because of only one vote he had cast—that the archdiocese was acting "in anticipation of the elections" to try to use its influence to defeat candidates with whose positions the Church disagreed.

The Cardinal revealed he had written Dearie in response to the assemblyman's charge that the archdiocese was trying to influence elections by its speakers' policy. The Cardinal told Dearie that his statement had been "grossly untrue, deeply insulting, and morally libelous."

In that letter, the Cardinal also said it was "categorically untrue" that he personally had ordered the silencing of Dearie. But he did not say he was sorry it had happened, or that the ban would be lifted.

Governor Cuomo had made a public point of saying: "I feel sorry about John Dearie—it's a touching, touching story."

The Cardinal, meanwhile, was only slightly less angry at "a great number" of unnamed critics of his Vicar General's directive. These were people, he said, who "know very little about the Church and have never lifted a finger to support the Church. But now they are taking up the cudgels with holy indignation to defend anybody and everybody who attacks the Church or disagrees radically with the Church on grave issues."

In his column on the subject in *Catholic New York*—a much longer column than usual—the Cardinal tried to set the matter straight. The title of the September 11, 1986, column was "A Matter of Common Sense": "So what is all this furor about? What is the nonsense I read about squelching 'free speech'? Where is the deep, dark, sinister political motivation that some choose to see? When did common sense, or a sense of appropriateness, become unconstitutional or un-American? Why the hysteria that leads a columnist to speak of the 'thought police' of the archdiocese of New York? (A rather nasty, Nazilike implication there, wouldn't you say?)"

It was time, said the Cardinal, for certain questions to be asked.

One such question I asked of a television reporter. . . . He told me there were people in high dudgeon that Bishop O'Keefe was denying our sacred constitutional and democratic principle of free speech. I asked him what his TV station manager would do if he, the reporter, attacked the manager while interviewing me. What would be his job future? More important, how likely would it be that the attack would be aired as part of the interview? He didn't answer, and I noted that even my question was not aired when the interview was shown. . . .

Still another question. Why do we have Catholic pulpits and classrooms? They cost an enormous amount of money to build and to operate. I am personally engaged at this very moment, and will be for years to come, in a constant round of fund drives to keep our Catholic schools open. I refuse to gouge our teachers. I worry and scheme day and night to find ways to improve their wages and benefits, because I have a passion for justice to working people.

Hundreds of thousands of Catholic families in the archdiocese of New York bear the burden of paying for our churches and our schools. Why? The answer should be obvious. When they go to church they want to hear what the *Church* teaches. When they make what are often inordinate sacrifices to send their youngsters to Catholic schools, they want them to be taught what the *Church* teaches.

Where are those who demand "free speech" in our Catholic schools when it comes to *paying* for those schools? In my experience, some of the strongest *proponents* of what *they* consider to be free speech are the strongest *opponents* of any kind of tax breaks or governmental support for parents who choose their own version of "free speech" when they pay to send their children to Catholic schools. . . .

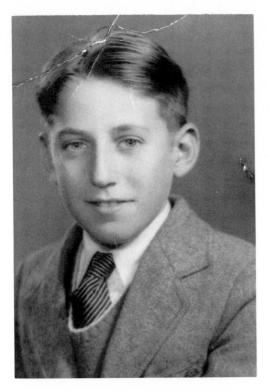

On days when they could afford it, John O'Connor *(center)* and his boyhood friends would buy a watermelon for a dime a slice. *From the collection of Cardinal O'Connor.*

John J. O'Connor as a student at Tilden Junior High School, Philadelphia. *Photograph from the collection of Cardinal O'Connor.*

At ordination, December 1925. *From the collection of Cardinal O'Connor.*

As a seminarian at St. Charles Borromeo Seminary, Philadelphia. *From the collection of Cardinal O'Connor.*

John J. O'Connor saying Mass on the USS *Canberra* (CAG-2), 1962.
U.S. Navy photograph.

John J. O'Connor as senior
chaplain at the United States
Naval Academy, 1972. *Photograph
by U.S. Naval Academy.*

Admiral O'Connor with the late Terence Cardinal Cooke at a press conference announcing O'Connor's having been appointed bishop of the military vicariate, 1979. *Photograph by Chris Sheridan*/Catholic New York.

Pope John Paul II lays hands on the head of Bishop John J. O'Connor, ordaining him to the episcopacy, in St. Peter's Basilica, Rome, May 27, 1979. *From the collection of Cardinal O'Connor.*

O'Connor saying good-bye to friends in Scranton at the University of Scranton Athletic Center after celebrating Mass there on March 11, 1984, prior to becoming Archbishop of New York. *Photograph by Chris Sheridan*/Catholic New York.

Mother Teresa visits O'Connor at the New York Catholic Center, May 1984.
Photograph by Chris Sheridan/Catholic New York.

Archbishop O'Connor and Joseph Cardinal Bernardin, of Chicago, in Central America, February 1985. *Photograph by Gerald Costello*/Catholic New York.

O'Connor with Nicaraguan President Daniel Ortega, Managua, Nicaragua, February 1985. *Reuters/Bettman News Photos*.

Receiving the red hat from the Pope, May 25, 1985. *Photograph by Chris Sheridan*/Catholic New York.

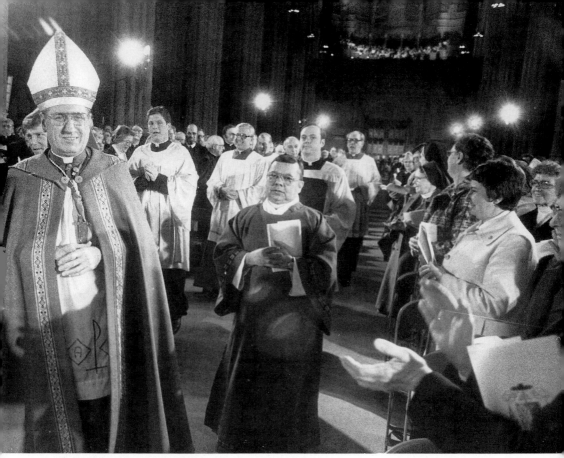

The Cardinal at St. Patrick's Cathedral, New York City. *Photograph by Chris Sheridan*/Catholic New York.

The Cardinal's throne, St. Patrick's Cathedral. On its back is the Cardinal's motto: "There can be no love without justice." *Photograph by Chris Sheridan*/Catholic New York.

The Cardinal's residence, on Madison Avenue. *Photograph by Chris Sheridan*/Catholic New York.

As for the smoldering issue at hand, the Cardinal continued to ask questions in his column:

Who is supposed to make the judgment in such matters? Our pastors, with the guidance of our Vicar General, are charged by Church law and by my delegation to provide guidance. Are we to have a Church in which everyone's judgment is equal to everyone else's? That's not a Church, it's chaos.

Who's obligated to set the tone, keep the "store" going, see that the bills get paid, build the schools, certify the teachers, provide spiritual, moral and religious leadership? Has there been a sudden declaration that the bishop no longer has responsibility for such? Or for Church teaching? Are our parents ready to have teachers teach what they will? Are our parishioners prepared to have preachers preach what they will? It's interesting to observe that the occasional angry letter I receive about teaching or preaching is almost inevitably from someone who believes that Church doctrine is being seriously violated.

Just one more note. The other day, when a reporter told me Bishop O'Keefe said it is necessary to avoid confusion, I told him that the Bishop was talking basically about what we technically call "scandal." In the subject under discussion, scandal could accrue in a number of ways. One way would be to permit or foster the notion that honoring a given speaker could be perceived as supporting that speaker's position—if the position is contrary to that of the Church in a grave matter . . .

Are our Catholic people deprived of hearing dissenting views simply because such views are not presented under Church auspices? Don't they hear them on radio and television, read them in newspapers and magazines? Can't they go to lectures and speeches elsewhere? Don't they see and hear an almost relentless attack against Church teaching and practice all over the place— even in advertisements and commercials such as those published by Planned Parenthood and others? Are there really many Catholics who don't know "the other side"? . . .

Question: Suppose I invited Mr. Farrakhan to preach in St. Patrick's Cathedral? Would there be protestors outside? Suppose I invited South Africa's Mr. Botha? Is my refusing to invite them or to permit their being invited a deprivation of free speech? . . .

Question: Should I invite to St. Patrick's Cathedral the nationally syndicated columnist who, a year or so ago, threatened that I was endangering our tax exemption when I preached in St. Patrick's Cathedral what he disagreed with?

Meanwhile, also in *Catholic New York*, the Vicar General noted sharply that Governor Cuomo was further making himself an illustration of the kind of speaker who, if invited into a parish, would confuse and divide people. "He equates abortion and birth control. These are not the same. Abortion is the taking of fetal life. Vatican II called abortion a 'heinous crime.' You can't minimize that."

Other kinds of confusion began to appear. The *National Catholic Reporter* observed that "neither the Brooklyn diocese nor the Rockville Centre [Long Island] diocese has issued a directive similar to that of New York, although Monsignor Francis Maniscalco, speaking for Bishop John R. McGann in Rockville Centre, said he would have a problem inviting [Governor] Cuomo or Geraldine Ferraro to speak at parish functions, and that pastors would not be encouraged to invite them.

"Earlier, Father Joseph O'Hare, president of Fordham University, said he would have no difficulty inviting Cuomo or Ferraro or, for that matter, Father Charles Curran to address a university audience, because the archdiocesan directive was 'not pertinent' to Fordham. He said, however, Bob Guccione of *Penthouse* magazine might be a different matter."

The case of Bronx Assemblyman John C. Dearie, barred from speaking in his own parish, was also cited in the *National Catholic Reporter*, which quoted a New York columnist as saying that the action against Dearie "also raises the question, buried we thought with John F. Kennedy, of whether an American Catholic can be a 'real American' and legislate, execute, or adjudicate laws with which he or she does not in private morally agree."

In an editorial, the *New York Times* claimed that the dispute between the Governor and the Cardinal—with Mr.

Dearie hauled in from the wings—was not really about the Vicar General's directive. It had to do, said the *Times*, with "how fervently Catholics in public office must oppose abortion."

Like Cuomo, said the *Times*, "many Catholic politicians have . . . distinguished their 'personal' acceptance of Church teaching on abortion from their 'public' obligation to respect and defend the rights of Americans to decide on abortions for themselves. The Cardinal may believe that this distinction trivializes religious belief, turning into a merely advisory opinion what should be a strongly felt imperative to guide action."

But Cuomo, the *Times* noted, addresses the quintessential dilemma of Catholic politicians: "How can they swear to uphold the law and the rights of others when, as with abortion, those rights interdict [the] teaching [of the Church]? Does the Cardinal know a better way to bridge this dilemma than by distinguishing between personal conviction and official duty?"

The *Times*, however, neglected to mention in this and in its other editorials on the subject that it is not necessary to sidestep conviction while carrying out one's official duty. Since elected, the Governor has referred to his "personal" conviction about abortion in only a perfunctory manner. Nor has he urged the reversal of *Roe* v. *Wade*, the Supreme Court decision declaring a constitutional right to an abortion. It is as if Cuomo had been Governor of New York in the 1850s and dutifully upheld the Fugitive Slave Act while merely whispering his opposition to slavery. It is one thing for a public official to uphold the law as, of course, he must. But this need not prevent him—if he is convinced the law is wrong—from forcefully and often saying so in an effort to persuade the citizenry to help change it. This Cuomo has not done with regard to abortion.

As for the Vicar General's directive, the *New York Times* noted that "the archdiocese has every right to invite the speakers it wants. Mr. Cuomo's protest that lay Catholics have a 'right to be heard' in church forums is a question for

canon, not civil, law. The Cardinal also has every democratic right to try to influence politicians politically."

But if the Cardinal does that, the *Times* warned, "Voters may well reject Catholic candidates rather than risk
electing someone who puts religious conviction ahead of
political tolerance."

If someone believes, whether out of religious or human-
ist conviction, that abortion is the killing of a developing
and quite innocent human being, is he or she—while
upholding the law—supposed to dilute that personal conviction out of "tolerance" for those with a different view?

The electorate will decide. Of course, it will. But is it
accurate for the *New York Times*—and many liberals, including Mario Cuomo—to pose the question as if it were
somehow a defiance of the democratic process to be a candidate who refuses to publicly abandon or mute conviction—
even religious conviction? By that standard, the religious
Abolitionists were not playing the political game in the
American way.

The *Daily News*, in its editorial on the uproar, focused
solely on the Vicar General's directive, which it found
"confusing, unrealistic, and open to charges of political ma-
nipulation."

Somewhat confused myself as to the sweep of the directive, I asked the Cardinal how it came into being, and how
he defined its scope. Also, who actually does compile the list
of those forbidden to speak in a parish?

"Ultimately," the Cardinal said, "it will be the prudential judgment of the local pastor, but we want the local
pastor to take into mind *most particularly* the degree to
which what we call 'scandal' might be created. We're concerned with confusion, with people not knowing where in
the world we stand when it's all over.

"The basic question is: Does a parish invite a person with
a reputation of being mightily hostile to the Church—hostile to what we consider to be really sacred values, absolutely indisputable values? In that case, our bringing that
person into a church or to some other kind of parish event

would confuse people because it would appear that he had the approval of the Church.

"And the pastor will decide this?"

"There is no way in God's world," the Cardinal said, "by which you can give a pastor a slide rule, a chemical measure, for making a judgment each time. But pastors have to make judgments every day on infinitely more important things than this. Now, if I were to disagree with a pastor on this matter, and if it were a serious and continuing disagreement, then we'd have to confront the issue."

I wondered why, if the ban were not so important, the Cardinal had made it look so important by his public comments—until he had come to appear to be closing the archdiocese to a broad range of differing but not necessarily "scandal"-making opinions.

Unexpectedly, as I asked this, the Cardinal laughed. "I'm going to tell you," he said, "what triggered this whole thing off. It really is funny. It's ironic." He chuckled. "It makes a good story, and it's not known. What is so funny is that so many of the politically oriented people jumped on this and said, 'Boy, there goes O'Connor again! There's an election campaign starting, and the Cardinal is out to make an example of somebody.'

"So here's what happened. There's an organization—I won't name it lest it embarrass the members—a group of Catholic ladies. Just by virtue of the nature of their lives, they are largely older women. Some are in their eighties. They do a great deal of charitable work and they're just the most wonderful, loyal, gentle people. They're devoted to the Church in every respect.

"They were planning a luncheon, and the priest who acts as the chaplain of the organization invited a speaker for the luncheon. The priest had no knowledge of the person he was bringing in. That speaker, I'm told—I wasn't there— then proceeded to blast Church teachings on masturbation, contraception, and homosexuality.

"After forty-five minutes of this, the Chancellor of the archdiocese, who was there, got up and said, 'Look, we've really had enough of this.' It was all very polite and so on, but the Chancellor ended it. The ladies were mortified. It was a debacle.

"All of this was in-house. There was no publicity about what had happened. But it really got Bishop O'Keefe thinking, after he was told about it. So he asked, 'What guidelines *do* we have? Apparently you can't just depend on everybody's common sense.'

"That luncheon speech," the Cardinal said, "is what really brought the Vicar General to the decision to issue that directive. The incident took place maybe four or five months before he wrote the guidelines, but it was shortly after it happened that he figured the next time he published his newsletter for the pastors, he'd put in some quiet, unobtrusive item for this sort of thing."

"Why," I asked the Cardinal, "didn't you tell this story when the storm broke to make clear how it had all started?"

"A very worthy question," O'Connor said. "But when the news about the directive broke, it was immediately necessary to confront all the allegations against Bishop O'Keefe. At first, he was on his own. So I felt that integrity required me to show that I supported him. It was essential for me to act and to speak on the immediate issue. And the more I watched what was going on, the more I saw that those who were criticizing him weren't simply criticizing that one action he took. They were criticizing our right to act in that way. They were denying the archdiocese's right to act in that way."

Referring to Governor Cuomo without naming him, the Cardinal continued: "One statement of criticism, for example, was that 'we laymen have a right to speak.' Well, within appropriate contexts, there are many opportunities for lay persons to speak, but is that the same as saying 'We politicians have a right to speak within a Church context'?

"So then I wrote what I thought. I wrote it in *Catholic New York.* I felt there was an important principle at stake, and I guess I got a little bit mad."

"You certainly did," I said. "Not only in your column, but

in your letter to John Dearie. I've never seen you so angry in print."

The Cardinal looked somewhat rueful. "I have an almost unbreakable rule," he said, "of never writing a letter of response the same day I frame it in my mind. I always sleep on it first. But the letter to Dearie went out the same day I saw his interview in the *New York Times.* I was rushing to Washington, I knew I'd be gone three or four days, and what he said to the *New York Times* did get me angry. Particularly, when he attributed to me the order that banned him for speaking. *And I just didn't do that.* I usually pay no attention when I'm accused of doing something I didn't do, but then, when he said it had been done with a *political* motivation to affect a *political* campaign, I really did get mad because I knew why the Vicar General had set up those guidelines. I just told you why.

"If I were dying within the hour, I could swear that the last person in my mind when I saw that directive—except for Mario Cuomo—was John Dearie. When I read what Dearie said about a political motivation being behind it, I thought, The man can't be serious. But he said it. At my age, charity should have taken over. But I sat down and scribbled that letter. I told him what he had said was deeply insulting and morally libelous and grossly inaccurate.

"He didn't answer the letter, but I understand he called and wants to see me."

"Are you going to see him?" I asked.

Without any hesitation, the Cardinal said, "Oh, of course. I see anybody who wants to see me." The Cardinal paused, and shook his head. "I am not saying at all that John Dearie has fabricated a story. It is clear that someone—and that someone turns out to have been one of my secretaries—evidently thought that I had issued some kind of edict directed at Dearie, and he passed on to Dearie's pastor what he thought that edict was.

"That's very unfortunate, because I just didn't do that. I was personally mortified. I wasn't going to blame my secretary. I was mortified, but it's my responsibility because I apparently had not spoken clearly enough to my secretary so that he understood what I was saying."

The Cardinal frowned. "I would really have to say honestly—and this may simply reflect my ignorance of Who's Who in the New York archdiocese—but I just wouldn't have thought of John Dearie. I don't think I even knew what his voting record was on various issues."

The meeting between the Cardinal and John Dearie was held in September 1986, but at the Cardinal's request, the exchanges between the two men were kept private.

32

SOME SIX MONTHS LATER, I asked John Dearie whether he was still banned from speaking at his own church and his own parish. After all, in the fall of 1986, Joseph Swilling, a spokesman for the Cardinal, had told the *New York Times*, "I don't think the Church wants to blacklist anyone or make lists of who can or cannot speak."

Dearie, however, felt there was still a list, even though it might be a list of only one.

"Yes, I'm still banned," he told me, "and not only in my own parish. I'm forbidden to speak in all 411 parishes in this archdiocese, although I could be invited to churches in Brooklyn and Queens, where Bishop Mugavero is in charge." (In the fall of 1986, the Cardinal's spokesman had told the *New York Times*: "Each parish will consider the guidelines and consider how it should be followed, without fear of repercussions from the archdiocese.")

"It looks like a confused policy," Dearie told me. "Yet, it

may be that the intent is to keep it vague. On the one hand, they say it's archdiocesan policy, but when they're pressed about a particular case, they say it's up to the individual pastor."

But according to the comments of Dearie's pastor, Monsignor Vier, at the time of the banning, had the decision been left to him, Dearie would have been allowed to speak.

The hour-and-a-half meeting with the Cardinal in September, said Dearie, had been "enormously frank and very warm." He had agreed to provide no details. At the end, the two men agreed to think on what was said and perhaps meet again. But there had been no further meeting, and Dearie was still out in the cold.

The way out of the impasse, Dearie felt, was for him not to speak about Medicaid funding of abortion at parish events, but to be allowed to talk about other matters in which he had special legislative competence. Like problems of aging.

So why didn't the Cardinal agree to that resolution? "I think," Dearie said, "that he didn't want to embarrass Bishop O'Keefe." (In the public mind, Dearie's banning had been inextricably involved with the Vicar General's directive which was issued later.)

"It's my own feeling," said Dearie, "that if the Cardinal had his druthers, he'd prefer that O'Keefe had never issued that directive."

Also, despite O'Connor's angry denial that the barring of Dearie was motivated at least in part by a desire to harm Dearie politically among Catholic voters, the Assemblyman still believes that was indeed part of the motivation of the action taken against him.

"It was like a warning—'We're letting you know we're watching you.'" A warning, Dearie believes, to other Catholic legislators as well.

"I also don't believe," said Dearie, "that the Cardinal didn't know anything about me and about my legislative record. He and I have worked on other things in the past. As for abortion, you know, I'm forty-six, I just got married five years ago. My recollections of childbearing are not vague. Three years ago, and then two years ago, my wife and I looked at a sonogram during her third month of pregnancy. 'There's the head,' 'There's the arm,' 'There's the leg.' It's difficult for me to cast a vote for Medicaid funding for abortion, all the more so because I am very much a practicing Catholic. But I do feel that if abortions are legal, the poor are entitled to Medicaid funding for them."

Presumably all of this was discussed during Dearie's meeting with the Cardinal, and, I was thinking as Dearie spoke, at least O'Connor had had a two-way talk with the man. Under Cardinal Spellman, Dearie might have also been barred from the very presence of the spiritual leader of the archdiocese. Still, O'Connor's rigidity in dealing with Dearie reflected a side of him that is part of the insular nineteenth-century American Catholic Church rather than the Church that opens its windows to the world.

I asked Dearie how news of the ban had affected his performance in the November 1986 election. "Well," he said, "my district is heavily Italian, German, and Irish—about seventy-five to eighty percent Catholic. Furthermore, of all four hundred and eleven parishes in the archdiocese, the one in my district is one of the eight or ten strongest.

"In going around the district before the election, I found that almost everyone was aware of my having been banned, and the consensus was that they were opposed to Medicaid funding for abortion but they were very upset by the way I had been treated by the archdiocese."

Dearie won the election—running against a Republican, a Conservative, and a Right-to-Life candidate—by 78 percent of the vote. It was his highest margin of victory in the district.

"It's not that I was in danger of losing," he said, "but if the voters had approved of the ban on me, they could have cut down my margin considerably."

Among the more than six hundred letters and telephone calls Dearie received after he had been made a "nonperson" in his parish by the archdiocese was this caustic comment from a woman in Westchester: "1986 or 1686? Have politician hunts replaced witch hunts? Who's next at the stake?"

On the other side, a Manhattan woman wrote: "Is Cardinal O'Connor wrong because he wishes to keep his parishes free from the Dearies of the world? The Bronx Assemblyman should be forbidden at any religious function until he reconsiders his views on Medicaid funding for abortion. If a child of mine was to seek an abortion, the first thing I would give her is a one-way bus ticket to Sodom."

A man in Westchester told Dearie: "My spiritual leader will always get my vote. God bless you, Cardinal O'Connor. I'll pray for you, John."

And a man from the Bronx: "If we allow the Church to lobby the government on a slew of different social issues and yet disallow those same government representatives with mildly dissenting views to address a Church-related function on those same social issues, then we have reached a very dangerous state of censorship and persecution by the Church. Under such circumstances, how far is the Church from trying Dearie under canon law?"

Another observer from the Bronx noted "When you are a forward-looking person, you will always be picked on by the Catholic Church. . . . Only bigots listen to Cardinal O'Connor."

A "mother in the Bronx" disagreed:

I am a practicing Catholic and a registered voter in your district. (I knew I would have to mention the latter to catch your attention.) I have voted for you each and every time you have run for office, and up until recently, I have never regretted it.

I was so disappointed to learn of your decision to vote favorably for Medicaid funding of abortions. I was disillusioned that you, as a Catholic, did not share my belief that abortion is murder. By voting for the funding, you have condoned abortion and abandoned your faith. To call yourself a Catholic now would be a total hypocrisy.

I understand your concern that all people should have the same rights, whether rich or poor, but what about the rights of that unborn child?

Now I see that Cardinal O'Connor is being taunted by the press to comment on your ban from speaking at Church functions. That was very clever of you, Mr. Dearie. You have succeeded in turning the tables and make the Church out as the "bad guy" once again.

I still believe in miracles, so I will continue to pray that abortion will someday cease to exist, and I will pray for you, Sir, that you may find the strength to denounce conformity to the political pressures that surround you.

On the other hand, a woman in Parkchester wrote:

I have known you for a very long time, and you have always been a family man with very deep concerns for our Parkchester community.

Your seeking to guarantee the rights of poor women to make the same painful choices more affluent women must sometimes make, represents nothing more than you as an elected official executing the law. It does not, as the Church believes, solely represent a personal view.

That is why it grieves me so that the Catholic Church would seek to bar you from addressing a parish function, especially one that is unrelated to the abortion issue.

I am not praying for you, John, but for my Church to reverse this stupid policy.

33

OF ALL THE REACTIONS to the archdiocesan banning policy as a whole—including the silencing of John Dearie—the most probing was a long cover story in the December 6, 1986, issue of the Jesuit weekly, *America*. The article was significant not only because it was so trenchant a rebuke to Cardinal O'Connor as the person responsible for archdiocesan policy but also because of the identity of the author.

Monsignor Harry J. Byrne had been Chancellor of the archdiocese of New York from 1968 to 1970 under Terence Cardinal Cooke—with supervisory responsibility for housing, job, and racial-justice programs. At the time of his article in *America*, he was pastor of Epiphany Church on East Twenty-first Street in Manhattan. The Byrne essay, "Thou Shalt Not Speak," is of particular value because it gets to the core of those residual elements of the nineteenth-century Immigrant Church—defensive, tight, unwittingly self-diminishing—in Cardinal O'Connor. As much a son of Vatican II and an admirer of Dorothy Day as he is in other respects, O'Connor can also, on occasion, take on the stance of the historic autocrats of the American Church.

There is no question, Monsignor Byrne began, "that critics who claim the Church is inhibiting free speech when it provides guidelines or regulations regarding its teachers or teachings, are guilty of improperly transferring a political principle into ecclesiastical government. A church has every right to instruct its members regarding its tenets."

But that's not the point with regard to the Vicar General's directive, its implementation, and the Cardinal's support of it. The point is *how* the Church instructs and disciplines its members. The point is the *spirit* of the Church, as revealed to its members and to the rest of the society.

"That a new authoritarian mode of Church governance has recently been in seems clear," Monsignor Byrne wrote. "The authoritarian style of today's Church, both in its internal governance and in its relations to the external society is in strong contrast with the earlier style of Pope John XXIII and the spirit of the Second Vatican Council, so well articulated in the 'no condemnations' policy set for the council at its outset.

"In his October 11, 1962, speech opening the council, Pope John XXIII declared: 'Today the Spouse of Christ prefers to use the medicine of mercy rather than severity. She considers that she meets the needs of the present age by showing the validity of her teaching rather than by condemnation.' Here is clear reliance on the persuasiveness of message and example rather than on the authority of the proclaimer."

But that was then.

"The present spirit in the Church," Monsignor Byrne continued, "is reflected in the Church in the United States by involvement of some bishops in the electoral process as they instruct people with messages, variously delivered, on who not to vote for. The issue is complicated by similar tactics on the part of other groups in our society: Fundamentalist Christians, with their portfolio of issues, keep scorecards on legislators, and Jewish groups—more subtly, with equal definitiveness—convey a message of defeat at the polls for legislators who would vote against even minor pro-Israel legislation. It is a problem for the three major faith groups."

Byrne focused on the Catholic dimension of the problem, with particular reference to Bishop O'Keefe's guidelines for the selection of speakers in the archdiocese of New York. Granted, said the Monsignor, that there is a difference between the principles of free speech in a political democracy and the right of the Church to set rules for the instruction of its members in matters of faith and morals. Nonetheless, the O'Keefe guidelines raise questions. Questions the Cardinal has not clearly addressed.

For instance, for the Church to "ban a speaker who dissents on one issue from talking on any issue, such as local housing legislation, at his parish communion breakfast, carries serious political fallout if he is running for office. Is this simply an exercise in the teaching mission of the Church?"

Then there is the matter of precisely what Vicar General O'Keefe meant when he said the criterion for banning people was whether their "public position is contrary to and in opposition to the clear, unambiguous teaching of the Church."

What of those Catholics, Byrne asked, who accept "civil divorce in our legal system?" What of those who accept contraception? "Is there a line? Where is the line? Or is any and every dissent from declared 'clear, unambiguous teaching of the Church' grounds for the ban?"

Ah, but it's up to the individual pastors in the parishes. With so broad and vague a directive, however, the archdiocese may well be faced "with 400 lists of prohibited speakers."

The Monsignor next addressed the troubling question of how Assemblyman John Dearie had been treated. Here is a man, Byrne pointed out, who "has been in the forefront of safeguarding the interests of tenants and owners of small homes. He has consistently sponsored and voted for legislation providing various forms of state aid to parochial school students—tuition tax credits, textbook loans, and transportation—and to the parochial schools themselves—reimbursement for state-mandated services such as attendance and test reporting.

"Except for his vote favoring Medicaid funding of abortions, he has voted conservatively on abortion-related matters, as, for example, his vote favoring parental notification if a minor has an abortion."

Byrne recalled that during the 1984 presidential campaign, the United States Catholic Conference—the nation's bishops—felt the need to clarify for Catholics and non-Catholics just what Church policy is concerning politics. The Conference had said: "We specifically do not seek the formation of a religious voting block; nor do we wish to instruct persons on how they shall vote by endorsing candidates . . . We hope that the voters will examine the positions of candidates on the full range of issues as well as their integrity, philosophy, and performance."

Well, now, Byrne asked, "Is abortion the single issue that bans a specific candidate? The single issue that triggers penalties? Is it applicable only to Catholic candidates?"

The only two people publicly banned at that point were John Dearie and—according to Monsignor O'Keefe—Mario Cuomo. Both are Catholics and both were barred because as Catholics they had not supported the Catholic position on

Medicaid funding of abortion. A further mark against Cuomo, according to the Vicar General, is that he is "so smart" he would confuse people.

The banning directive, Monsignor Byrne said, raises a serious theological problem. If a Catholic, in conscience, takes a position that Church authorities consider erroneous, at what point does he lose "the right to represent himself or herself as 'Catholic' [having become] subject to a sort of partial excommunication by being declared less than Catholic and by being banned as a speaker in Catholic circles?

"Such a penalty can have serious political ramifications in an area with a heavy Catholic voting constituency and can constitute an extrinsic pressure on the officials' conscience."

After all, Vatican II had said of the right of religious freedom: "This freedom means that all men are to be immune from coercion on the part of individuals or of social groups and of any human power, in such wise that no one is to be forced to act against his conscience privately or publicly, whether alone or in association with others, within due limits."

The directive banning speakers, and its affirmation by Cardinal O'Connor, also raises serious pragmatic political difficulties—difficulties that John F. Kennedy had appeared to render obsolete until this directive.

As Monsignor Byrne put it, "Kennedy perceived that personal conscience was the mediating link between one's church and the act of a public official. He affirmed the right of a religious body to instruct its members 'in the area of faith and morals,' but disavowed the propriety of a religious body trying to bind directly a public official in his public duty."

Contrary to the expectations of many non-Catholic Americans, including not a few bigots, John Kennedy clearly proved that a Catholic elected official would not be a mere agent of his or her Church.

What greatly worries Monsignor Byrne is that directives

like the Vicar General's may blur the evidence of the Kennedy presidency in this regard.

The Vicar General's directive, with no criticism of it from the Cardinal, brings back the specter of the Church trying "to coerce a particular position of an official who voted 'the wrong way' by banning him or her from speaking on any topic at a church affair."

This move by the Archdiocese of New York, says Byrne,

is fraught with enormous risk. The question will always arise as to Catholic candidates or officials who carefully follow a Church position: Do they do this for reasons intrinsic to the issue or for fear of the ban if they do not? Just raising the question damages both a candidate and the political process. . . .

Inflicting punishment seems to be the dynamic at work here, regardless of counterproductive effects. . . . Assemblyman Dearie, the Catholic, must be punished for his one adverse vote.

If the preservation of clear Church teaching is the intended goal, as is claimed, simple declarative statements by Church officials would suffice, or perhaps at most forbidding the dissenter to speak under Catholic auspices on the subject of his or her dissent.

The totality of the ban, with its obvious political consequences, carries the unmistakable aura of punishment and penalty . . .

Monsignor Byrne then underscored the fundamental, lurking dangers in the archdiocesan directive: the "speakers' ban with its political effects has the potential of violating a candidate's conscience, of improperly intruding on the political process, and of disqualifying Catholics from public office in the minds of significant portions of the electorate."

According to Byrne, "adverse reaction to the speakers' ban was immediate among great numbers of New York priests, religious, and lay people."

Yet the Cardinal made no move to rescind or more narrowly define the ban, and John Dearie remained a pariah so far as being able to speak in his own church—or any church in the diocese.

I have written about this episode in the history of the Cardinal because it reflects his own conflicted personal and ecclesiastical personality—his concern with opening himself and the Church to all of New York, and all the world, on the one hand, and his occasional regression to the "fortress mentality" of the Immigrant Church on the other.

The directive also indicates that the Cardinal, usually a very clear thinker, is unable at times to gauge the potentially harmful effects of his sometime stubbornness. If he remained rigid about the directive so as not to embarrass the Vicar General, his loyalty turned out to be costly to how Catholics and non-Catholics perceived his understanding of the spirit of Vatican II.

If he himself saw nothing wrong with the vagueness of the directive's wording—and worse yet, with the pressure it put on both individual conscience and the democratic process—then he did not fully understand what Monsignor Byrne understood very clearly indeed: "American democratic political principles are not to be imposed on Church governance. But Church authoritarian procedures in the name of protecting its teaching are not to be imposed on the democratic governmental process.

"This principle works both ways. It is a fact of life that American voters will never elect someone whom they view as politically subservient to a religious body. For churchmen to cross the line between, on the one hand, instructing and informing conscience and, on the other hand, trying to force a legislative position on an officeholder by a speakers' ban is a very dangerous political game. It can result in the nonelectability of Catholics. . . ."

There was no public response from the Cardinal to Monsignor Byrne's blunt analysis. The directive of the Vicar General remained in force.

Governor Cuomo, on the other hand, said the archdiocese had made it clear that the speaking ban did not apply to him. Not so, said Bishop O'Keefe. The Governor would still not be allowed to speak at his church—which is part of the Catholic Center, the headquarters of the Archdiocese of New York.

⚜

34

THE SAME PRELATE who appeared to be so unbending in the punishment of John Dearie—which he affirmed, if not ordered—is, however, an enthusiastic admirer of the life and works of that devoted Catholic troublemaker Dorothy Day. In her lifetime, she scandalized a fair number of those in the hierarchy of the American Church. By contrast, John Dearie is the mildest of Catholics.

Long before Vatican II, this convert, who had started as a journalist and political radical, acted on her conviction that the Church must go into the world. At war with all violence, including that commanded by her nation, she helped organize abandoned workers, continually lived as well as worked among the poor, and did all this because, she said, her Catholic faith instructed her to.

O'Connor recalls: "I was a very young seminarian in Dorothy Day's early days in the Catholic Worker Movement. Her name was really a household word with us in our zealous youth and got more of us concerned about the poor and the homeless than she ever dreamed of. For years I read [her paper] the *Catholic Worker* avidly. It fit my own father's philosophy and what he passed on to me about the worth and dignity of working people, remarkably.

"I visited a number of [Catholic Worker] Hospitality Houses back in those days, but I'm afraid I have visited the

Catholic Worker folks here [in New York] only once since I have been in New York. They were doing precisely what I remembered their doing more than forty years ago, and I must confess they made me ask myself if the current Archbishop of New York has the same zeal that young seminarian had way back then."

Not long after he came to New York, the Archbishop urged that a study of Dorothy Day's life be started with the aim that she eventually be canonized.

There is a clear linkage between Dorothy Day and John Cardinal O'Connor. On May Day, 1933, in the first issue of the *Catholic Worker*, Dorothy Day spread the news that there are people of God who are working not only for the spiritual needs of the dispossessed but also "for their material welfare."

And in his Christmas Day message in 1986, Cardinal O'Connor said: "There's no point in simply talking to people about filling their souls if you don't fill their bellies."

Dorothy Day's favorite saint was Teresa of Avila, a vivid sixteenth-century Spanish mystic who occasionally observed with a not-too-gloomy sigh that "life is like a night spent in an uncomfortable inn." Cardinal O'Connor has felt that way more than once.

There was also a direct line between Dorothy Day and many of the current bishops of the changing American Church. In their 1983 pastoral letter on war and peace—on the drafting committee of which Archbishop O'Connor had served—the bishops cited Dorothy Day as a powerful witness for Christian pacifism for a very long time. And surely, the bishops' 1986 pastoral letter on the economy, *Economic Justice for All*, had been influenced little by little as a result of some of those bishops', as young priests, having read the *Catholic Worker*—a paper that spoke to their own American roots. In a 1983 study of American bishops in the Jesuit weekly *America*, Father Thomas J. Reese disclosed that: "Sixty-four percent of their fathers did not graduate from high school, and only 12 percent [of their fathers] graduated from college. Their roots in the working class may partially explain why the American bishops have taken 'liberal' positions on economic policy questions, especially when these positions have accurately reflected papal encyclicals."

Such encyclicals, for instance, as Pope Leo XIII's *Rerum Novarum* (1891), which stoutly supported workers' rights to organize while excoriating capitalistic greed. And the present Pope, John Paul II, has emphasized that the dignity of workers demands they have a part in the decisions that affect their lives. And this Pope has also claimed that workers deserve a share in the profits of their work.

In the 1986 pastoral letter on the economy, it could have been Dorothy Day speaking: ". . . the justice of a society is tested by the treatment of the poor . . . we say it is a social and moral scandal that one of every seven Americans is poor. . . . In 1983, 54 percent of the total net financial assets were held by 2 percent of all families . . . Eighty-six percent of these assets were held by the top 10 percent of all families."

In December 1946, in writing of a coal strike in Derry, Pennsylvania, for the *Catholic Worker*, Dorothy Day spoke both of workers' rights and of an American Church that was not nearly as concerned then as it is now with economic justice: ". . . when we read of the inhuman suffering of the workers, when we remember the blood that is on our coal, we know what the Holy Father means when he says that the world has lost a sense of sin. Not personal sin, but *social sin.* When priests do not cry out for the workers, try to share with the workers their poverty, then surely this is what the Holy Father means when he speaks of the devitalization of the Church. They are dead branches indeed."

There are fewer dead branches in the present Church, among priests and bishops, and Cardinal O'Connor—when it comes to the poor and the unorganized—is certainly not one of them. In his way, as have other American bishops in their ways, O'Connor has redefined what it is to be a Catholic bishop.

As the American bishops—in part because of Vatican II, in part because of their own family backgrounds, and in part because of the American ethos, however bent, of democracy—became more liberal in social and economic matters, one of them did a great deal to integrate their religious and social priorities.

At Fordham University on December 5, 1983, Joseph Cardinal Bernardin, of Chicago, built on what previous Catholic thinkers had designed as a consistent ethic of life. Bernardin called it "the seamless garment," a term first used by Eileen Egan, a friend of Dorothy Day and Mother Teresa.

Bernardin made the point that "those who would defend the right to life of the weakest among us must be equally visible in the support of the quality of life of the powerless among us: the old and the young, the hungry and the homeless, the undocumented immigrant and the unemployed worker.

"Such a quality of life [approach] translates into specific political and economic positions on tax policy, nutrition . . . and health care."

And more. "I submit," Cardinal Bernardin continued, "that the Church should be a leader in a dialogue which shows that the nuclear question itself is part of the larger cultural, political, moral drama . . . The range of application is all too evident: Nuclear war threatens life on a previously unimaginable scale; abortion takes life daily on a horrendous scale; public executions are fast becoming weekly events in the most advanced technological society in history; and euthanasia is now openly discussed and even advocated. Each of these assaults on life has its own meaning and morality; they cannot be collapsed into one problem, but they must be confronted as pieces of a larger pattern."

John Cardinal O'Connor has supported the "seamless garment" approach in public meetings with Cardinal Bernardin and in his newspaper columns. He does, however, place special emphasis on the meaning and morality of abortion in this design, and in that respect sometimes calls himself a "single-issue" man. But O'Connor also speaks out against poverty, the excesses of the defense budget at the expense of woefully inadequate health care and housing for the poor, and the rest of the seamless garment. For another example, O'Connor, unlike many of his flock, unequivocally opposes capital punishment.

The effect of Cardinal Bernardin's concept—which later became part of the official policy of the National Conference of Catholic Bishops as "the consistent ethic of life"— was quite divisive among Catholics. Some were fearful that abortion would be neglected amid all these other issues. Others said that the hierarchy ought not to get involved in such "political" issues as nuclear disarmament and the American economy.

Interestingly, and, some said, ominously for the liberal bishops, sociologist Dean Hoge of the Catholic University stated in 1986 that research showed "the greatest threat to future unity in the American Catholic Church" could come less from dissonances surrounding women's ordination and priests' celibacy than from opposition among the laity to bishops taking stands on political or social issues. In the survey, only 39 percent of Catholic adults surveyed supported bishops taking public stands on such questions as the economy and the arms race. By contrast, 80 percent of the priests surveyed did believe the bishops should speak out on public issues.

Despite that research, there has been considerable evidence that many younger, well-educated Catholics in particular have been buoyed and even inspired by "the seamless garment" concept.

Robert McClory of the *National Catholic Reporter*, for instance, wrote in the December 30, 1981, *Chicago Sun-Times:* "For too long the pro-life movement has been held captive by the most reactionary forces in American religion and politics. If you thought abortion was wrong, and said so, everyone assumed you must be carrying all the other overstuffed baggage of the New Right. You were supposed to hang on to every word of Representative Henry Hyde, Senator Jesse Helms, and the Reverend Jerry Falwell. You had to oppose affirmative action . . . environmental protection controls, economic planning, anti-handgun legislation, the Equal Rights Amendments, and every conceivable social welfare program."

But many Catholics opposing abortion opposed the other political positions of Hyde, Helms, and Falwell. And Cardinal Bernardin's way of illuminating the whole continuum of pro-life priorities has, in a way, rescued some of these Catholics from the stereotypical equation: Catholic = pro-life = Right Wing.

No longer would it be quite as easy as before to categorize Catholic antiabortionists in the ways listed by Robert McClory: "You were expected to endorse more military spending, prayer in public schools, prompt U.S. intervention in trouble spots all over the world, unlimited freedom for big business and industry, unquestioned support for every repressive Third World dictatorship so long as it wasn't leftist, and, of course, the swift execution of convicted murderers."

And, of course, these invidious stereotypes were not applied solely or primarily to pro-life Catholics. Through the decades, to many American liberals—ignorant of the diversity of Catholic thought—practically all Catholics have fitted neatly into the categories listed by McClory. And that's part of the still deeply embedded anti-Catholicism among a good many Americans, especially liberal and "radical" intellectuals.

This Know-Nothingness about Catholics does not appear to have lessened significantly, but Catholics are less and less on the defensive. And for some Catholics, the "seamless garment" has helped reilluminate their definitions of themselves, and their faith.

Even those liberals and radicals who hold on to their anti-Catholic stereotypes as part of *their* orthodoxy might have been surprised at the following exchange at the 1985 annual meeting of the National Conference of Catholic Bishops in Washington. They were discussing a draft of a pastoral letter on the economy that had already greatly irritated the White House and lay Catholics of the rich right. Bishop Anthony Bevilacqua, of Pittsburgh, rose to urge that the letter be more upbeat in tone so it would remind the faithful and all others that, after all, our economic system is the best in the world.

The man who headed the committee writing the letter, Archbishop Rembert G. Weakland, of Milwaukee, looked at the Bishop of Pittsburgh and said that, in truth, the American economic system may be the *worst* of all those in the developed world in terms of how it distributes its wealth. Quoting a Brazilian economist, the Archbishop spoke of "economic apartheid" in American cities.

The Bishop of Pittsburgh, clearly bereft of any significant support among his colleagues, sat down.

35

A PARTICULARLY VIVID EPIPHANY of the changing self-definition of an American bishop—manifested in a way that would have been unthinkable a half century and more ago—took place on May 9, 1987.

William Casey, former director of the Central Intelligence Agency and for many years a powerful presence at the highest echelons of public and private life, was being buried in St. Mary's Church, Roslyn Harbor, Long Island. This was his home diocese of Rockville Centre, and delivering the homily was Casey's bishop, John R. McGann.

In the church were President Ronald Reagan and his wife, Nancy Reagan; former President Richard Nixon; Secretary of State George Shultz; Defense Secretary Caspar

Weinberger; Attorney General Edwin Meese; and FBI Director William Webster, who was to succeed Casey as head of the CIA.

In the homily, Bishop McGann spoke warmly of his longtime friend and took grateful note of Casey's long service to the diocese. He ended by emphasizing his differences with Casey concerning American policies in Central America, including this nation's use of violence there as a means of foreign policy.

McGann said that Casey's "conviction about the fundamental moral purpose of American actions, I'm sure, made incomprehensible to him the ethical questions raised by me as his bishop about our nation's defense policies since the dawn of the nuclear age.

"I'm equally sure," the Bishop continued, "that Bill must have thought us bishops blind to the potential for a Communist threat in this hemisphere as we opposed—and continue to oppose—the violence wrought in Central America by [the Administration's] support of the Contras.

"These are not light matters on which to disagree. They are matters of life and death. And I cannot conceal or disguise my fundamental disagreement in these matters with a man I knew and respected.

". . . my prayer is that Bill Casey, once our country's director of Central Intelligence, will now live forever in the presence of Creation's central intelligence . . . who we believe is also universal love and everlasting peace."

Outside the church, as if to accentuate Bishop McGann's criticism of the famous deceased, the Reverend William Brisotti, pastor of Our Lady of Loretto in Hempstead, led three other protesters against the Reagan Administration's Central American policies.

"As a priest, I believe," Father Brisotti said, "you must encourage people away from supporting the Contras. I hope some compassion will touch the heart of Ronald Reagan and bring about a change."

Bishop McGann's criticism of William Casey at his very funeral made the front pages and television news broadcasts throughout the country. His spokesman explained, reported *Newsweek*, that the Bishop "felt that if he omitted any mention of the Contra issue, it might appear that the Bishop had changed his position and [it] would raise questions about where he stood. He said McGann felt he could not ignore the issue, and felt it was possible to separate the moral character of Casey from his political decisions."

McGann's decision to speak his mind and spirit at the funeral astonished and angered a good many Catholics. The Bishop has been a vigorous pro-life activist, and so, in the abstract, has President Reagan. But McGann's outspokenness in front of the President should not have been entirely surprising because he had also opposed the Vietnam War. That opposition, however, had been behind the scenes. Now, as the American Catholic Church kept getting bolder, becoming more involved in political issues, McGann had also become bolder.

Many angry letters, however, were written to Catholic newspapers about the Bishop's criticism of the dead CIA Director. In the *Long Island Catholic*, the newspaper of McGann's own diocese, a reader called the Bishop's remarks "appalling, amazing, and alarming to us of the Catholic laity who share neither his views, nor those of the bishops to whom he refers, nor agree upon the occasion during which he chose to express them."

Yet, in *Catholic New York*, the paper of Cardinal O'Connor's diocese, a reader, probably representing another considerable segment of the Catholic laity, wrote:

. . . I had been reflecting with particular sorrow on that Sunday, Mother's Day [when William Casey was buried], on the mothers of Nicaragua, who have been so cruelly bereft of so many, many children in these last six years, in satisfaction of our prevailing, obsessive, anti-Communist ideology.

A missioner from Esquipulas had written me recently of a single mother in his parish who has lost five sons in this vicious war. The raw statistics are dreadful: a country of 3 million; 15 thousand killed; median age 15. Think of it. Thousands of children . . . have died because our leaders, so tragically limited, so incapable of perceiving nonpolar alternatives, have judged that Nicaragua's children are better off dead than Red.

In crafting his thoughtful, balanced eulogy, Bishop McGann remained faithful to Pope John Paul II's injunction "to call by name every social injustice, discrimination and violence inflicted on man."

In the time of Francis Cardinal Spellman, had such a letter been written it would almost certainly not have been printed in the equivalent then of *Catholic New York*. Indeed, in the time of Cardinal Spellman, it would have been highly unlikely that any bishop, no matter what he thought privately, would have dared criticize a prominent former official of the government while officiating at his funeral—and especially not in the presence of the President of the United States.

In an editorial, the *Brooklyn Tablet*, a diocesan paper that was quite jingoistic thirty and forty years ago, not only supported Bishop McGann but added: "The church must exercise its freedom to express itself in a pluralistic society. That task is not to be taken lightly, nor can it be limited to general aphorisms."

While the majority of responses to the editorial were critical of the *Tablet* and of Bishop McGann, a priest, Father Edward F. Doherty, exemplified the criteria of moral political action that an increasing number of American Catholic priests share: "Had Bishop McGann's remarks omitted all reference to the discrepancy between Mr. Casey's views and the position of the U.S. bishops on our government policy in Central America, his silence, not his words, would have been the scandal. When history has closed its books on the murderous policies of the CIA in Central America, let us hope it mentions the courageous moral leadership of a bishop who was not cowed into silence by the presence of the mighty, but who instead used the pulpit to place God before Caesar. He deserves more than admiration from his fellow bishops. He deserves imitation."

And a lay Catholic, a woman, wrote about the Bishop's closing remarks: "It is so refreshing to see that morality can and should extend 'beyond the bedroom.' Bishop McGann did a courageous, moral thing, and I applaud him for it."

A particularly perceptive comment on the historic significance of the Bishop's farewell to his friend appeared in the *National Catholic Reporter* (May 22, 1987):

Let's pause to reflect a few moments on a mainstream U.S. bishop, vintage 1987, the kind of bishop so solid and solidly middle [and "mainstream"] you rarely hear he's around. I'm thinking of Rockville Centre, N.Y., Bishop John R. McGann, the man who had the courage to look down at President Reagan, sitting in the first pew of St. Mary's Church in Roslyn Harbor, Long Island, and boldly tell him his nuclear arms and Central American policies are ethically marred. . . .

McGann is generally not a nationally known bishop, just one plodding forward in his journey with his vision of the Church, a vision that now routinely includes calls to aid the poor, to end the warfare in Central America, to build more public housing, to open one's home to the poor—all McGann pleas in recent months.

So let's recognize courage when we see it. McGann, even believing as he does, did not have to speak as he did. Or did he? How far *have* we come? Of course, the Bishop is catching flak for speaking up. It's coming from the press and even from some in his diocese. They're saying he was out of place, that raising ethical questions before the President and the Casey family was not what was expected from the Catholic Church. So where have they been? But it shouldn't surprise us they still don't understand. All the more reason to know that McGann, "bishop mainstream," is on target.

So to him and the rest of the "mainstream" out there, hats off.

Not long after Bishop McGann became nationally and controversially known, I asked John Cardinal O'Connor what he thought of the Bishop's remarks at William Casey's funeral.

"Well," O'Connor said, "when Bishop McGann made his remarks, gee whiz, there were a lot of phone calls and letters addressed to *me.* They wanted me to fire him. People think I have all sorts of authority I don't have. They don't understand the separation of the dioceses.

"Now, as for what I thought. I personally would not have said what he did at a funeral."

It was the place, rather than the content, of the remarks?

"Oh, yeah," said the Cardinal. "I've said what he said in many other contexts, but not at a funeral. That's a matter of temperament, of personal judgment. But Bishop McGann is such a fine, gentle, and sensitive man, certainly not someone who engages in rash statements or arbitrary statements or in hurting people.

"If I were in a position of authority on this matter, and I am not, I certainly couldn't and wouldn't take any action against the Bishop on the basis of what he said."

The Cardinal was not being diplomatic; he seldom is. Although it would have been against O'Connor's grain to take issue with a dead man at his own funeral, he agreed with what McGann had said about American policy in Central America.

I asked the Cardinal about another member of the hierarchy who had become a national figure, Archbishop Raymond Hunthausen, of Seattle. Not because of what he had said at a funeral but because he had been criticized by the Vatican for, as some put it, being too casual an archbishop in matters of doctrine. Those "weaknesses" included being overly liberal in the liturgy and in accommodation of homosexual groups, allowing sterilizations to be performed in Catholic hospitals, a looseness in the use of general absolutions, improper education of priests, improper selection of priesthood candidates, the admission of non-Catholics to communion at Mass while also allowing Catholics to receive communion at Protestant services.

Hunthausen, though he had a number of fierce critics among conservative Catholics in Seattle, was much admired by the majority of the laity, the priesthood, and members of the religious orders. He also had won the respect and affection of peace and antinuclear activists of all religions—and none. Some of Hunthausen's supporters believed that the Vatican's crackdown on the Archbishop had to do with the militancy of his peace work, but it is much more likely that Hunthausen's troubles came essentially from the alleged doctrinal divergences from the Holy See that he had allowed. Yet, as the *New York Times* noted on November 10, 1986, "many practices for which . . . Hunthausen . . . was reprimanded by the Vatican are common across the United States."

In 1986, Hunthausen was humiliated by having to turn over, under Vatican instructions, all his authority as Bishop in a number of key areas under dispute to a new Auxiliary Bishop, Father Donald Wuerl, a Vatican appointee.

Although Cardinal O'Connor chooses to deny that a quiet rebellion against the Vatican among many American bishops followed the disciplining of Hunthausen, there is no question that during the November 1986 meeting in Washington of the National Conference of Catholic Bishops, much displeasure at the Holy See was expressed behind closed doors. And a final statement of support for the Vatican's handling of the case was eventually so attenuated as to send a clear message to Rome that the Pope and his advisers had made a serious mistake. The bishops deleted a phrase characterizing what Rome had ordered done in Seattle as "just and reasonable." The bishops substituted a cooler statement that Rome's actions were taken "in accord with general principles of Church law and procedure."

The Holy See got the message and also recognized that unless some kind of reversal of Hunthausen's lowered status took place, the Pope's September 1987 visit to the United States might well be marred by additional lines of pickets.

Accordingly, in January 1987, the Vatican appointed a three-member panel to "review" the situation in Seattle. According to a number of experts on the inner politics of the Church whom I interviewed, the task of this extraordinary pontifical commission was to get the Vatican off the hook. Church historian Monsignor John Tracy Ellis told me, "You notice, for instance, that the Holy See appointed three top-notch bishops, not ordinary bishops." The three were Joseph Cardinal Bernardin of Chicago, Archbishop John Quinn of San Francisco, and John Cardinal O'Connor of New York.

In the spring of 1987, the commission recommended, and the Pope personally approved, what appeared to be a signal victory for Archbishop Hunthausen. All his powers were restored to him, Auxiliary Bishop Wuerl was sent away, and a new, more congenial coadjutor archbishop, Thomas Murphy of Montana, was appointed instead. The special commission was told by the Holy See to continue monitoring the situation, but that may have been a way of face-saving for the Vatican.

There had been strong rumors before the decision was announced that a deal had been struck whereby there would be an appearance of victory for Hunthausen but within a year or so he would resign. Hunthausen, showing no signs of having been pressured into any deal, said, after being restored to his full authority, "I have no intention of resigning or retiring."

Monsignor John Tracy Ellis was very pleased with the resolution of the Hunthausen affair. Quite clearly, he told me, the American bishops had gotten their point across to the Holy See that Rome had gone too far with regard to Hunthausen. The solution had been a conciliatory move by the Vatican, Ellis said.

I asked Cardinal O'Connor if he agreed. "I'd be more inclined to say," O'Connor responded, measuring his words, "that it was made clear to the Holy See that that way of sharing power in Seattle was not going to work. It was my personal conviction that it was not working. So much confusion had been generated, so much bitterness had developed. There had been so much conflict and so much tension that even if the arrangement had been a good idea, it didn't have a chance of working."

And all of this tension had been magnified, the Cardinal went on, "by all the reports in the newspapers, on television and radio, and from letters flooding in from all over."

At this point, O'Connor, the quintessential loyalist,

stressed: "There came to be a great deal of confusion in Rome as this situation continued, but in Rome they never felt they had acted unjustly to Archbishop Hunthausen in any way. And I would agree with that."

O'Connor would not agree with Monsignor Ellis that in November 1986 the National Conference of Catholic Bishops had sent a clear message to the Holy See to back off. He did concede that at the meeting, "there was considerable anxiety that the tension and confusion about the Seattle affair was going to keep on expanding, and people were beginning to hold their breath in apprehension of when the next explosion was going to take place."

However, O'Connor continued, "Monsignor Ellis is certainly right in saying that once the Holy See appointed the pontifical commission, it was clear that the Holy See wanted to look for other possibilities."

At that point, O'Connor revealed, as he sometimes does, that his loyalty to the Pope can cloud the customary clarity of his judgment: "Maybe I'm just too supportive of the Holy See, I don't know, but I don't think the appointment of the commission was a signal on the part of the Holy See that it felt it had made a mistake. The Holy See was confronted by a very very complicated situation, and I think it was an act of great integrity on their part to say, 'We have to clear the smoke and try to find out where we are in this matter at this moment. We can't depend on the newspapers to tell us, so we'll appoint a commission.'"

O'Connor and the other two members of the pontifical commission made an insistent and public pledge that it would not be secretive. The reason for stressing this was that Hunthausen and his supporters had bitterly resented the secrecy with which the previous investigation of the archdiocese and its bishop had been conducted by the Holy See.

In his November 1986 statement to the conference of Catholic bishops in Washington, Archbishop Hunthausen had told his colleagues that the entire process by which he had been investigated had been "performed in a shroud of secrecy." Indeed, he said, he had not even been notified of the charges against him. "Secrecy," he said, "does not work in matters of this sort, and [it] should not work." Moreover, Hunthausen added, that secrecy had led to "confusion and serious scandal for many of our people."

Then, as if that secrecy had led to contrasting the American Church today with the "pay, pray, and obey" Immigrant Church, Hunthausen said, "Our people have 'come of age,' and they deserve to be treated as adults. They are capable of dealing maturely with problems where they exist and they take seriously the 'ownership' of the Church that is their birthright as baptized members of the Body of Christ."

In January 1987, as the turmoil in and about Seattle intensified, the Vatican's ambassador to the United States, Archbishop Pio Laghi—who had been a frequent harbinger of good news to Cardinal O'Connor—tried to explain to Americans the differences between their criteria of fairness in an investigation and the standards of the Vatican.

Speaking to Joseph Berger of the *New York Times* (January 30, 1987), Laghi said that Americans, with their "complex of Watergate," believe that "when something is behind the door, there is the impression that something is wrong."

But Berger reported Laghi as emphasizing that "the Vatican believed more in 'the principle of charity' and in being sensitive to the privacy of a person under investigation."

The Vatican, Laghi noted, only revealed some of the details of its investigation of Hunthausen at the urging of a number of American bishops who, being American as well as Catholic, felt strongly that it was fundamentally unfair that Hunthausen did not have a clear sense of the charges against him.

Laghi believes, nonetheless, that secrecy is beneficial to those being investigated. "We cannot expose, because for us, when a person testifies, we have to respect that person."

But how does the Vatican respond when complaints are made that it is acting as if Franz Kafka wrote the script? "In defending itself," says Laghi, "the Holy See would have offended somebody."

But the Holy See, in its secretive procedures, profoundly offended Archbishop Hunthausen and his many supporters. And a good many Catholic bishops of the American Church.

At the end of the interview with the *New York Times*, Archbishop Laghi—in view of the persistently discordant aftermath of the Holy See's initial Seattle decision—said that it was his "duty to convey to Rome the kind of expectations of an open democratic system" that characterize many American bishops.

Rome had already heard.

And the three-member pontifical commission kept that expectation of openness very much in mind.

"Our very first decision," Cardinal O'Connor told me, "was that we would do absolutely nothing that had to be kept secret. We said among ourselves and to Archbishop Laghi and to Hunthausen and to Wuerl that we would not use any documents that were not available to Hunthausen and Wuerl. We would not write any reports that we could not give to them. I think that decision for openness was tremendously important."

"And," said O'Connor, "this was a most unusual thing— for a papally assigned commission of this sort to complete its work and then universally distribute its report. Now, it has to be said, if the Holy Father asks you to assess something and give him that assessment, that assessment belongs to him. He could have told us, 'This report will not be publicized.' So we said to ourselves, 'Let's write this report in such a way that when we take it to the Holy See, we'll be able to convince them that it's publishable. That way people will see that we have nothing up our sleeves, and that the Holy See has nothing up its sleeve.

"We were very happy when the Holy See agreed. There was no question about it. They agreed completely about publicizing the report, as they did with our recommendations. So, to my knowledge, there is not a single piece of paper or oral agreement to connect with this report that is secret. It's all out. There was no sense of this being a trial involving faceless accusers."

After the Hunthausen inquiry was all over, or so it appeared, it was still unclear why the Holy See had focused on Archbishop Hunthausen—and what that meant in terms of future relationships between the Vatican and the American Church.

One thing was clear. A continuous, heavy barrage of letters ferociously criticizing Archbishop Hunthausen had been directed at the Vatican over a considerable period of time by exceptionally aggressive conservative Catholics, particularly the staff and readers of *The Wanderer*, an American Catholic newspaper of fiercely orthodox views. Those criticisms concerned both doctrinal matters in the Seattle archdiocese and the Archbishop's continually outspoken opposition to nuclear arms and nuclear reactors. Accordingly, Hunthausen had become considerably more visible to the Vatican than most other bishops in the United States, including those who were engaging in many of the same doctrinal practices that later resulted in Hunthausen's being brought up on charges.

Another theory as to why Hunthausen was targeted is that while the Holy See recognizes that the American Church—by the very nature of American society and traditions—has to be somewhat diverse, limits have to be placed on that diversity. And Hunthausen had strayed too far— both in doctrinal matters and in the manner in which he protested nuclear war—from the reasonably normative behavior that Rome expects from even American bishops. He had called the Trident submarine's base there "the Auschwitz of Puget Sound." Accordingly, an example had to be made of him.

In any event, as Monsignor John Tracy Ellis told me, American bishops, at least some of them, were personally much disquieted by the attack on Hunthausen, even though he was eventually restored to his full powers. As Father Richard McSorley, director of the Center for Peace Studies at Georgetown University, said: "If they can do it to Hunt-hausen, they can do it to any one of the bishops."

But the Vatican would appear to have learned a lesson from its mishandling of the Hunthausen affair. If they go after another American bishop, it is likely to be done openly, not secretively, and with a good deal more due process in other respects as well. What happened in Seattle may have taught the Vatican something of the distinctly American elements of the American Catholic Church. And liberal American Catholics have learned that if they make their displeasure evident to Rome, they can have an effect. Rome does not listen only to the orthodox among the American faithful.

As the *National Catholic Reporter* put it, "It was . . . clear to the Catholic community that strong, unrelenting, pro-Hunthausen pressure from priests, and religious, and lay people had much to do with the Vatican's change of course."

"Hopefully," said a priest in Seattle, "Rome will never treat another diocese the same way." And a Holy Name Sister added that the outcome demonstrated that "it's *our* Church."

The ownership of the Church, however, is still not that clear.

What is clear is that while Rome may have to change its strategy in keeping the American Church in line, the Holy See nonetheless intends to do just that. In the November 17, 1986, *U.S. News & World Report*, David O'Brien, professor of American religious history at Holy Cross College in Worchester, Massachusetts, said: "The Pope and a lot of European Church leaders feel that we are a kind of libertarian, hedonistic, loose kind of society. They simply don't understand this culture, and don't really want to."

O'Brien and other historians of the American Church point out that Rome also does not understand the growing influence and, equally important, the collegial procedures of the National Conference of Catholic Bishops—including the way it carefully involves members of the laity in preparing such of its pastoral letters as those on nuclear arms and the economy.

This kind of policy-making national conference of bishops, each bishop equal to the others, is, Professor O'Brien emphasized, "revolutionary—a new way of being a Church that can't be controlled or predicted."

As William Bole of the Religious News Service observes: "At one time, the Catholic hierarchy in this country was identified almost exclusively with the major archdioceses on the East Coast, in Chicago and Los Angeles, and with the imperial cardinals who presided over them. They wielded the greatest influence and were, in the eyes of many, the Church.

"Today, much of this influence is in the hands of the national conference of bishops, which was revitalized in the wake of the Second Vatican Council reforms during the 1960s. Because of this structure, a bishop from Youngstown, Ohio, who becomes president can speak for the hierarchy in a way that the cardinal of Boston, New York, or Philadelphia can't." (And in November 1986, Bishop James Malone, of Youngstown, Ohio, as president of the National Conference of Catholic Bishops, was able—with the support of this institution—to say at the annual meeting of his fellow bishops: ". . . no one who reads the newspapers of the past three years can be ignorant of the growing and dangerous disaffection of elements of the Church in the United States from the Holy See.")

It is now possible, therefore, for a "provincial" bishop to be for a time as influential among his colleagues as—or more than, let us say—a cardinal from Boston. And also, as William Bole notes, this shift away from the "power centers" of the past, "gives the national structure an independent identity which the bishops, notwithstanding their sincere loyalty to Rome, jealously guard." (It is also the best financed and organized national structure in the entire Church.)

And, as a *somewhat* independent entity with regard to Rome, the national conference of American bishops was

able—at the end of its discussion of the Hunthausen affair—to offer Rome "any assistance judged helpful and
appropriate by the participants involved."

Quietly, the offer was accepted, and the Holy See appointed the extraordinary pontifical commission of the
three American bishops including John J. O'Connor.

Still, the National Conference of Catholic Bishops has
yet to be fully challenged by the Holy See, and there is fear
among American bishops of what might happen if the Vatican were to insist on greatly tightening its control over the
Church in America. That fear has been expressed by Joseph
Cardinal Bernardin. Characteristically, the careful Chicago prelate framed his apprehensions through a history
lesson, "The Church in the United States: Where are we
going, where have we been?" in the May 3, 1987, issue of *Our
Sunday Visitor*, a conservative Catholic weekly.

Bernardin was explaining the rise and precipitous fall at
the beginning of the century of a doctrine called Modernism. As explained by Martin E. Marty in *An Invitation to
American Catholic History*, the Modernists, first in Europe
and then in America, consisted of theologians and other
Catholic intellectuals who were drawn to, among other
things, "scientific biblical scholarship. They believed that
faith would be strengthened through analytical knowledge.
Some, for instance, saw no necessary conflict between evo-
lution and orthodoxy.

"The Modernism that reached American shores," Mary
emphasizes, "was very moderate and always loyal," but in
Europe, some of the Modernists took positions edging toward heresy—questioning, for example, whether Jesus had
consciously intended to found a church.

In 1907, the Holy See condemned Modernism, cautioning
the Church throughout the world to resist "all systems to
thought by whatever name which . . . threatened the validity and stability of dogma."

In *The Now and Future Church*, Eugene Kennedy reports the reaction in America to Pope Pius X's indictment
of Modernism: "Intellectual martial law was declared

throughout the Roman Church: committees of vigilance were established in every diocese to sniff out the acrid scent of heresy, teachers thought sympathetic to Modernism were to be discharged 'without compunction,' books and magazines, periodicals of every kind were to be censored if necessary, priests were forbidden, except in the safest circumstances, to gather in congresses."

And Cardinal Bernardin, writing in *Our Sunday Visitor* decades later, when the Vatican had again been punishing dissenters and the insufficiently orthodox in the American Church, says of the crushing of Modernism:

while Catholic discipline was greatly strengthened, the progress of Catholic scholarship in the U.S. and elsewhere was inhibited. In fact, Catholic thought did not show convincing signs of new vigor and creativity until 40 or even 50 years later.

As an elderly priest-theologian once told a much younger confrere, "You don't know what it was like to teach theology in those days. You had to keep your creative thoughts to yourself and worry about the state of your soul—unless you didn't think at all."

Bernardin is hardly the only bishop, or priest, in America who wonders, at times, whether those days of darkness will return. John J. O'Connor, however, is apparently not concerned, for he sees perpetual light in the canons of orthodoxy.

36

IN ADDITION TO Archbishop Hunthausen, another member of the Catholic hierarchy was involved in controversy in 1987, and surely would be again. On May 5, for the first time in the history of the American Catholic Church, two bishops were arrested for civil disobedience in the course of a protest against nuclear war—and preparations for nuclear war.

One of the prelates was retired Bishop Charles Buswell of Pueblo, Colorado. The other, Detroit Auxiliary Bishop Thomas Gumbleton, is a longtime peace activist, a critic of American policy in Central America, and national president of Pax Christi, an organization of Catholic pacifists. He served with Cardinal O'Connor in the preparation of the 1983 pastoral letter on nuclear arms by America's Catholic bishops.

The arrest of the two bishops marked only the second time in American Catholic history that a bishop had been arrested for an act of civil disobedience of any kind. The first had involved Emerson Moore, Auxiliary Bishop of New York, for his involvement in a protest against South African apartheid. Bishop Moore is black. At the time, Cardinal O'Connor strongly supported Bishop Moore's action.

The May 1987 protest took place in Mercury, Nevada, and was directed at American nuclear weapons testing. In his invitation for others to come and join the protest, Bishop Gumbleton said: "It is time to resist our participation in government policies that conflict with the Gospel. We must change public policy in accord with the clear teaching of the [1983] peace pastoral. On the fourth anniversary of [the 1983 pastoral letter] *The Challenge of Peace*," I invite all of you to come to the Nevada desert to pray at the place where all U.S. nuclear weapons are tested . . ."

Before the demonstration began, Gumbleton made clear that he was not acting as a member of the American Catholic hierarchy but rather as "a disciple of Christ." Still, he added, he was pleased that the day's action had the support of twelve other bishops, thereby perhaps strengthening the credibility of that and future actions.

"We must stop this madness," said Cardinal O'Connor's former colleague on the pastoral letter. "We cannot allow the arms race to propel us to physical and spiritual self-destruction. There is no longer, for me at least, any moral alternative. I must actively resist . . ."

In the *Catholic Agitator*, a Los Angeles paper published by local members of the Catholic Worker, Ciaron O'Reilly, an Australian poet, described the events of that historic day in the desert that led to the two bishops' being handcuffed and taken away by police from the Nevada Nuclear Test Site, which, over the years, has become the center of national resistance to nuclear arms.

O'Reilly wrote: "Shosone tribal elder, Bill Rosse, spoke to us of the history of his people on this land and the spirituality that had developed in relation to it, the pain of invasion and the final sacrilege of seeing [this land] destroyed by nuclear weapons testing."

Bishop Gumbleton spoke of the hopes that accompanied the 1983 pastoral letter on war and peace. The hopes, he said, "that the President would be influenced by the moral demands of that 1983 statement and make specific moves to limit the production of nuclear weapons leading toward eventual disarmament." But instead, "the escalation of the arms race has kept rising."

During the speeches, O'Reilly saw around him "scores of nuns, parish priests, Oblates, Franciscans, Jesuits, Holy Name Society members, mothers of four, brothers of many. They were here at this place of death, this state-sanctioned denial of Christ in the Nevada desert. They were here with their Roman collars, sensible shoes, occasional veils, crucifixes, rosary beads, a banner depicting Our Lady of Guadalupe, holy water, and T-shirts with messages. They were here from twenty-eight U.S. states and three countries to break bread, break their silence, and break the law."

A letter was read from Bishop Maurice Dingham of Des Moines. Bedridden as a result of a recent stroke, he asked those who had been able to come to the desert "to consider this witness an opportunity to fill the expectations of the pastoral letter [of 1983]. For me, to remain silent would be a sin of omission. In my powerlessness to physically move, I experience the powerlessness of all those who are paralyzed in the face of this evil. I ask you to carry me across the line in a broken, fragile world that desperately seeks peace."

A banner was up: "THE CHURCH IS CROSSING THE LINE."

A captain from the county sheriff's department told all those assembled: "First, I am going to ask you not to do this. Second, if you do cross the line, I have to tell you that you will be arrested and transported to Beatty [a town sixty miles from the test site]."

Ninety-eight Catholics crossed the line. Handcuffed and singing hymns, they were taken off to Beatty.

Something happened before the arrests that reflects the kinds of dialogue about "ownership" of the American Catholic Church that have been increasingly and insistently taking place. As noted in the *National Catholic Reporter* (May 15):

While many will rightly focus on the historic nature of the protest, another story relating to that protest should not get lost, because it speaks to the maturing way in which U.S. Catholics see themselves as Church.

Before the ninety-eight demonstrators crossed the line, a discussion developed. Initially, there was talk that the bishops should go first, as they were the focus of much attention. After further discussion, the thinking was that the bishops, viewed as representing the Church hierarchy, should go last—because in speaking out against the arms race and risking arrest to stop it, the bishops were following the lead of many others who had gone before . . .

Upon further reflection, however, political symbols and ecclesial symbols gave way to spiritual symbols. "It was quite a spiritual moment," one participant later reflected. "We really came to realize, to see, we were one as Church. And that the bishops were one with us."

It was finally decided the bishops, one with all the other protestors, and accepted spiritual leaders, would lead the group, crucifix before them all, across the line.

(Later, the National Federation of Priests Council supported the antinuclear act of civil disobedience, by a vote of 119 to 2.)

A few weeks after his arrest in Nevada, Bishop Gumbleton was in Linz, Austria, participating in a celebration of the eightieth anniversary of the birth of Franz Jagerstatter, an Austrian executed in August 1943 for refusing to serve in Hitler's army.

Gumbleton said that Jagerstatter's refusal to participate in evil is a reminder "that believers of God's word should *not let other believers die alone* ... His death reminds us that we all ought to be there, God's people together, resisting together what we know to be evil. When the public authority leads us away from truth into nightmares of human destruction and then persuades us that they are doing good, the believing people who [have] known something ... of God and of human love, must stand in *the public arena* and say no."

Bishop Gumbleton is a member of the National Conference of Catholic Bishops Committee to Assess the Moral Status of Deterrence. This committee is charged with determining whether to recommend that the American bishops go beyond the 1983 pastoral letter on war and peace. That letter had called for "a strictly conditioned moral acceptance of nuclear deterrence"—provided that real advances were subsequently made toward disarmament, because otherwise, the bishops said in 1983, what they had agreed to for the time being would not "be adequate as a long-term basis for peace."

It is not inconceivable that after the deliberations of the Committee to Assess the Moral Status of Deterrence, America's Catholic bishops may decide that if the use of nuclear weapons is immoral, then the possession and stockpiling of them is also immoral, and therefore the policy of nuclear deterrence is immoral.

Cardinal O'Connor had originally been assigned to the Moral Status of Deterrence Committee, but he resigned because of the press of other work. Should Bishop Gumbleton's views prevail on the committee, Cardinal O'Connor may regret his decision not to stay.

Not long after Bishop Gumbleton and the other ninety-seven Catholics had been arrested in Nevada in May 1987, I asked Cardinal O'Connor what he had thought of the historic event.

Cardinal O'Connor took pains to remind me that one of *his* bishops, Emerson Moore—not Thomas Gumbleton—had been the first American bishop to have been arrested for civil disobedience. "It is a tactic," said O'Connor, "that is open to a bishop, as it is to anyone else."

Gumbleton, the Cardinal continued, "is a deeply, deeply sincere and passionately dedicated person, and I certainly do not rebuke him for what he did. It is not my way of doing things because it is not my temperament."

I asked O'Connor if he could conceive of the possibility that something might strike him as so unjust that he might commit civil disobedience in protest.

"Oh yes, sure. I don't think you can rule it out. But I would have to be convinced that there would be a reasonable degree of probability that my doing it would be effective. That it wouldn't be just a gesture. I'm always trying to weigh everything in terms of the lesser of evils. Being arrested is not a good in itself. I don't like the idea of being arrested, and I certainly wouldn't like the idea of being thrown into jail. So I would have to convince myself that what I did had a reasonable chance of being effective and that it wouldn't do more harm than good."

"You think you might consider," I asked, "an act of nonviolent resistance against the American Civil Liberties Union?"

There was loud laughter from the priests in the room, and a smile from the Cardinal. "No, I really don't see myself doing that. For example, I don't know that anyone has stronger feelings than I have about abortion. But I can't imagine that my getting arrested for civil disobedience in connection with abortion would do any real good. I'd get my name in the papers if I had myself thrown into jail for trespassing at a clinic. But to what good?

"As for Bishop Gumbleton, he clearly feels that nonviolent resistance does some good. And he has been one of the major driving forces in the pacifist movement in the United States. I disagree with him in that I disagree with absolute pacifism. I think selective conscientious objection is certainly something the Church teaches and which I support strongly. But I don't see the position of the *absolute* pacifist as logical and defensible. But more power to Bishop Gumbleton. Who knows what good his position may bring?"

I asked the Cardinal how he might react if the bishops' committee reviewing the pastoral letter on war and peace— the committee on which Bishop Gumbleton serves—decided to follow the lead of the United Methodist Church, the third-largest church body in the country. (The Catholic Church and the Southern Baptist Convention are the largest.)

On April 29, 1986, the Methodist Council of Bishops voted unanimously to release a pastoral letter emphasizing the bishops' "clear and unconditioned" opposition to any use of nuclear weapons. Said Bishop John Warman of Maryland: "No one can imagine Jesus using the nuclear weapon."

C. Dale White, the United Methodist Bishop of New York added: "We are challenging the policies of the government of this nation, and we are doing so in the name of Christian justice. And the pastoral letter itself declared: "We conclude that nuclear deterrence is a position which cannot receive the church's blessing."

Indeed, a draft of the letter had said: "The creation itself is under attack. God's sovereignty is denied. The most blasphemous evils are committed and prepared by the policies of government. . . . U.S. arms are now being purchased with food stamps, welfare checks, rent subsidies, Medicare payments, school lunches, and nutrition supplements for poor mothers and their children."

What if the Catholic bishops' review committee came to a similar conclusion?

The Cardinal paused before answering. "I'd be surprised if that were to happen," he said. "But I've been surprised before."

I asked him how strenuously he would object to such a decision by a committee of Catholic bishops.

O'Connor looked at me. "I wouldn't have myself arrested over it."

Much laughter from the priests in the room.

"The Holy Father," O'Connor said, "has continued to speak simply and straightforwardly that nuclear deterrence is supportable until, through negotiations and other means, we can bring about total disarmament or a significant degree of disarmament so that nuclear weapons become far less meaningful.

"Now, when we first went into the committee hearings that resulted in the 1983 pastoral letter, the American strategic doctrine unquestionably included, in my judgment, a first-strike capability and we had unquestionably targeted Soviet cities. Now we do not target Soviet cities, so that's a change."

"That is," I said, "if our government's statements to that effect are credible. I don't mean only the present government, but any administration."

"That's right," the Cardinal said. "And the credibility of not only our government, but any government, is at issue."

I told O'Connor it seemed to me that much of the argument on all sides about nuclear disarmament ignored the danger—not of a first strike or a nuclear escalation coming out of conventional warfare, but the danger of an accident. An accident that could lead to what is still the unthinkable—a nuclear holocaust.

O'Connor leaned forward. "I never could get the possibility of an accident taken seriously in all the various arguments I've had about nuclear weapons systems. During twenty-seven years in uniform, I saw technical breakdowns and human breakdowns so frequently that I've always been far more concerned about an accidental start of a nuclear war than a deliberate detonation. I mean, something that starts by accident could wind up being a deliberate war in the sense that the people on the receiving end of what looks like an attack by the adversary will react against it because that's what their instruments tell them to do.

"To me," the Cardinal said carefully, "the possibility of an accident is the *key* issue, and I personally don't think we have been demanding enough of the government or the military authorities on that single question."

O'Connor then told me something that is more than somewhat at variance with the view some of his critics have of him as the Genghis Khan of the American Catholic hierarchy—as the bishop who, because of his many years in uniform, is most likely to be receptive to the most aggressive military projects.

"I was asked a couple of years ago," the Cardinal said, "to go to a White House briefing on the so-called Star Wars nuclear defense system. [A space-based defense against ballistic missiles.] I knew the briefer—a fine man, a very fine man. He's a devout Lutheran and convinced of the rightness of what he's doing.

"I made two points during the briefing and, as a result, I was made to feel by some of those present as if I were Benedict Arnold. I said first of all, 'I do not know how you can create a delivery system for antinuclear weapons that cannot be created into a delivery system for nuclear weapons. So you can have the most glowing ideals, and the President can be very sincere in his belief in what he has been sold—a concept that there will be no nuclear detonations except the detonations in outer space of *incoming* missiles. And on that basis he further believes that eventually this destruction of an adversary's missiles in space will make it impractical for the adversary to fire them.'

"Yet," the Cardinal continued, "the lesson of the whole history of warfare leads to the conclusion that once you've developed a delivery system for antinuclear purposes, there is no particular trick to putting a nuclear warhead on it for offensive purposes."

I asked the Cardinal if any convincing rebuttals had been directed at him at that White House briefing.

He shook his head vigorously. "No."

The Cardinal had gone on at the White House briefing to raise the possibility of accidents.

"I've written about this," O'Connor said, "when I was in uniform. And I've given speeches about the kinds of accidents that have been experienced in ordinary military life. Over in the Mediterranean a few years ago, off the coast of Spain, we lost a live nuclear warhead. Please God it's at the bottom of the ocean, and maybe somehow it will be degraded. I don't know what will happen or how many fish will be killed. But that was an accident.

"Out in the West a few years ago, there was an accidental firing of a missile that fell someplace harmlessly. It did not explode, but it's also an accident that it did not explode.

"I have great, great respect for those I served with in the Navy and Marine Corps—services I know best, having spent twenty-seven years in them: at sea, in a hole in the ground. I would certainly never denigrate or condemn those in the Navy or the Marine Corps in any way.

"But if you live that life, then you know you're dealing with ordinary human beings and you know you're dealing with equipment that's dependent on a manufacturer. And you know that so many weapons systems have been created under the equivalent of laboratory circumstances—out on a flat table in the desert, for example; not on a pitching, tossing, rocking ship with the salt air eating into the mechanism, and with the radar down as much as it's up. So, if you live that life, you know about the possibility of accidents."

"Although you're not a pacifist," I said to the Cardinal, "I gather that this kind of knowledge, out of your own experience, might make you particularly eager for what you'd call responsible disarmament."

"I'll tell you this," O'Connor said. "The only thing that ever really got to me in those arguments, those debates, during the roughly three years we were trying to develop the pastoral letter on war and peace—and the only thing that has gotten to me since—is that I am so often accused of being the *militant* member of any body concerned with disarmament. That itself doesn't bother me. But overlooked was the fact that as the only member of that committee who had experience in military uniform and in combat, *I was therefore more frightened than anybody else*."

This is not to say John Cardinal O'Connor is on the edge of pacifism. "What I do say," he emphasized, "is that we have to keep our objective in mind. Our objective is to try to assure peace with justice. Now, can we do that by getting rid of all the weapons in the world? That's a gross unlikelihood because of the weaknesses of human nature. Can we do that by getting rid of nuclear weapons? Well, maybe we can do it by incremental decreases in nuclear weapons. Or it's possible we can do it by research and testing that could conceivably result in a generation of nuclear weapons with far less fire power, far less destructive potential, and therefore, far less possibility of being used in an all-out war.

"I'll probably be battered for saying this, but there is no good, there is no evil, in any particular weapon. The evil lies in the use that's made of it, and in the costs, if they're disproportionately high. Again, the objective is peace with justice, and it may be that getting rid of a particular weapons system may actually enhance the possibility of war."

O'Connor smiled. "You know, in the pastoral letter on war and peace, we had an anomaly—I won't call it a contradiction. That's always the risk when you try to turn from being a moralist to being a strategist or a tactician. In the pastoral letter, we call for an increase in conventional forces in Europe in order to be able to do away with some nuclear weapons. That's hardly a pacifist approach."

"Did Bishop Gumbleton agree?" I asked.

O'Connor smiled again. "Every one of us is responsible for everything in that pastoral letter."

In the same collegial spirit, Bishop Gumbleton had told me earlier that for all the objections O'Connor had expressed during the drafting of the 1983 pastoral letter on nuclear arms, "once we voted for the letter, O'Connor accepted it and worked for it."

37

ONE AFTERNOON in early summer 1987, I told the Cardinal that I had heard from New York State Assemblyman John Dearie, who claimed he was still banned from speaking in his parish.

"Mr. Dearie feels much aggrieved," I said.

There was a pause. The Cardinal did not look entirely comfortable at hearing of Dearie's distress. "Yeah, I know," O'Connor said. "Some time ago, I suggested we have a further meeting and not focus on where he could speak, or whether he could speak, but rather on why in the world he takes the position he does on Medicaid funding of abortion. He agreed to think and pray more on the subject, and we promised each other we'd get together again."

The Cardinal looked into the middle distance. "Since then, I must confess that I had put that whole question out of my mind. But I think I have to reevaluate it. Out of consistency."

The priests in the room looked surprised.

"The need for reevaluation," said the Cardinal, "sprang into my mind when a majority of the faculty council at Brooklyn College recommended against giving an honorary degree to Brooklyn Bishop Francis J. Mugavero because he is against abortion. And earlier, some college or university refused to give Jeane Kirkpatrick an honorary degree because there was opposition to her views.

"So I thought to myself—and I'm still thinking about it—am I right in maintaining this position on who shall speak and who shall not speak in the archdiocese? Am I doing the same thing those people are doing who voted against giving Bishop Mugavero an honorary degree and who prevented Jeane Kirkpatrick from receiving an honorary degree? I haven't convinced myself yet one way or another."

"In the meantime, John Dearie still can't speak at a parish function?"

"Yeah. Well, I don't think we said from here that the Archbishop of New York says no one who has said this or that can speak in your parish. I think we asked pastors to evaluate the people they were bringing in to see if there were inherent contradictions between what they were known for saying and Catholic beliefs. I'm going to have to read again what we did say about speakers in the parishes."

I reminded the Cardinal: "John Dearie's pastor told him that the call to ban Dearie had come from your office."

Monsignor Finn, the Cardinal's director of communications, broke in. "The Dearie case," he said, "was considerably earlier than the *suggestion* that went out from the Vicar General to pastors that they be aware of who is being scheduled in their parishes. And the Vicar General's suggestion didn't mean that if there were election forums or debates, candidates couldn't be invited in to face the music."

"Yeah, but the policy is *murky*," the Cardinal said impatiently. "And I'm not comfortable with it."

Finn nodded.

O'Connor frowned, and spoke as if to himself. "What was my concern in not having someone come in and talk to our Catholic people in an attempt to convince them of the validity of a particular position that we think is immoral? I guess my Irish temper has been tested to the fullest by the fact that so many politicians can purport to be such devout Catholics but then publicly take positions they know are categorically opposed to the positions of the Church.

"Yet these politicians can find a theologian—they might even find a bishop—to agree with them. But, for example, about abortion, the Pope is saying time after time after time that abortion is a heinous crime. And then there is the Second Vatican Council. Everybody who pretends to be a liberal says we should be following the Second Vatican Council. But the Second Vatican Council says abortion is an abomination. It's an abominable sin.

"Yet a political figure can get himself a theologian or two to say, 'Right on, you're doing exactly the right thing, don't pay attention to the O'Connors of the world.' And our Catholic colleges practically compete with each other to give people with such views an honorary degree. All that was part of my concern in setting this policy.

"I haven't really figured out in my own mind," O'Connor went on, "whether we went at it the right way in coming out with this edict. Yeah, it was Bishop O'Keefe's edict, but he is the Vicar General, and anything the Vicar General does is my responsibility. I supported him. But I have to look at it again to see if it should be changed.

(Six months later, the Cardinal said he still had "a growing fear that I was wrong, and I intend to come up with a more just and equitable policy.")

"But I tell you, I still want to make it clear to all of our institutions that we should not honor a person who has really publicly rejected a very serious teaching of the Church."

"It would be like the American Civil Liberties Union honoring an advocate of the death penalty?"

"I think so."

I asked the Cardinal about another dimension of dissent that affects not only New York Catholics but all the other Catholics in America. A few weeks before, there had been a documentary on public television, "Catholics in Crisis," and most of those speaking were young, devout, critical of the hierarchy and the Pope on a number of fundamental issues, and *determined to stay in the Church.* I read some of the passages in the documentary to the Cardinal:

A woman: "The Church is the most sexist male-dominated institution, I think, in our world today."

A theologian, Marikee Martin: "We are looking at the birth of a new church, [a kind of birth] which never took place in the Roman Catholic church. What has happened up to now is that people [who disagreed] said, 'Good-bye, I can't stand you, I'm getting out of here.' Never before has a sizeable portion of [Catholic dissenters] said, 'We are the Church. We are the real Church. You [other] people are out of date. You don't know what to do with the message of Christ.' These are sincere people. You can't accuse them of being vicious and insincere and bad. No, their intentions are good."

A nun for 38 years, Connie Martin, who left her order for the secular world but says she was "enormously happy, very fulfilled" while in the convent: "If I had to to it over again, I would do it over again. What changed me was, I think, a growing feminist awareness. The church excludes women at every possible level. It excludes them from . . . administering the sacrament. It excludes them from even being altar girls. I cannot accept from the Pope his exclusion of women in almost every aspect, every important aspect of the institutional Church. That to me is not only inappropriate; it is sinful. Sexism is a sin. It is excluding people based on their sex. There's no question it is an evil. It is a sin. So in that case I cannot obey nor accept those kinds of teachings from my Church.

"I do consider myself a Catholic and I have no intention of leaving the Church. The phenomenon of what's happening today is a growing group of women and men who refuse to have themselves defined by a white male establishment that is extremely oppressive of women."

Theologian Marikee Martin: "In the last twenty years, the majority [of American Catholics] have found out that in order to live like their fellow Americans . . . they could not, would not at least, follow the rules of the Church which had been observed by their fathers. And [observed] by themselves up to this time. They wanted to be able to divorce like an American. They wanted to be able to practice contraception and limit their families as Americans do . . . [some] wanted to practice abortion. Also the homosexual community within the Catholic [community], which had always existed, wanted to come out of the closet like the American homosexuals have been doing . . . So you have the effect of the emergence of a new Church because one other fact is sure: Rome will not change. And what we're heading for is something completely different from what we've had for 1900 years.' "

Sheila Murphy, a Legal Aid Society attorney and a mother, along with her husband, Dennis Carney, are members of Young Families, a spiritual and social group of Our Lady of Sorrows Church. So are their friends, Liz and Vinnie McMahon.

Vinnie McMahon: "I think there's definitely a difference between the American Church that my children will grow up in than the old Catholic Church that I grew up in, in several ways. I definitely think they will have more say. I also think that the role of women has to change in the Church."

Dennis Carney: "This kind of comment about sexism in the Church was never raised in my house. It was: 'The Pope says!' And you go to Church and men become priests, you sing those little songs. We tip our hat to the priest . . . That was a whole different ballgame. [But] now, we're coming home after Church, sitting down, and talking about 'Why can't my three-year-old daughter aspire to be a priest?' "

Sheila Murphy: "Catholics are no longer motivated by fear, and that is a wonderful thing to experience."

Liz McMahon: "We're motivated by hope."

Sheila Murphy: "Right, so you're no longer joining a churchful of frightened, unquestioning people. You're joining a dynamic group. It's unsettling, but it's great."

Toward the end of the documentary, Pio Laghi, the Vatican's Ambassador to the United States, said: "I admit that the Church cannot exist without the people, because that is a constitutional element of the Church. But if you exclude the Pope, if you exclude Peter and the successor of Peter, what kind of Church is that? It's just an assembly. You cannot call it the Catholic Church."

But an unidentified man emphasized: "It's the end of blind faith. It's going to be a questioning Church. It's going to be a Church that wants more information. But on the other hand, it's going to be a better Church. It's going to be a more spiritual Church. We're going to grow together. We're all in this pilgrimage together. And along the way we're going to have a lot of questions. Of course, we're going to have a lot of questions for which we don't have answers."

After I had read those passages to Cardinal O'Connor, I asked him if he considered this dimension of dissent, so intense and confident, a significant phenomenon.

His answer came slowly and softly. "I think," he said, "it is an actual phenomenon, but how extensive it is I don't know. Nor do I have any idea what the future of it will be. However, I guess I'm hopelessly optimistic. I believe in the apostolic succession from Peter onward. I believe in the promise of Christ that has established this Church, and I believe that nothing is going to prevail against it.

"I believe you can't have it both ways. If a Council, Vatican II, that was greeted with such wild enthusiasm has enunciated the basic teachings of the Church and then you reject those teachings or you look at them eclectically and you become, as it were, a very selective Catholic, I think that sooner or later you're just going to wither away [as a Catholic]."

O'Connor paused. "Now is that withering away going to be soon or late? And is it desirable? Of course, it is not desirable. Our Lord Himself says that a branch cut off from the tree cannot live.

"This is a new phenomenon in our age, but I don't know that it's historically much different from the heresies of the past."

"Except that in the past," I said, "the heretics left the Church."

"Ultimately they did. Ultimately they did. But not initially. And therefore, that's why I ask if what's going on now is remarkably different from then. Will people holding these views ultimately leave the Church? I have no way of knowing, but I think that if Church teaching is true and if we are articulating the teaching of Christ, then by definition, they will leave. The branch will die; it will not remain with the tree.

"Is that what we want? You know, the scriptures say: 'I desire not the death of the sinner but that he be converted and live.'"

The Cardinal looked down at his hands. "I go to bed with this every night. Long before I became a bishop—and I don't know why becoming a bishop ever happened to me—I worried a great deal about the Church Universal. I shuddered at the things I would read, the attacks on the Church from within. Not that I thought the Church was going to fold up, but that people were destroying themselves. And in doing that, they were confusing a lot of other people and thereby robbing them of the richness that they deserve. I always took those attacks on the Church from within very seriously. And very personally.

"Then I became a bishop. I probably exaggerated my own importance and thought it was my responsibility to worry even more about the Church. That was even when I was an auxiliary bishop.

"Since I became a member of the College of Cardinals, and, you know, kind of a quasi adviser—no more or less than other cardinals—to the Holy Father, I take even more seriously and more painfully the attacks that I think are ultimately masochistic in that people are destroying themselves, they're destroying their own faith."

Many of these attacks, I told the Cardinal, seem to have, as a starting point, the ban on birth control. They go forward to, among other things, the resentment by a rising number of Catholic women at their inferior place in the Church. As forceful as the attacks are, they seem to be based on a genuine, deep, and almost desperate devotion to the Church. "These dissenters," I said, "very much want to be part of the Church."

"Yes," said the Cardinal. "It creates great pain. That's why I feel sorry for people in this situation. And God knows, I could be in their shoes so I can't criticize. It's very painful, very painful.

"I hesitate to say this," he continued, "because it sounds noble or it sounds martyrish, but I'm not awake half the night simply because of inherited insomnia. I go to bed worrying about these things. I do too much reading in bed at night and maybe the wrong reading, because most of it is professional reading, and who wants to see the chaos? Who wants to see the confusion?

"If only it were in a constructive cause that these things were being done. If the criticism were that we [bishops] are being bad, are being unjust, that would be constructive. Maybe I'm being a bad bishop, and that's very possible. Maybe I'm not serving the people as I should.

"Then let the pickets come. Let the protest marches deluge us. Let people come into St. Patrick's Cathedral and object to what I say or object to what I do. Or expose me. That's the way it should be. Getting an evil bishop out of there. Sometimes I think they should look at me a lot more closely than they do. I mean that very sincerely.

"Or, if somehow or other there had developed among the bishops of the United States a very ambiguous teaching that is clearly or commonsensically erroneous, then you can have a constructive reform movement. We've had so many of such reform movements in the Church, but I hate to see what so often seems to me a destructive tendency—if *suicidal* is too strong a word. In terms of what's going on now, so many people are going to be misled.

"St. Paul says in his Letter to the Colossians that the day is going to come when your ears are going to itch for novel teachings, and that's when you're going to have to teach the faith consistently in season and out of season, when convenient and when inconvenient."

The Cardinal paused again and then talked about his own experiences at being a target of the "new" Catholics: "Anybody who thinks that it's a joy to have people, who think *they're* right, attacking you because they think you're unjust and that you should be impeached—" He shook his head. "Above all, anybody who thinks it's a joy when people either believe or pretend to believe that you're being deceitful and phony and fraudulent—or even that you're a politician rather than a priest—I find no joy in that.

"Of course, you must always question your own conscience and your own motives. Are you standing there trying to defend teachings of the Church because you believe they're valid, good for the Church, and good for the world? Or are you standing there in your arrogance? Are you just standing there because you're the authority figure?

"The psalms say, 'Every man is a liar and you can deceive yourself.' "

There was no doubt in my mind—nor, I believe, in the Cardinal's—that careful as he is to question his own conscience and motives, he believed he knew precisely who was right and who was wrong, as to the teachings of the Church, between the current reformers who would not leave the Church and John J. O'Connor, who would also not leave the Church. And the Cardinal also appeared to be free of all doubts as to who would continue to "own" the Church.

38

THE CARDINAL'S VIGOR of body and spirit is such that I had put off any questions about retirement, but I was curious, and I asked him one afternoon.

"The way it works," he said, "is that on his seventy-fifth birthday, a cardinal, or any bishop, is asked to submit his letter of resignation to the Holy Father. It says, 'I am seventy-five, I am at the disposition of the Holy Father, and prepared for my retirement. It is up to the Holy Father to accept or reject that letter of resignation. Cardinal Koenig of Austria, for example, is eighty-two, and Cardinal Krol of Philadelphia is seventy-seven."

"So you could go on another thirty years?"

"I'm torn on that," the Cardinal said. "Many days, I wish that I were retiring tonight. Wishing that I were retiring tonight is very cowardly, but I never pretended to be a hero, even when I was in uniform. Especially when I was in uniform. But whether I retire or not is up to the Holy Father.

"However, I do not like our current diocesan policy on retirement. The way it is now, with rare exceptions, a *priest* is asked to retire at seventy-five. I've come up with a new approach. I invite a priest who at seventy-five is in good shape to take a position as what I call a senior priest and be available for a different assignment than he has now. And some have done that. The life span has expanded so that certainly a man of seventy today generally has the health that someone of sixty had some years ago. Now, should that mean an older retirement than seventy-five? I don't know. You have to allow for young blood with better ideas, and, thank God, we're getting more young blood as there are more vocations now in the archdiocese."

With regard to the growth in new vocations, I asked the Cardinal about celibacy. Some of those critical of the Church but insisting meanwhile that they *are* the Church feel that the requirement of celibacy is one of the reasons why, in many places, there is such a shortage of priests. There is also a sense that celibacy is unnatural and thereby limits a priest's or a bishop's capacity to empathize with some of the most basic life experiences of his flock.

"There was for a time," the Cardinal said, "an erosion of the sense of the intrinsic value of celibacy as a liberating force. By liberating, I mean celibacy involves making a decision, a commitment, once and for all, that you are not going to be distracted. You might be tempted by this woman or that woman, but you aren't going to take that seriously. You would suffer the temptation but you wouldn't say, 'Well, why should I stay with what I'm doing? I can get dispensed from my vows and lead an honorable, productive

life outside the priesthood. Well, that sense of celibacy declined over the past couple of decades.

"There has now been, despite the criticism of celibacy,
a rethinking in the Church in general about the intrinsic
value of celibacy, and seminaries are reacting accordingly.
Now, recruiters, seminary rectors, and others who have to
make the decisions as to who is potentially a priest look
much more carefully at the attitudinal makeup of each individual. Certainly, in our seminary we rely pretty heavily
on psychological screening."

"What do *you* look for?"

The Cardinal paused. "I used to do a lot of psychological
testing myself. Some of it is worthwhile, some of it is virtually useless, and some of it in the wrong hands is worse than
useless. But we have a good psychologist at our seminary
who tries to look for balance. He doesn't look for, and I don't
look for, a future priest who doesn't want to get married.

"As a matter of fact, the future priest has to convince me
that he's normal, well balanced, and would like very much
to get married and have his own family. But he's prepared
to sacrifice that to become a priest. That's what we're really
looking for. I'm scared to death of the individual who has
no sexual desires, no romantic desires, no fantasies. I think
that kind of priest is going to be completely isolated among
the people. He's going to have no understanding of human
beings. He's going to have no sensitivity. He's certainly not
going to understand the most common of all sins. He's not
going to have any patience with married people, with single
people. He's not going to have any patience with his brother
priests, most of whom are 'full-blooded' American men.

"Especially, I guess—and I'm not sure I've ever clearly
articulated this even to myself—I think that the need for
legitimate companionship, a legitimate emotional relationship with others, is crucial to a healthy psychological life.
And if an individual, a potential priest, doesn't feel he needs
that, or even wants it, then I worry about his overall stability. He's going to bust in some other way, I think."

The Cardinal leaned forward again, waving away a

priest who told him that a roomful of people were waiting for him. The Cardinal turned to me. "You know, I need people," he said. "I wish I had more privacy than I have at times. I wish I could spend more time alone just reading, just listening to music, just playing golf, just praying, just studying, I don't have that kind of time in this job. But I wouldn't want privacy all the time.

"I need people. I need not only people in general, but I have to have a friend. For example, I have to be able to associate normally with women. I like to be able to talk to a woman intelligently, and with a certain emotional warmth, without fear, without— But you know, I'm not going to—I'm dedicated to celibacy. Neither at my age nor in my state now am I going to run off with a mother superior or even a mother inferior."

There was loud laughter from the priests in the room. One of them, a secretary to the Cardinal, reminded him again that many people were waiting, and so, smiling at the image of his running away with a mother inferior, the Cardinal said good-bye.

39

ONE OF the most difficult periods in John O'Connor's years as a Cardinal started in June 1987. It had to do with Pope John Paul II's decision to receive at the Vatican Kurt Waldheim, Austria's head of state, who had been accused of war crimes as an accomplice of the Nazis.

Although I was greatly disappointed with Cardinal O'Connor's behavior during and after Pope John Paul II's "rehabilitation" of Kurt Waldheim, I was not surprised. He has never been able to say a critical word about the Pope. When he does not understand an action by John Paul II, O'Connor substitutes trust and faith for reason. He considers this unquestioning loyalty to the Pope one of his greatest strengths.

There are times, however, when this is O'Connor's greatest weakness, for inside the changing American Church, as has been evident, the Pope is far from automatically obeyed or trusted by a growing number of Catholics who are not going to leave the Church. And they will be skeptical of Church leaders who do unquestioningly accept *everything* the Pope says and does.

One basic belief of these "new Catholics" who are trying to claim ownership of the Church is that the Pope, like any Church leader, must continually *earn* the trust of the faithful.

In the November 7, 1986, *Commonweal*—which has for many years been a journal for and by critical Catholics— William Shea, past president of the College of Theology Society and formerly associate professor of theology at the Catholic University of America, wrote:

The Pope and the bishops are not God, they are not the incarnate Son of God, nor are they the church of God. They are simply brothers in the Christian family who, more often than they should, take themselves more seriously than they can afford to do. The family belongs to God, and we ought to resist as the plague the pronounced tendency of our leaders to identify their wishes and beliefs with those of God.

With God we must be as the lilies of the field and the birds of the air in obedience, loyalty, and trust; with popes and bishops we must keep at least one eye open, for our failures are more than likely matched in number and quality by theirs.

Only God deserves our unconditional loyalty, trust, and obedience. Anybody else must earn a measure of each and must hold them by being worthy of them in action. If . . . Peter is to be trusted, he must be trustworthy. History displays a solid number of [Peter's] successors whose denial of their Master, although sometimes more subtle than Peter's, was far more radical and disastrous in its consequences. They did not prove worthy of our trust. The present bishop of Rome [John Paul II] is, to my mind, perilously close to losing his claim on our trust, obedience, and loyalty.

The present bishop of Rome managed to antagonize Jews all over the world by meeting with Kurt Waldheim. True, it is of small consequence to John Paul II if the Jews do not trust him, but as a result of that meeting, bishops and priests in Europe publicly rebuked this Pope. But only a few in the United States. And not John Cardinal O'Connor.

This Pope, this successor of Peter, had said earlier in the year, on his way to Chile: "I am the evangelizer of the Gospel. To the Gospel message, of course, belong all the problems of human rights."

Yet, on June 25, 1987, John Paul II had become the first head of state in the world to officially receive Austrian President Waldheim, the former Nazi *oberleutnant*, an intelligence aide to Wehrmacht General Alexander Lohr (executed as a war criminal). Waldheim, who had tried for many years to erase his past, had finally been charged with, among other things, implication in the execution of Serbian Christians along with involvement in the shipping of Yugoslav and Greek Jews to be consumed in the Holocaust. So said the Yugoslav War Crimes Commission. And the American government has placed Waldheim on a list of those who are persona non grata here.

Watching the repellent scene on television—the smiling Pope, the fawning Waldheim—I was again a boy in Boston, reliving the fear, the anger, and the silence.

Back then, the newsreels of Nazi street games with the Jews had moved out of the movie theaters and into our own streets. Gangs of feral youths, Catholics, came roaring regularly into our ghettos, smashing heads and windows.

We were not surprised. We knew what these invaders were being taught, and not only by Father Charles E. Coughlin of the Church of the Little Flower in Royal Oak, Michigan, in his Sunday network radio broadcasts. This

Cardinal O'Connor gives a homily on New Year's Day, 1987, at St. Saviour's Church, in the Old City of Jerusalem, that later made headlines in New York. *Photograph by Chris Sheridan*/Catholic New York.

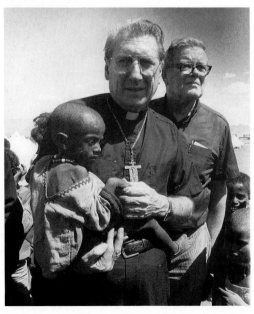

A visit to an Ethiopian camp at Mekele, with Monsignor John G. Nolan, director of the Catholic Near East Welfare Association, January 1987. *Photograph by Chris Sheridan*/Catholic New York.

At Jerash, a Roman ruin near Amman, Jordan, the Cardinal relaxes in the wind. *Photograph by Chris Sheridan*/Catholic New York.

The Cardinal at prayer, the
Wailing Wall, Jerusalem.
Photograph by Chris Sheridan/Catholic New York.

At Yad Vashem, the Museum of the Holocaust, Jerusalem, with
Mayor Teddy Kollek. *Photograph by Chris Sheridan*/Catholic New
York.

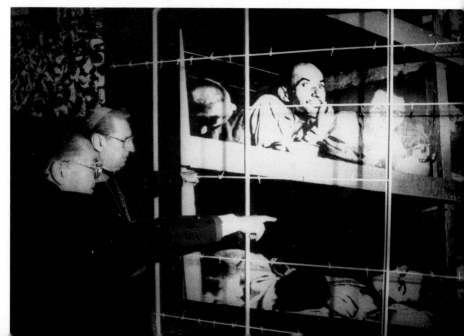

After returning from his trip to the Middle East, the Cardinal met with several American Jewish leaders at his residence, January 19, 1987; here, Theodore Mann and Morris Abram join him for a press conference. The calm is only apparent. The painting is of Terence Cardinal Cooke. *Photograph by Chris Sheridan*/Catholic New York.

Jesse Jackson visits the Cardinal at his residence, June 1987, to collaborate in a strategy to raise the pay of home health-care workers. *Photograph by Chris Sheridan*/Catholic New York.

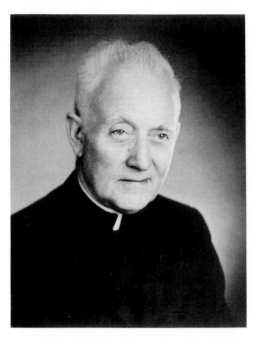

Monsignor John Tracy Ellis, the preeminent historian of the American Catholic Church and an admirer of Cardinal O'Connor. *Photograph by Chris Sheridan for* The Catholic News.

The Cardinal's niece, Attorney Eileen Ward. She brings cheer when few others can. *Photograph by Chris Sheridan/* Catholic New York.

Cardinal O'Connor at a center for the handicapped. *Photograph by Chris Sheridan*/Catholic New York.

The Cardinal greets handicapped children at St. Patrick's Cathedral. *Photograph by Chris Sheridan*/Catholic New York.

Church and State: The Cardinal and Governor Mario M. Cuomo in front of
St. Patrick's Cathedral. *Photograph by Chris Sheridan*/Catholic New York.

was before Vatican II, when a prayer in the liturgy of Holy Week called for the condemnation of "the perfidious Jews." Why were we "perfidious"? Because century after century, we persisted in denying that Jesus is the Messiah.

And we knew, or some of us knew, that in that part of the Good Friday liturgy that was called the Reproaches, there we were—all Jews—condemned by God "for what you have done to my Son." For centuries, the Catholic Church had been engaged in—as French Jewish historian Jules Isaac put it—"teaching contempt for the Jews."

As the brawny youths—who punched out our teeth and shoved old men and women from the Old Country out of their swaggering way—used to remind us, we were "Christ-killers."

But all those years ago, it was the silence that was most frightening. Not a Catholic priest, not a bishop, in Boston said a public word of admonition to their insatiably anti-Semitic flocks. The Cardinal, too—the man with such refined taste in music and in painting—he was silent. William Cardinal O'Connell, who could not bear anything vulgar, had nothing to say as these bounding Irish lads pushed Jews into the gutter in our ghetto.

Finally, one voice was heard. Frances Sweeney, the young editor of a muckraking Boston paper of uncertain frequency, and a fiercely devout Catholic, attacked the silence of the Cardinal and the priests. She would not let up, and she stirred other members of the Catholic laity to join her.

In the summer of 1987, I was listening for a resounding Catholic voice of protest as Pope John Paul II opened his doors to the pariah from Vienna. Maybe, I thought, loyalist though he is, this would be too much for John Cardinal O'Connor. After all, he had said from his first day as Archbishop of New York that he considered all the people of New York to be his concern. Most certainly including Jews. My mother would never have believed he would have protested, but I waited.

In Europe, a number of Catholic voices criticized the

Pope. For receiving Waldheim, and then for not saying a single word about Waldheim's past. Indeed, John Paul II, looking warmly at this remnant of the Third Reich, had actually praised Waldheim as a man "dedicated to achieving peace among peoples" and had asked him to lead Austria "in the defense of human rights."

Austria, where anti-Semitism is an intractable part of the national heritage, figured in the Vatican's communiqué on Kurt Waldheim's meeting with the Pope. The Catholic Church, the Vatican said, must "consider and respect Austria, [an] ancient and noble Catholic country."

The Pope's welcoming of Waldheim was too much for Albert Cardinal Decourtray of Lyons, France, where the trial of Klaus Barbie was being held. The Cardinal, as primate of Gaul, is considered head of the Catholic Church in France, and he is in charge of Jewish-Catholic affairs in that country. "I experienced a certain suffering on hearing that Pope John Paul II was going to receive Mr. Waldheim," the Cardinal said. "I am still trying to understand the reasons for this visit, but I must say that I have not understood." The Cardinal added that the meeting "shows a total misperception of Jewish sensibility."

Jean Marie Cardinal Lustiger of Paris, who was born Jewish, and a number of other French bishops, who were not born Jewish, signed a letter of accusation, noting that "Pope John Paul II, with his action [receiving Waldheim], has forgotten that the rationality of politics must never supersede moral obligations."

And Uli Schmetzer, in the June 28 *Chicago Tribune*, quoted the Reverend Ivan Florianc, a Yugoslav priest who was among those in St. Peter's Square protesting the Waldheim visit: "In Argentina and in Chile, the Pope gave communion to generals and dictators, but he would not receive the mothers of the *desaparecidos* (the disappeared victims). For me and many priests, these are gestures that cannot be reconciled with the spiritual and moral role of a Pope."

In Europe, then, not all were silent within the Catholic Church. But in the United States, there were exceedingly few voices of protest among the bishops and cardinals. An especially dismaying disappointment—because he had criticized the Vatican's disciplining of Archbishop Hunthausen of Seattle—was Rembert Weakland, Archbishop of Milwaukee. Principal architect of the Catholic bishops' pastoral letter on the economy, with its insistence on social justice for the poor, Weakland is one of the most humane of American prelates. A man of many parts (he is an accomplished classical pianist, for instance), Weakland almost radiates sensitivity. And what happened when he was asked about the Pope and the *oberleutnant*?

Archbishop Weakland declined to comment.

A monsignor did speak up. The labor priest George Higgins. In his weekly column for the Catholic press, Higgins quoted the Archbishop of Lyons' bewilderment at what the Pope had done, and added his own.

And there were voices from the laity, Eva Fleischner—a Catholic theologian and a member of the National Conference of Catholic Bishops' advisory committee for Catholic-Jewish relations—criticized the Pope, saying: "Anyone who takes Judaism seriously has to be shocked." Fleischner, born in Austria, came to the United States after Hitler annexed her country, and she teaches a course on the Holocaust at Montclair State College in New Jersey.

When she was asked about Jewish demands that there be a real, not a ceremonial, meeting of Jewish groups with the Pope when he came to America later in the year, Eva Fleischner said: "The Pope should consider himself lucky that the Jews are willing to talk with him after what the Church has done."

Tom Fox, the editor of the *National Catholic Reporter*, told me that in addition to being very disturbed at the Pope's decision to legitimize Waldheim, he was equally dismayed that "this Pope sees no need to explain himself, nor to explain why he says nothing. And in this case, he remains silent even despite the record of the Catholic Church concerning the Jews over the centuries."

In New York City, John Cardinal O'Connor—who had

repeatedly spoken for the release of Soviet Jews, had visited synagogues, and had spoken often of the Holocaust—was not silent. Indeed, he said a great deal about the Waldheim visit to the Holy See—on national and local television, to newspapers, and in statements from his office. But what he said was words, just words.

For example, on a New York NBC television program, the Cardinal said: "I am so convinced of the integrity of this Pope, his concern for human rights, that I truly believe that he determined to do this for motives that he believes to be highly meritorious, *and my suspicion would certainly be that in the private session with Mr. Waldheim he had some pretty stern things to say* [emphasis added]."

Whatever the Pope said privately in his meeting with the *oberleutnant* clarifies nothing, of course, so long as the words remain private. In any case, there is nothing whatever to indicate that Waldheim was even mildly chastised in that private session. When he had returned from the Vatican, when the visit of state was all over, the *oberleutnant* was asked if he had been disturbed by the protesters with their shouts and signs.

"I did not hear them," said Waldheim. "I did not see them. I only saw smiling faces and people waving to me on the way to the Vatican."

By contrast with Cardinals Decourtray and Lustiger in France, who felt they had no choice but to openly criticize the Pope's bestowing on this man the prestige of the Vatican, Cardinal O'Connor tried in every way he could to justify what had happened.

The Pope, said O'Connor, "was doing what he saw as his duty in receiving Mr. Waldheim. Who could respect *any* Pope who refused to carry out what he saw as a duty, simply because others, whether one community or the entire world, believed he should not act?"

Was it also the Pope's duty to act as if Waldheim was simply another head of state, without a history of involvement with the Third Reich and its crimes? O'Connor often speaks sardonically about Catholic politicians who say they are personally against abortion but, as public officials, must follow the law. This should not prevent them, O'Connor correctly emphasizes, from speaking out in opposition to abortion as they carry out the law.

So, too, if the Pope believed it his diplomatic duty to receive any head of state, no matter what the rest of the world believes, why did he then not say a single public word to Waldheim about his past in the Wehrmacht?

In a full-page advertisement in the *New York Times* (June 26, 1987), the American Jewish Congress, in an open letter to John Paul II, said that Waldheim "has become the symbol not only of an evil Nazi past, but of current efforts to diminish, falsify, and forget the Holocaust." Accordingly, in view of the Pope's refusal to speak to that dreadful twin symbol, when receiving Waldheim, "how is one to explain so profound an insensitivity to the meaning of the Holocaust, so painful a failure of the moral imagination, by the custodian of the Catholic conscience"?

The American Jewish Congress went on to say: "How paradoxical, and how deeply disquieting, that secular governments like the United States were determined to put politics aside to take a stand on moral principle by isolating Waldheim, while the Vatican was guided by political considerations, and put moral principle aside!"

The best Cardinal O'Connor could do was to ask that Jews share his faith in the goodness of the Pope: "I personally know nothing of any motives the Holy Father may have had for receiving Mr. Waldheim other than the motive reported by the media. [His duty to receive other heads of state.] My trust in Pope John Paul II, however, is unconditional. I am absolutely convinced that he would not deliberately or arbitrarily cause pain to our Jewish brothers and sisters or to anyone else. His motives are his motives. I trust them completely."

The phrase "His motives are his motives" cannot possibly be any part of any real dialogue. Yet, the Cardinal's

utterly uncritical loyalty to the Pope deluded him into believing that he himself was indeed conducting a dialogue
with Jews on this matter.

The Cardinal continued that statement by saying: "As
Archbishop of New York, home of the largest number of
Jewish people in the world, I cannot be indifferent to their
anxiety." But to keep repeating that the Pope can do no
wrong hardly alleviates anxiety or anger.

Still trying to reach across a chasm that he had only
managed to deepen, O'Connor then proposed that a group of
Jews and Catholics meet in St. Patrick's Cathedral or in a
synagogue "simply to pray together quietly—not to dialogue, not to give speeches or argue or debate. But simply to
pray for increased mutual understanding and a peaceful
resolution of a regrettable difference."

That proposal, to begin with, omitted Orthodox Jews. As
Rabbi Milton Polin, president of the Rabbinical Council of
America, sharply reminded the Cardinal: "We are opposed
to joint prayer and he is very well aware of it."

Howard Squadron, past president of the American Jewish Congress, which welcomes all Jews, responded to the
proposal caustically: "If the prayer is for the redemption of
Waldheim's soul, it might be of some value."

O'Connor was floundering, an affliction that can beset an
honest man who is also an unswervingly loyal man and so,
on occasions like this, is caught between honesty and loyalty and cannot keep his moral balance.

Another aftermath of the meeting between the Pope and
the former Prisoner of Vienna, as some called him, were
irate calls to the Cardinal's office by Catholics furious at the
Jews for having the chutzpah to criticize the Pope. After all,
if John Paul II—as the Cardinal keeps saying—can do no
wrong, then these Jews have no basis for being so cruel to
the Holy Father.

On television, in interviews, and in a formal statement,
the Cardinal proclaimed: "I remind all Catholics of the sin
of anti-Semitism. Let no Catholics believe they are honoring our Holy Father or defending our faith if they engage

in verbal attacks on our Jewish brothers and sisters, thinking such to be justified because the Pope has been criticized. The Pope is accustomed to criticism. His record on the defense and advancement of the human rights of all people, of all races, creeds, colors, and ethnic backgrounds, is impeccable. There is no warranty for conflict between Jews and Catholics; Jews are indeed our elder brothers and sisters. They deserve the respect of every Catholic. They know they have mine."

Since no cardinal or bishop had said anything like that in my growing-up years, when Catholic attacks on Jews in Boston were hardly only verbal, I felt somewhat guilty at first in not being able to respond with proper gratitude to the Cardinal's attempt to cool the backlash. But then I realized that, without intending it, the Cardinal was sending a double message. One was to Catholics to restrain their anger (and, in some cases, their anti-Semitism). And the second message, probably hidden from the Cardinal himself, was to Jews: Don't provoke Catholics into being anti-Semitic by your baseless criticism of our impeccable Holy Father.

"I don't want to exaggerate," O'Connor said at one point, "but [the backlash] could be disastrous."

In an editorial during the tumultuous debate on the Pope's having received part of the remnant of the Third Reich, the New York *Daily News*, after criticizing the Holy Father, noted: "Nazism was a triumph of moral passivity."

The silence of the American bishops all these years later when the *oberleutnant* was welcomed by Pope John Paul II did indeed take me back to when I was a boy, surrounded by the silence of bishops and priests as gangs of the Catholic faithful regularly invaded our ghetto. This time, Cardinal O'Connor was not silent, but he might as well have been.

On September 1, 1987, John Paul II, surprised and somewhat shaken by the reaction of Jews throughout the world to his meeting with Kurt Waldheim, met for seventy-five minutes with a delegation of Jewish leaders. It was the first such open conversation by a Pope with Jewish leaders in the modern history of the Vatican. The Jews spoke to him about his audience with Waldheim, but John Paul II never mentioned that meeting in his remarks.

After the Jewish leaders left, the Vatican said it would prepare a document on the Holocaust and other evidences of anti-Semitism.

But Kurt Waldheim was spared from embarrassment.

40

FLANNERY O'CONNOR has noted that "a Catholic has to have strong nerves to write about Catholics." A non-Catholic, and indeed a Jewish atheist, has to muster considerable chutzpah to write not only about Catholics but also about the "Cardinal of the Capital of the World."

Yet, since the Church—and certainly the American Church—has been very much in and of the world, particularly since Vatican II, I feel no constraints in writing about that part of its work. Matters of doctrine have also figured in this book insofar as they affect the deep and deepening clashes within the American Church. Clashes, for example, on the ordination of women, on "creeping infallibilism," and on the place of homosexuals in the Church and in the world.

The clash connecting all others, of course, is the degree to which dissent from Church teachings can be effectively suppressed by the Holy See in the American Church. American Catholics, after all, are shaped, to greater or lesser degrees, by the same expectations of openness, of self-expression, and of sharing in decision making that are at the core of growing up American.

John Cardinal O'Connor, himself, for example, is quintessentially American in, among other things, his zest for speaking his mind. Although he claims not to relish the controversies this zest pulls him into, the Cardinal takes manifest delight in jousting with public officials and public figures. (Most of the time, it is his ripostes that are remembered from such exchanges.)

He is also an impassioned democrat (lower case) in his conviction that *all* members of the polity must be treated with respect and fairness. There is no trace of elitism in John Cardinal O'Connor. Some have charged him with a leaning toward the powerful and well-placed, but I have never seen him more out of place than during an evening he once spent with a group of prominent conservative intellectuals in a private room of a university club on Manhattan's East Side.

The first draft of the American bishops' pastoral letter on the economy had recently been released, and O'Connor's interrogators wanted to know what business it was of the Church to get involved with matters of economic justice for the poor, the minimum wage, maximum employment, and such secular matters—particularly when this pastoral letter seemed to them to be unabashedly socialist in its outcome, if perhaps not in its intent.

The interrogators were also distressed at the earlier pastoral letter by the bishops on nuclear weapons and peace. Here was the Catholic Church, so long a bulwark against world Communism, and now recommending that the American government weaken its nuclear defenses against that evil empire.

O'Connor told of the agonizing—as he put it—time he had put in as a member of the committee that drafted the pastoral letter on war and peace, and said that in the end he had approved of the letter because he had been greatly educated through all the months of listening to witnesses and through the debates with his fellow bishops. Though he did not say so explicitly, O'Connor implied that his listeners might do well to study more about war and peace rather than stick to their rehearsed responses.

As for the letter on the economy, O'Connor said in a soft voice that nonetheless carried remarkably well, "The Church is concerned with the life of the individual. About nine hundred thousand individuals in New York City live in substandard conditions, including overcrowding, with all the attendant evils of that kind of life. And bishops all over the country are seeing more of this. That's why we bishops are concerned with the economy.

"The question I go to bed with—and wake up with in the morning—is 'Am I failing the people in the parishes? Am I fulfilling my religious and moral responsibilities?' I would be failing if all I did was to say Mass and carry out the customary religious duties of my office."

O'Connor did not persuade his interrogators, and at one point in the evening, I said to him across the table that I expected he now had a much keener appreciation of the value of some of the thinking on the left than he had before he came into this plush room with its hunting prints on the walls.

O'Connor laughed, and kept laughing for quite a while.

That night, and during the rest of the time he has been in New York, O'Connor has continued to justify what the *New York Post* said on May 25, 1985, the day he became a Cardinal: "O'Connor does not say what the world wants to hear. He is no smooth modern churchman who excuses the fashionable and flatters the powerful. [And] unlike certain other religious leaders, he could never be mistaken for an agnostic."

O'Connor tried to define himself in an interview with Charles Bell in the New York *Sunday News* when he first came to town: "I don't like the word *conservative.* I prefer *orthodox*, and I am thoroughly orthodox in Church doctrine. And progressive—even, heaven forbid! liberal—on social issues."

He has, for further example, been continually and consistently censorious of any form of racism or insensitivity to the rights of blacks. Including in his own Church. There are around 1 million black Catholics—about 2 percent of the total American Catholic population—and the number is increasing, having grown by 41 percent between 1975 and 1985.

A forceful application of O'Connor's homilies and columns on racism has been his support for economic justice for the largely black and Hispanic working force in the hospitals and in home-care health services. On June 4, 1987, he held a press conference with Jesse Jackson. (Imagine Cardinal Spellman holding such a conference.) The two clergymen, in the presence of members of health-care union locals 1199 and 1707, urged that attention be paid the indecent wages being paid to home health-care workers.

The Cardinal emphasized to the press that 51 percent of these 52,000 workers, most of whom are minority women, earn less than $7,000 annually and 80 percent of them live below the poverty level. Three-fourths, moreover, are the principal support of their families.

The goal of the workers was a modest raise from $4.15 to $6 an hour—along with better health-care benefits and training. Jesse Jackson noted that this battle for just wages was a political issue. "The government," he said, "changes only when the people from the bottom up decide to change."

The Cardinal, familiar with complaints that the Church has no business being involved with political issues, vigorously agreed with Jackson, and said: "Political life today is fraught with moral issues, and I have to be concerned with them. What kind of leader would I be if I did not talk about the poor, the homeless, or the hungry?"

Another index of the Cardinal's unflagging support of labor was an ad in the September 28, 1986, *New York Times*. Placed by a health-care union, Local 1199, the ad listed a number of New York hospitals that, the union claimed, were reneging on a wage increase agreed on more than two years before. Among the exceptions—employers that had honored "their commitment to social justice and fair-

ness"—were the city's Catholic hospitals. The ad then proclaimed: "We salute Cardinal O'Connor and the Catholic
Archdiocese, not only for living up to their ideals of fairness
and social justice for all working people, but also for their
commitment and cooperation and progress in reaching a
fair and decent new settlement covering future years."

The contrast could hardly have been greater between
Francis Cardinal Spellman breaking the grave diggers'
strike by outfitting his seminarians with shovels and John
Cardinal O'Connor being celebrated in a union ad that in-
cluded as its credo: "Honoring Our Commitment to Social
Justice Is What Has Made America Different. Let Us Never
Forget."

During a Labor Day Mass in September 1986, the Cardinal said at St. Patrick's Cathedral that those employed by
the archdiocese, including hospital workers and teachers,
had to have a living wage because "they cannot live on air,
prayer, and holy water." Further, "The nature of work is the
continuation of God's creation. This magnificent cathedral
would not exist were it not for the work of architects, engineers, and most particularly those working with their
hands."

In the course of another Labor Day sermon, O'Connor
would have made his father particularly proud: "There are
some who think that unions have seen their day, and there
are some who seem to be applauding this idea. But pray that
such is far from the case. With God's help, we can assure
that for the union movement, the best is yet to come."

The Cardinal's allegiance to the principle of unions was
revealed again during the summer of 1987, when members
of the National Association of Broadcast Employees and
Technicians went on strike against the National Broadcasting Company. A news conference had been announced for
the Cardinal's residence, and when the nonunion "scab"
crew from WNBC-TV arrived at 452 Madison Avenue, a
secretary of the Cardinal, Monsignor James McCarthy, told
the crew that while the Cardinal was not taking sides on the
issue, he does have a respect and high regard for unions and

would not allow this nonunion crew through the door. The Cardinal's precise instruction to the Monsignor was "Just tell them they're not invited."

Quite apart from unions, it was characteristic of the Cardinal to say during that same summer that he would become, for a time, a volunteer at St. Clare's Hospital, a Catholic institution that has a good many AIDS patients. O'Connor decided to do this, he said, "to understand better what services are offered AIDS patients" and to get a direct sense of their needs. At the same time that he revealed his plan to work as a volunteer at the hospital, O'Connor dedicated and blessed a dental clinic at St. Clare's—the first of its kind in the country, for it treats AIDS patients only.

The Cardinal's concern for AIDS patients—and his publicizing of that concern—are part of another of his primary concerns. He is angry and fearful at the increasing rate at which certain people are being written off because their "quality of life" is such, according to some, that their lives are not worth continuing. Handicapped infants, for instance, patients in a vegetative state, the elderly who have become senile.

O'Connor calls this burgeoning phenomenon the "consistent ethic of death," and it is one of his most insistent concerns. The slide toward putting "useless" people to death started, he believes, with the legalizing of abortion. And now, "the inexorably consistent ethic of death continues with life at the other end of the spectrum. . . . 'Death with dignity' has become the polite description for putting elderly people out of their misery, determining that the 'quality of life' of the cancer patient has deteriorated to an unacceptable point, deciding that an individual can no longer live 'productively.' It's a fancy term—like 'terminating pregnancy' and 'pro-choice.' 'Living wills' are springing up all over the place.

"How long will the death march continue to be voluntary? If the baby in a mother's womb is given no choice about being put to death, will the day come when the elderly or the 'prematurely senile' are considered to be in their second childhood and given no choice about being put to death?"

In a message read at all the Masses in all the parishes in the archdiocese on October 5, 1986, the Cardinal said he was "frightened and chilled" by the "clamor throughout the United States for legislation that will lift any restrictions whatsoever in regard to sustaining the life of a terminally ill patient. Indeed, the move is toward authorizing the deliberate speeding up of the deaths of vulnerable patients by starvation or dehydration—denying them even food and water. . . .

"I plead with you to reflect with utmost urgency on what is happening. Do not think that *your* life or that of your aging parents, or the lives of the handicapped, the cancerous, the so-called useless will be secure if the proponents of 'euthanasia' have their way, even if they never use the term. Who is to decide who lives and who dies, if the so-called quality of life becomes the determinant?"

In this vital area—respect for life and for the value of every individual—the Cardinal has been a powerful teacher, and his views are consonant with those of most other American Catholic bishops. On this subject, and in their pastoral letters on such issues as the economy and nuclear arms—and often by personal actions—these bishops exemplify the Church in the world. Thereby they are in marked contrast with those of their predecessors who lived as autocrats behind fortress walls.

Today's bishops, as O'Connor says, are of necessity in frequent tension with the world because their attempts to apply the values of the Church are often resisted by those in the world with different values. There is also tension between some of the bishops and a number of Catholic politicians who separate what they call their "private" convictions from their "public" responsibilities.

It is as a Catholic priest in the world that O'Connor is at his most resounding. In the March 20, 1986, issue of *Newsday*, Eugene Kennedy, the perceptive chronicler of American Catholic bishops, noted:

O'Connor . . . has invaded the metropolitan imagination, taking on its street-wise Jewish mayor, not to mention its glove-smooth Catholic governor, clashing with the principalities and powers of the media and stirring up controversy and criticism over his forthright stands on abortion and homosexual rights.

The self-congratulating New York establishment has always preferred its major churchmen to pray for peace and rain, to offer untroubling invocations at black-tie dinners, and not otherwise to speak unless spoken to. Its new Catholic archbishop arrived as confidently as John the Baptist out of the wilderness, not asking anybody's permission to preach or to apply his deeply felt religious convictions to the human misery he senses beneath the piled-up statistics about urban America's social ills.

When attacked out in the world by those who say preachers have no business in the business of daily life, O'Connor does indeed respond with unblinking confidence, and he never fails to make his point effectively, if controversially. Where his deeper problems lie, although he seems unable fully to admit this to himself, are in the attacks against him and other bishops from within the Church. From more and more of the laity.

I have found much resentment against the Cardinal from some Catholics who go to Mass regularly and believe they are more serious than he is when, at St. Patrick's Cathedral, he turns to them and says, *"You* are the Church!"

These Catholic critics exemplify a truism of this stage of American Catholic history that has been underlined by Russell Shaw, the encyclopedic communications expert at the National Conference of Catholic Bishops. In the May 31, 1987, issue of *Our Sunday Visitor*, Shaw wrote: "In significant ways the problems of the past were different from the worst problems of the present. Back then the worst threats to the Church came from outside: now they come from within."

Many of these problems in America center on John Paul II, and since Cardinal O'Connor is regarded correctly as an American prelate who is utterly loyal to the Pope, O'Connor also becomes the target of those who accuse the Pope of "creeping infallibility." This is the notion, as explained by Bernard Cooke, chairman of the department of religious studies at the College of the Holy Cross, that "even though certain doctrines are not infallible, people are obliged to accept them as if they were being taught infallibly."

The Pope, in sum, must be obeyed in all things. Or, in almost all things, and the official options for disagreement continually shrink.

Archbishop Pio Laghi declares: "The strength of the Church is the Pope of today."

That puts a great burden on whoever is Pope, and on those Catholics who agree with Pio Laghi. And it puts a great burden on Cardinal O'Connor—so far as critics of the Pope within the American Church are concerned. They see, as O'Connor surely does not, what Catholic theologian William Shea underlined in a November 1986 issue of *Commonweal*: "[Pope John Paul II] appears the sort of man who is not plagued by self-doubt. His predecessor, Paul VI, who taught quite forthrightly, was able to hold together a church in turmoil at least in good part because we all knew he suffered with the Church and that he would not break the bent reed. A good belt of hesitation and doubt might not be a bad thing for this pope, for he throws the church into turmoil by his determination to calm it, and thinks he can calm it by his command."

On the one hand, this Pope has traveled widely in the world. But he has also, as noted by Father John B. Breslin, director of the Georgetown University Press, "clearly and frequently indicated his intention of maintaining stricter discipline within his own camp, or curbing what he and several of his closest advisers see as dangerously centrifugal forces released in the wake of Vatican II. The tension between contraction and expansion, between insisting on internal cohesiveness (the spirit of orthodoxy) and exhibiting a sweeping universalism (the pastoral journeys) has been the hallmark of John Paul's papacy. And its effects are being felt."

They certainly are. The tension between contraction and

expansion has become an integral dynamic within the Church. I have been told by Catholic historians that this tension must exist inside John Cardinal O'Connor. If this is so, being a man of remarkable self-discipline, he has not given any public indication of differing one whit from the Pope's curbing of the centrifugal forces within the Church.

And there—as striking a figure as O'Connor is in the world—is his vulnerability in the changing American Church.

For instance, he is in spirit and letter at one with Sister Joan Chittister, prioress of Mount St. Benedict Priory in Erie, Pennsylvania, and a social activist, when she says: "You don't have to be an economist to look at American society and see that we are ourselves facing a rising number of poor and that we are drawing back from the obligation of the state to care for those who cannot care for themselves.

"You don't have to have a Ph.D. in economics to be concerned about that. All you have to do is read the beatitudes and look at Jesus's compassion for the poor. The [American] bishops are showing us the social sins that can happen when privatized Christianity sinks into itself and has a spree. They're telling us that the Gospels have to be held up to society and to its structures and institutions."

But the American bishops, very definitely including O'Connor, are not at one with Sister Chittister and rising numbers of Catholic women (and their male allies) in this unsparing illumination by Sister Chittister from the 1987 Houghton Mifflin collection *Once a Catholic: Prominent Catholics and Ex-Catholics Discuss the Influence of the Church on Their Lives and Work:*

The ordination issue is central because it has something to do with the quality of a woman's soul and the nature of women as God sees them, not the nature of women as men see them or as other people see them. It brings into question the credibility of all the best doctrines of the Church: baptism, grace, redemption, incarnation, creation. Everything is wrapped up in that package called the female soul—and is it qualitatively different from the male soul? All of this talk about you can't ordain a woman because Jesus was male has got to be patent nonsense. Jesus did not come to be male. Jesus came to be flesh—"And the Word became flesh." You know, we have never said in any of the Christian churches that I know of, "And the Word became male."

They say you've got to have a male in order to be a sign of Jesus. *No* male can be a sign of Jesus, any more than a woman can be. If you have to have a male who is like Jesus to be Jesus—then one of the criteria ought to be that the person has to be Jewish—that has a great deal more to do with being Jesus than being male because the Redeemer was to have come from the line of David."

So long as John Paul II is Pope, Cardinal O'Connor will give no encouragement, on this question, to the many, many Sister Chittisters in the Church.

Nor, as he has indicated, is O'Connor comfortable with those dissenters who insist on staying in the Church and fighting from within. These "new Catholics" are growing in numbers. (See *The American Catholic People* by George Gallup, Jr., and Jim Castelli [Garden City, N.Y.: Doubleday, 1987]). Their spirit is distilled in an editorial in the September 19, 1986, *National Catholic Reporter*:

The pope and the Roman Curia are not the final arbiters. They merely recreate as best they can what they think Jesus meant and the Creator wanted. Conscience is the final arbiter. . . . [Pope John Paul II] pulls, as we all do, on what he knows. Much of what he seems to pull on does not respond to the needs of a Western church like ours, *the* most questioning and best-educated mass society in history.

There are more Catholics in the United States today than lived in the times of the first 200 popes (John Paul II is the 264th) of church history—and most Catholics who lived then were illiterate and quiescent.

The Vatican is afraid of U.S. Catholics. True but sad. Rome does not like our democratic and pluralistic experiences, our social sciences, our style of church. . . .

So why not try some other Christian church?

Because finally, for all its faults, this one most struggles with all the world's and every community's questions in the light of its most remarkable history. Because this is the sacramental one. This is the oh-so-slow teacher gradually educated by the students.

And the students at the same time are educated by the teacher, and both, as Augustine said, are educated by the word of God. . . .

Alas, the current Vatican administration appears sexually fixated, much to the detriment of John Paul's magnificently radical economic and social message. . . .

We remain faithful to the church as we preach the truth in it as we understand it. Sometimes by example. Sometimes with an open ear and closed mouth. Sometimes—and these are such times—by sticking out our necks and boldly saying where we are on the tough issues. . . .

It is enough, for today, that we are alive, plugging away for what, in formed conscience, we believe the church is to be.

Which Church? Archbishop Pio Laghi says of American Catholics: "You talk about the people of God, and you expand" the concept of the Church. But in Europe, Laghi continues, "our view of the Church is more biblical. Your view is more peoplehood."

Indeed it is, notes Sister Joan Chittister: "Rome, it seems, sees the Church as a place to which people come. American religious have come to see the Church as a people to whom the Church must go."

And some of the people who consider themselves the American Church do increasingly believe the Holy See has become distracted from the basic teachings of Jesus as it focuses so fixedly on sex. In a letter to the *National Catholic Reporter*, Jim McRae cites an editorial in the British Catholic journal, *New Blackfriars*: ". . . as far as the Church is concerned, *in practice*, is there anything more important than how we are to behave sexually? The shadow of the nuclear holocaust, the advancing of social justice, the conquering of human greed, interfaith dialogue, even promotion of the fundamental truths of the Faith in day-to-day Church life—are any of these as important, in the eyes of the men of the Vatican and of the mass of ordinary Catholics, as is the fight over what is orthodoxy in the area of sexual ethics?"

In the American Church, however, a good many of "the mass of ordinary Catholics" disagree with Rome on sexual ethics and practices. In 1986, the Notre Dame Study of Catholic Parish Life—a survey of representative parishes across the country—focused only on "core Catholics," those deeply involved in the Church and in parish life. On an index of support ranging from one to four, only 2.23 percent of those questioned believed that "the Church should remain strong in its opposition to the use of contraceptives." Other surveys indicate a much higher rejection of Church teaching on this matter among all Catholics, including those who are not "core" members of the Church.

This area of dissent has been present since Pope Paul VI's 1968 encyclical, *Humanae Vitae*, forbidding artificial means of birth control. The depth and extent of that disagreement with Rome is generally regarded as the beginning of what has come to be the widespread phenomenon of Catholics selecting which teachings of the Church they will obey.

Or, as the Notre Dame Study of Catholic Parish Life says of the negative reaction to *Humanae Vitae*, "its long-term effect may have been to develop a loyal opposition within the American Church—an educated and active laity who feel it is appropriate for the Church to offer moral teaching and who will weigh it, but who in the end will consult their conscience and experience in deciding to accept it or reject it."

America's bishops, quite aware of the rejection of *Humanae Vitae* by so many Catholics, seldom preach extensively or with particular intensity on the subject. This is also true of Cardinal O'Connor. He has told me at length of his total support of the Holy See's ban on artificial means of birth control, but he very seldom speaks of *Humanae Vitae* in his homilies or in his column in *Catholic New York*.

The Notre Dame Study also revealed, as have other surveys, that most Catholics still oppose abortion on demand, but would allow it under "certain extreme circumstances" (a threat to the mother's life, rape, incest).

In a broader 1987 survey, *The American Catholic People*, George Gallup, Jr., and Jim Castelli have found that while

72 percent of American Catholics believed in 1969 that premarital sex was wrong, only 33 percent of those surveyed in 1985 held to that view. By a 3-to-1 margin, Catholics felt that "divorced Catholics should be allowed to remain in the Church," and by a 2-to-1 margin, they favored a married priesthood.

With regard to the demographics of American Catholics, Gallup and Castelli reported that of the approximately 52 million Catholics in the United States, "29 percent are under thirty, 36 percent are between thirty and forty-nine, and 35 percent are over fifty." By contrast, "only 18 percent of Methodists, Presbyterians, and Episcopalians are under thirty."

As the authors say, American Catholics are sure to "have a profound impact on the shape of American society a quarter century from now." And beyond. As they do now.

Already encompassing a sizable "loyal opposition" to certain Church teachings as well as to the autocratic attitude of the Holy See, American Catholics are very likely to include even more dissenters in the years ahead. In a January 2, 1987, letter to the *New York Times,* Mitchell Kelleher wrote:

One cannot, after all, expect the Holy See, which sees itself as the custodian of divinely revealed truth, to trim its sails to the winds of public opinion. But neither can Rome expect to change the minds of those who believe its moral strictures are unduly harsh and unrealistic, not to be taken seriously. Hence this impasse will last indefinitely . . .

It is clear that papal authority is no longer enough to command general obedience from the laity (or even from some theologians and clergy members) on the issues in dispute; and equally clear that the Pope has no feasible way of imposing his will on the dissidents.

He can forbid a liberal theologian like Charles Curran to teach, and he can discipline a bishop like Raymond Hunthausen for alleged laxity. But he can hardly excommunicate tens of millions of Catholics for whom personal conscience, not official teaching, has become the arbiter of morality.

Papal authority today is more nominal than real—because in-numerable Catholics have withdrawn their consent to it.

It is impossible, utterly impossible, for Cardinal O'Connor to agree with the conclusion of that letter. He cannot help but recognize that dissent exists, but to him papal authority has never been more compelling. What is most troubling, in terms of his future peace of mind, is that the Cardinal will not admit that a Mitchell Kelleher speaks for large numbers of Catholics in their twenties, thirties, and forties. And they, or most of them, are going to stay in the Church. Much as they may admire such of the Cardinal's positions as those on economic justice, they will pray against him with regard to his support of the Holy See's "creeping infallibility."

In many respects, O'Connor is attuned to "the new Catholics." For example, according to Gallup and Castelli's *The American Catholic People*, the majority, unlike their parents, grandparents, and great-grandparents, support cuts rather than increases in defense spending. And instead of the automatic "patriotism" of the members of the Immigrant Church, these Catholics oppose their government's policies in, for instance, Central America.

Indeed, O'Connor is quoted in the book concerning Central America: "To pursue a military solution . . . is to fail the test of political realism and moral action." But on other matters, such as the ordination of women and certain aspects of sexual morality, O'Connor is not a priest many of these American Catholics would prefer in their parish church.

With all this dissent, the American Church is strong. In a *New York Times* interview in 1987, the Papal Nuncio, Archbishop Pio Laghi, says of the Church here that it is "a very dynamic, very young, very vibrant Church." Except for the growing number of Hispanic members (now 40 percent of the American Church, it has a higher rate of attendance than is the case in most countries; its members give generously to Church projects and are committed to the survival of Catholic schools. Its bishops operate in an open, collegial system—sharing power in a democratic way. And, as Tom Roberts, news editor for the Religious News Service, points out: "The change [since Vatican II] in the way the bishops govern themselves has had a lasting influence on all levels of Church life. Extending the principle of collegiality, or broad participation, to the parish level meant inviting the laity onto parish councils and an array of other committees and organizations that were given unprecedented authority for shaping the life of faith in the parish.

"Americans accepted the invitation perhaps more seriously than any other national group, dug into the task at hand, and, in so doing, established a new sense of what it meant to be a Church."

Now, with the laity accustomed, in many parishes, to be greatly involved in the Church, the declining number of vocations is making the power of the laity all the more crucial to the very survival of the Church in certain areas.

Bishop James Malone, of Youngstown, Ohio, former president of the National Conference of Catholic Bishops, has pointed out that by the year 2000 the number of priests in the United States will have declined by 50 percent. But Pio Laghi, though regretting the decline, does not consider it catastrophic. The priest, he says, "was supposed to do so many other things that now the lay people and sisters are doing. And the sisters—yes, they are fewer in quantity, but the quality is higher, I would say.

"There are 70,000 fewer sisters teaching in the Catholic schools today [than in the 1960s], and the Catholic schools here are . . . the backbone of catechesis. In many other countries, the Catholic schools would have collapsed if you were to take away 70,000—suddenly in 20 to 25 years—of your best teachers. What happened in the United States? The laity took over little by little [until] tens of thousands of lay teachers [came into the schools]."

What Pio Laghi and Cardinal O'Connor may underestimate is the strength that the increasingly visible and vital laity is likely to give to the already strong currents of dissent from Rome within the American Church.

The American bishops have now become accustomed to sharing power among themselves and, perforce, they will have to share power with the laity as well. Already, Pio Laghi has said that it is his "duty to convey to Rome the kind of expectations of an open democratic system that many American bishops have."

Rome already knows, and the crucial question in the years and decades to come is whether the Holy See is prepared to share any of its power with the bishops of America. In November 1986, the *New York Times* quoted a senior aide to the Pope: "In the past the disagreements have been posed in terms of disagreements on several different moral issues like abortion and contraception. Now everyone seems to realize that something much more fundamental is involved: the structure of the church and in particular the bishops' allegiance to the Pope."

This Pope has already laid down the line. In a message read at the opening session of the 1986 annual meeting of the National Conference of Catholic Bishops, John Paul II said: "You are, and must always be, in full communion with the Successor of Peter . . . [who, as the Pope,] is the first servant of the Church's unity and universality."

It may be that American Catholic reaction to the disciplining of Archbishop Hunthausen, the banishing of Father Charles Curran, and other instances of the Vatican's imposing a heavy presence in the affairs of the American Church, had something to do with the Pope's choice of language in that message.

Meanwhile, an epiphany of the Vatican style of dealing with dissent—as contrasted with that of the contemporary American Church—is in this 1986 report by Tom Fox, editor of the *National Catholic Reporter*:

Margaret Hebblethwaite, wife of Vatican affairs writer Peter Hebblethwaite, attended a papal audience Dec. 10. When Pope

John Paul neared, she took out a poster she had prepared that said, "English Catholics Support Hunthausen."

Peter [Hebblethwaite] said policemen grabbed the sign and tore it in two, without even looking at it. Then they grabbed Margaret and carried her out horizontally. Margaret said she was placed on the floor in the foyer. A cop stood over her and cried, "Get down! Do not move!" She asked, "Why are you afraid of me? I have come in peace. I have done nothing more than hold up a piece of paper."

She said they led her to the police office inside the Vatican, saying demonstrations are not allowed in the Vatican. Margaret then asked, "Is not the Pope allowed to know what Catholics around the world are thinking?" The cop replied, "The Pope knows everything." After about an hour, one of the cops brought a statement for her to sign. She said she noted inaccuracies and asked the police to rewrite it. She was threatened with a trial and possible imprisonment if she did not sign the statement.

Eventually, they permitted her to add a few explanatory phrases to the prepared agreement but refused to give her a copy. She was then escorted across the square by a cop, who wished her "Buon appetito."

In New York, homosexuals protesting John Cardinal O'Connor's appointment to the Presidential Commission on AIDS and his opposition to the passage of the city's Gay Rights Bill, have stood silently in dissent on some Sundays inside St. Patrick's Cathedral. They unfurl insulting banners during the Mass and turn their backs on the altar during his homilies. O'Connor has not had them dragged out, though he has successfully appealed to the courts. He would not act unilaterally.

But O'Connor is not the Pope. However, it is intriguing to speculate how O'Connor would have reacted if he were Pope and had been told of what had been done to Margaret Hebblethwaite. My sense is that she would have been allowed to stand peacefully with her poster. Certainly, she would not have been manhandled by the Vatican police. Not more than once, anyway.

"There's no question that he's personally democratic," a historian of the Church says of Cardinal O'Connor. "As are practically all of the American bishops. You can't be reared here in the democratic tradition and not have it affect you. And in these past twenty years, the American Church has been moved by the democratic ethos more than ever before. That's the way the Church has got to keep going."

In the years ahead, the American Catholic Church is likely to become more lively, more contentious, more democratic, and more questioning—of the world as well as of itself.

As Bishop James Malone said in a 1986 address to the National Conference of Catholic Bishops: "We Catholics have grown beyond the need to prove ourselves to the nation of which we are a part. We have moved into a new willingness to criticize our culture in its economic inequalities, its military posture, its foreign interventions, and in its countenance of a massive slaughter of the unborn.

"We are insistently willing to respect genuine difference and the rich pluralism of our nation, but this allegiance has not stopped whatever isolated but prophetic stand the Gospel demands. Some of these will be popular with one group, some with another.

"But there is scarcely another group in the United States which couples a horror at abortion with a preferential option for the poor [in the economy], a concern for a more generous immigration policy with a recognition of what easy divorce has done to the family, the resettlement of refugees from Southeast Asia with a condemnation of military aid to the Contras. The Church in the United States has become something of a sign of contradiction . . . and this may well be one of the signs of her health."

Whatever happens in the contentious, contradicting years ahead, John Cardinal O'Connor may lose political battles in the world and in the Church, but his faith will not waiver, and so he will never recognize defeat.

In April 1985, Cardinal O'Connor's column in *Catholic New York* illuminated that faith and thereby the life of this not-so-simple priest:

Weeks of the year come and go, shortening to days as the years mount, till they move so rapidly they become trains rushing by each other in a continuing blur, trains peopled with memories.

It must have been so with Christ, as even the days became hours running out of minutes during the week that began on a donkey, seemed to all the world to have ended on a cross, and started all over again in a garden.

All the days of His years must have kaleidoscoped through His mind, the years of His mother's widowhood, of the water into wine, the loaves and fishes and blind men and lepers and Lazarus and the alabaster box of precious ointment. Then the hosannas and the palm and olive branches and only a day or two to sort it all out and be ready for Gethsemane and a bloody sweat, for night lanterns and rough guards and a searing kiss of betrayal.

Everything chaotic now, minutes tumbling over one another, time racing onward and backward simultaneously, splintered by shrieks and giggles and lashes and thorns and questions that don't make sense because the answers are already known, or feared, or twisted into a sentence of death . . . better that one man should die for the people.

Do some tricks for me, make me some miracles. What is truth, are you a king, where are your armies? Better that one man die for the people. He makes Himself out to be the Son of God. Better that one man die for the people. Tear your garments, tear His flesh, hosanna to the Son of David, crucify Him and give us Barabbas. Let me wash my hands. It is better that one man die for the people.

My God, My God, why hast Thou forsaken Me? O Lord Jesus, is that the way it was with You? Did You get all mixed up and ask Yourself how it had all happened—where had all the flowers gone and the people who thought You were so wonderful? Did the pain shoot way past Your head and Your hands and Your feet deep, deep, deep into Your soul, so that You could no longer feel the touch of Your Father's love in the numbness of it? Did the blood run into the eyes of Your heart so that You could no longer see the wonder of His glory in You?

Is that why You know our pain so well, our suffering, our loneliness and desolation, and how we get all mixed up about life? Is that why You understand how our faith falters and we're not always sure of what we believe or why, and how much it hurts to be misunderstood or ridiculed or slandered or deserted or divorced or unwillingly pregnant or emptied by an abortion? Is that why we can lay on You the insecurity of our dwindling years, the confusion of our adolescence, the broken dreams of our middle age?

"Is that what Your having become a human being is all about?"

And, in a June 1987 column in *Catholic New York*, John Cardinal O'Connor wrote, as he often does, of his childhood:

We were not a collegial family. There was no consultation on whether or not we should pray the rosary together, or, if so determined, it should be specifically on a Friday night and on our knees. I don't think my father actually *decided* such things. He simply *did* them. So *we* did them. The difference is that he did them voluntarily.

My father had iron knees, and he was no leaner. He didn't need Gertrude Stein to tell him that to kneel is to kneel is to kneel. So leaning on the arm of a chair or a couch was out. You knelt, and if you were 10 years old you squirmed and shifted your weight at every Hail Mary. . . .

Many psychologists would expect me to hate the rosary today. I love it. I'm not sure why. Maybe it's that I used to see what it did at wakes, when I was a young priest. You didn't just *go* to a wake then, nor did you read some unfamiliar prayers out of a book. As soon as you arrived, you started the rosary. Everybody knelt and remembered that death was no stranger—not necessarily a friend, but no stranger, someone you had met before and would meet many times again, one day arm in arm with yourself. The rosary didn't take the pain away. It just made it seem all right; heartbreaking, but all right.

There is no question in my mind that John Cardinal O'Connor would be happier, much happier, as a pastor, starting the rosary at wakes, making a retarded child smile, visiting the sick, and giving Sunday homilies that other priests might consider too long, but there'd be few complaints from the laity.

He has come to be another kind of pastor, however. And though he often relishes the battles he gets into as a very public figure, during his long, insomniac nights, I expect he could do without the wounds of those battles because he does not scar much.

What cheers up the Cardinal is the sunny painting over his bed of Jesus riding into Jerusalem on a donkey. What cheers him up is his faith, and the Pope who prevented his being a simple pastor. He will not say a word against this Pope, and so part of the American Church is passing him by even as he remains one of its most prominent, outspoken, and valuable voices, particularly concerning economic justice and the dark forces of the "consistent ethic of death."

One Sunday during Holy Communion at St. Patrick's Cathedral, a group of homosexuals came to the altar rail. They had signs around their necks: "I don't receive communion from bigots." Then they turned and walked away.

Not long after, some 300 demonstrators stopped outside the cathedral. Pointing their fingers at the great bronze doors, they shouted "Shame!" in protest at O'Connor's presence on the national commission directed to stop the spread of AIDS.

Held high was a sign: "CARDINAL O'CONNOR LOVES GAY PEOPLE . . . IF THEY ARE DYING OF AIDS."

In the same July 27, 1987, *New York Times* story that told of the demonstration, an AIDS patient at St. Clare's Hospital, which is operated by the archdiocese, had a somewhat different view of the Cardinal. Al Herz, thirty-seven, a homosexual, said that the Cardinal had visited him twice in the past week, each time for about twenty minutes. The patient said he had had hostile preconceptions about the Cardinal, but he said, "I found him to be quite straightforward. He made a firm statement to me that he would quit the commission . . . if it turned out to be a political body that was there only to make Reagan look good."

"I'm going to let him prove himself to me," said Herz.

Not long after, to make himself a more useful member of the national AIDS commission, O'Connor spent a whole day with more AIDS patients as well as with representatives of the Gay Men's Health Crisis.

When the dust has settled, as Monsignor John Tracy Ellis puts it, John J. O'Connor will have proved himself—to Al Herz and to anyone else who looks beneath the caricatures—an honest man who actually does believe in the value of every single life, including the lives of those who turn their backs on him. And he does not deceive. And he does know that "there's no point in simply talking to people about filling their souls if you don't fill their bellies."

The Cardinal will be remembered a long time—with curses and with love. And some will mix the two, for John J. O'Connor is not an easy man to sort out, simple priest though he would like to have been.

*From the Speeches
and Writings of*

JOHN
CARDINAL
O'CONNOR

Why Are You Dancing, My Children?

A little midrash [a rabbinical commentary], one of the thousands of the many beautiful midrashim that are built on the sacred Torah. We're told that God saw a group of angels dancing in heaven.

He asked why they are dancing, why do they celebrate.

They said, "Because your children the Israelites have just safely crossed the Sea of Reeds, Dry Shadda."

God said, "Why are you dancing? My children the Egyptians are drowning."

—Pace University,
March 9, 1986

Is You Is or Is You Ain't My Baby?

Dr. Jacob Bronowski, who became best known for his television series "The Ascent of Man," was considered a value-free scientist. The value-free school of science teaches essentially that it is for the scientist to research, hypothesize, theorize, discover principles, and then turn everything over to engineers and others to do with as they will. The value-free scientist, in other words, assumes no responsibility for the use to which his work is put.

After the atomic bomb was dropped on Nagasaki on August 9, 1945, Dr. Bronowski was asked by the United States government to assess the damage. He entered the harbor and took a small boat to the fleet landing where the sailors come in. On the landing was a group of American sailors singing the nonsense ditty of the day, "Is You Is or Is You Ain't My Baby?"

The words meant nothing to Dr. Bronowski. They went in one ear and out the other. Then he made his way around a grove of trees still there, and he came upon the city. He looked down, and there was utter horror, total destruction, complete devastation.

He was absolutely stunned. Then those words, "Is You Is or Is You Ain't My Baby?" began pounding through his very being.

And he asked himself: "Can I, can anyone, call himself a value-free scientist? Can any scientist disclaim completely the work of his hands, his mind, his very being?

"Can I, as a scientist, through my explorations, my hypotheses, my theoretical formulations, present concepts to the world which can then be taken by the engineers and converted into death and destruction [while I] wash my hands of the whole thing and say that science is completely value free?"

—Naval War College,
April 7, 1986;
Harvard Law School Forum,
April 15, 1986

If the Church Is Not Living in the Everyday World, Then It Might as Well Not Live at All

Should I be speaking out on matters in the secular world? Should the Church play that role or should the Church remain within the Church? Do I feel compelled to thrust myself into the secular world of everyday living in New York?

First, I think we'd have to define our terms. If the Church is not living in the everyday world, then it might as well not live at all. That's what we're here for. We are part and parcel of the everyday world.

There will always be conflicts between the Church and secular society. There will always be conflicts between church and state, and there should be. There are a number of reasons, but one that should be very obvious is that the Church is dominantly geared to another world, to a hereafter, to eternity. And by definition, the secular society is geared to this world. The Church has two responsibilities. One, to try to help people get to that other world for all eternity. That world we hope for them will then be a world of endless happiness.

At the same time, however, the Church must try to help people here. There's no point in simply talking to people about filling their souls if you don't fill their bellies. We have thousands of people living in the streets; we have thousands of people who are just outrageously hungry; we have a lot of crazy, mixed-up, chaotic situations in society. We have an economy which is in many ways the greatest and the most just in the world and in other ways is very badly

245

structurally flawed and can just crush an awful lot of people and bring about great turbulence in the world.

You know, I've lived much of my life arguing the morality of legitimate defense of a people when this is necessary. And yet I think it would be absurd to say that the whole world is not overstocked with weapons, and who's going to talk about that? And who's going to talk about housing that is not fit for pigs that is used for people—and is not even available for people? Who's going to talk about a lot of these issues if the Church doesn't?

I really have two positions from which to speak. I speak, one, as a citizen. I never gave up my rights as a citizen when I became the Archbishop of New York. I have the same right everybody else has to address civic issues. I have an additional responsibility as Archbishop of New York—not because of any merit of my own—in fact, it's crazy I am where I am, I have no idea why I'm in this job. So I'm in a highly visible position. I live in a goldfish bowl. And if I ignore some of the nightmares, the moral nightmares, of society—those things which are so devastating to people—if I say, oh, I get my cuffs of my trousers dirty and I don't want to get my hands dirty, then I shouldn't be here.

My number-one priority is always the dignity of life, always the dignity of the human person in every phase of the human person's existence—from the child waiting in its mother's womb to be born to the old woman lying ridden with cancer in a hospital bed or, even worse, in the street. To people who are being shattered with drugs, to people without homes, to the people who sleep to my great shame in the street outside my house at night, to the wars that we fight, to everything that involves the human person.

This is not just a broad, bland, nebulous, ambiguous statement that I'm making. I believe that our primary problems in this city stem from contempt for the human person. The only reason we should have—not the only reason, that's stupid—but you can't simply worry about improving your transportation system because it's better for business. Then you might as well have cattle cars. You have to improve your transportation system because human beings deserve it. And that has to pervade everything you do.

I've talked with the Mayor. I've talked with many other people about this in this city and in the surrounding environs. That there is a deep-rooted contempt for the human person that runs through all of society. And you see it in so many ways. This is what we have to break through.

Break it down into its component parts. Let's put it positively. When we try to design buildings, when we try to provide housing, when we look at our transportation system, when we look at our criminal justice system, when we look at the number of people in the streets, do we ask ourselves what the bishops have asked through this latest pastoral on the economy and social justice? And that's a very simple question. What does this do *to* people? What does this do *for* people? That's the acid test of any society and any economy.

If you're building a building and you're asking yourself: How much money am I going to be making on this building? then there is no way in the world that you're concerned about the worth and the dignity of the human person. If you start—with your architectural design and everything else—asking: What will be best for the human beings that are going to occupy this building? then you're on the track. That's when you're creating constructive societies.

—"Let's Find Out,"
WCBS Radio, New York,
December 21, 1987

Are the Bishops Also Citizens?

In our country, in our tradition, *every* citizen is invited—indeed, urged by the imperative of citizenship itself—to join the debate in any crucial issue of public policy.

Yet questions have been raised about the involvement of the bishops of the United States in the matters at hand, and there have been allegations of undue intervention in the political process, including even the charge that in a programmed and conspiratorial fashion, some bishops, at least, are trying to destroy the so-called wall between church and state; that the bishops are "perilously close" to threatening the tax-exempt status of their churches, or even more crudely, that the bishops are simply lusting for power.

What is the story as I see it?

The bishops have been saying substantially the same thing about abortion for years. Likewise, for years the bishops have been challenging the state and joining the public policy debate on a broad spectrum of laws and policies—economic, racial, social, military. The challenge was addressed to issues of war and peace with the widely publicized . . . pastoral letter "The Challenge of Peace: God's Promise and Our Response." While much was made [of nuclear war] in that letter, even more was made—and has been little noted—of the *causes* of war: injustice, oppression, economic and other forms of violence and exploitation and indignities against the human person. . . .

What would those who criticize the bishops' speaking out during an election campaign have the bishops do? Were those holding or seeking public office expressing explicit support for racism, for drug abuse, for pornography, for rape, for nuclear war, would the bishops be expected to keep silent? Or would they be damned for doing so? . . .

Are the bishops to be silent, then, on the question of abortion, if we are convinced that it is the taking of human life? Why would we be free to indict racism—indeed, be generally applauded for doing so—but damned for indicting abortion?

Why would we *not* be "imposing our morality" on others when we oppose rape, but "*imposing* our morality" on others when we oppose abortion? What a strange democracy it would be that would encourage bishops to cry out their convictions so long as these were popular, but to remain mute when so ordered.

—Harvard Law School Forum,
April 15, 1986

The Joy of Teaching Mimi

In 1962 [while in the Navy], I had begun a First Holy Communion class for retarded children. We had quickly gone from the local conviction that "there are no retarded children around here" to about twenty youngsters, some with Down's syndrome, some with brain damage, some with other difficulties. Mimi would usually stay in her seat for about two minutes, then be up and running around the room, stamping her feet, screaming, banging anything that would make a noise. Routinely I would evict her, routinely she would return, quietly, after all of a minute outside the classroom.

Mimi had never eaten a meal at her family's table, despite their overwhelming love and desperate desire to help. Her eating habits matched her classroom behavior—dishes slammed to the floor, food thrown at the ceiling.

. . . After six months I received a telephone call which thrills me as much in the recollection as in the event. It was Mimi's mother. She had called me many times. I knew immediately this time was different. "Father, you'll never guess." I suggested she try me. "Mimi ate dinner with us last night at the dining room table."

There is not one of you who ever spent so much as a half hour working with retarded children who doesn't know what that call meant. . . .

It's almost 24 years since Mimi's mother called me. I wish I could say that everything has changed since then for families with retarded children. Some wonderful research has been carried out. . . . But there is still so much public fear, so much public ignorance. There are still parents who feel guilty, who imagine God is punishing them for some long-ago sin. There are still those who are so very lonely, who don't know whether to keep their child at home or to turn to an institution. There are still those who refuse to believe that their child is, in fact, retarded. It's all still there today, 24 years later.

—Catholic New York,
January 30, 1986

The Abortion Mentality

Abortion is *the* pivotal legal and public policy issue of our day because . . . if the womb is no longer the safe refuge that surely nature and nature's God intended it to be, nothing, absolutely no *thing* and no person in our society can be assured a safe refuge until the tomb. . . .

Deeply as we feel the pain of the individual, and aware as we are that many, many women have abortions because that seems to them their only choice, we cannot, we *must* not, treat abortion as though it were a matter of concern only to an individual woman or man or family. We are already seeing cruel signs of what an abortion mentality can mean for all society.

We must ask, for example, how safe will the retarded be, the handicapped, the aged, the wheelchaired, the incurably ill, when the so-called quality of life becomes the determinant of who is to live and who is to die?

Who is to determine which life is "meaningful," which life is not? Who is to have a right to the world's resources, to food, to housing, to medical care? The prospects are frightening and far too realistic to be brushed aside as "scare tactics."

—Harvard Law School Forum,
April 15, 1986

My Very Poor Book

Even if it was justified for the United States to enter the war, as I suggested in a very poor book that I wrote on the subject and would like to rewrite today, or hide, even if it was justifiable for the United States to enter Vietnam, it is quite conceivable in accordance with Just War teaching that the manner of waging the war, what we would call the "jus in bello," do we have the right to use the particular means that we used in the war itself? . . . It would appear from the experience of Vietnam that even if we had started out justifiably, if we had begun to use more and more unjust means, then we rob ourselves, if you will, of a justification of being in the war at all.

—Pace University,
March 9, 1986

Tomorrow Is a Day Uncertain

My father had the liveliest sense of death of anyone I have ever known. For the more than fifty years I knew him, he never planned seriously for more than a day ahead, and then only with the very specific provision that he be alive, a possibility he never took for granted, and indeed rather doubted.

Management consultants would have viewed my father's attitude as a sure sign of organizational dysfunction that must inevitably have led him and the family onto relief rolls (welfare of the day). They couldn't be expected to understand that irresponsibility had nothing to do with it. On the contrary, every night I would see him lay out the beloved tools of his craft and arrange them meticulously for the next day's work. When he came home at the end of the day, nothing on earth could have kept him from cleaning those tools as though they were diamonds and putting them once again in order for the day ahead. No, it wasn't irresponsibility, or laziness, or inability to organize that precluded planning *seriously* for anything in the future; it was that he considered such planning to be very presumptuous!

Since the days of King David ("there is but a step between me and death"), no one was ever more conscious than my father that he might very well die tonight, or an hour from now. "Tomorrow is a day uncertain, and how knowest thou if thou shalt have a tomorrow?" That's out of Thomas à Kempis's *The Imitation of Christ*, but if my father had been a bishop, it could have been the motto on his coat of arms.

As a result of this cheerful uncertainty, my father would never issue an unconditional commitment to the future. Any commitment would begin "If the Lord spares me." He did have variations, such as, "God willing" and "If I'm alive" (sometimes rendered "If I'm around"). There was nothing morbid about this. It was a straightforward belief that "the Lord giveth and the Lord taketh away. . . . Blessed be the name of the Lord"—and that was that.

The whole business permeated our entire family. We grew up quite uncertain about whether we would. One of us would be sixteen years old tomorrow, if the Lord spared him. Another would pass algebra, God willing. It all seemed quite supernaturally natural. Rather than generate insecurity, it kept life on an even keel. . . .

Of course my father could get a bit excessive about it all, like when my mother would be after him to get a new suit, or at least a new tie. At 50, he would resist, telling us he wouldn't be around long enough to wear it. He was telling us the same thing when he died—at 86!

. . . I ask myself what my own attitude toward *life* would be today if it weren't for his attitude toward *death*. Pope John XXIII was said to have told his associates as he was about to die that his bags were packed. That's the way it seemed every day with my father, and I suspect it's why, among other things, I have a healthy respect for frequent confession! . . .

I'm sure it is my father's attitude toward the ever possible proximity of death that keeps me from getting puffed up about living on Madison Avenue, with all that such implies.

Swanky as it is, it's only a wayside inn on the pilgrimage.

My father died enviably. All of us were around the bedside praying quietly when he slipped into a coma, where he spent a day or two, I suspect, in telling God quite calmly that he had been around a lot longer than he had expected to be, never did buy that new suit, and felt that God willing, it was time. God was willing.

—*Catholic New York,*
February 27, 1986

How Is It Possible to Completely Separate Issues from the Persons Who Espouse Them?

It is, after all, an individual or a group of individuals—real live persons with names—who deliberately espouse, campaign on, or execute various public policies. It is not the Church that attributes such policies to them. Are they to be exempt, then, from public questioning or public criticism on issues they publicly espouse? Is it even possible to exempt them? . . .

Moreover, many concerns do not emerge as major public policy issues until an election campaign begins, and the identification of particular candidates with particular issues does not come into focus until then. If we are precluded from addressing given issues because they are identified with given persons, it could happen that we *never* address certain issues.

I think it is not out of context to look . . . at events in the Philippines. The bishops of the Philippines wrote a series of pastoral letters, one to be proclaimed each Sunday for an extended period prior to the recent election. They carefully and repeatedly disclaimed political partisanship.

It would be extraordinarily naive, however, to pretend that either the downfall of President Marcos or the ascendancy of President Aquino was unrelated to the activities of the bishops—and notably the activities of Cardinal Sin, who has been lauded throughout the free world for his courage and leadership.

Could the bishops [in the Philippines] have seriously dissociated the *issues* from the *persons* of President Marcos or his wife? . . .

One can be criticized for "imposing" the morality of the Church in one instance, lauded in another for courageous moral leadership—in accordance with whose ox is gored. . . . For the Church to influence public policy can be a rough-and-tumble business. . . .

And there is the fear of dividing the members of God's household into hostile camps (when the Church tries to influence public policy). It's a risk . . . we must take . . . if public policy is to be affected. . . .

For me, [the Church influencing public policy] is one of the most difficult of all problems in our efforts to make a transition from the theoretical to the practical. It categorically must be confronted by a Church that would appropriately influence public policy in the real world. . . .

—Address before the Catholic
Press Association, Columbus,
Ohio, June 4, 1986

The Anti-Abortion Mentality, I

I am convinced that as a nation, somehow, we know that there has to be something wrong when human life at any stage of its existence is wantonly destroyed. We know, somehow, whatever our religious persuasion, that there is something wrong when one and a half million unborn human lives are taken every year in our beloved country. . . . Our society must, surely must, have more support for the woman torn with conflict over a pregnancy than to point her toward an abortion clinic.

Is this simply a religious perspective? Is my own grave concern over abortion born merely of what I have been taught as a Catholic? I can't believe that. I know that millions of Jews, Protestants, Muslims, people of many other religious persuasions—and people who profess no religious faith at all—grieve as I do over this destruction of life.

Or, is abortion *not* the destruction of life? Are we, in fact, *not* putting babies to death?

If we are not destroying human life, of course, then our concern, our anxiety, our pain over abortion virtually disappears. There is a dramatic difference between removing four thousand pieces of tissue each day from the bodies of four thousand women and taking the lives of four thousand babies. . . .

What *is* abortion, then? . . . It is difficult, I think, to find a better source for an answer than in the commonsense experience of daily living and in the scientific evidence readily available, the same commonsense experience and scientific evidence that we find in a Planned Parenthood publication of 1963, which warns teenagers: "An abortion kills the life of a baby after it has begun."

That is quite plain, commonsense language. . . .

In our own day, miracles of modern science confirm what we have known all along—that life exists in the womb. Reporting on an article called "Healing the Unborn," the *1963 Medical and Health Annual of the Encyclopaedia Britannica* says: "Prenatal medicine is now beginning to be able to intervene before birth to alleviate, and even cure, conditions that previously would have severely compromised the fetus. This promises survival for thousands of threatened lives. . . . The concept that the fetus is a patient, an individual whose disorders are a proper subject for medical therapy, has been established."

—Harvard Law School Forum,
April 15, 1986

I Personally Will Defend the Union Movement with My Life

The first thing that Lenin and his party did when they went into power in Russia was to suppress the union movement.

The first thing that Hitler did when he and his party went into power in Germany was to suppress the union movement.

What little freedom had been won in Poland had been won by Solidarity—the union movement now suppressed by the Marxist government.

This should tell us something: that so many of our freedoms in this country, so much of the building up of society, is precisely attributable to the union movement, a movement that I personally will defend despite the weakness of some of its members, despite the corruption with which we are all familiar that pervades all society, a movement that I personally will defend with my life. . . .

Despite the growth, despite the accomplishments now of many years since the initiation of the labor movement in this country, we still have special problems which *result* in a situation completely contradictory to the concept of the Mystical Body of Christ and of Christianity itself. . . .

It has to be admitted, we cannot avoid it, that blacks among us are still poorer, still among the greater number of unemployed. Women among us—working women—are still among the poorer, still among the greater number of unemployed. (I'm speaking of those who want to work.) They are still victims of discrimination. This is true, as well, of the disabled. Most particularly, we have done virtually nothing in our society to support those who are critical to the continuance of our society—our mothers. Mothers who stay at home to take care of children receive no support whatsoever specifically as mothers. . . .

I know that there are a variety of reasons why many blacks, Hispanics, members of various ethnic groups, women, and others are still more commonly at the poverty level, or below, than others. But there is one fundamental reason that we *can* come to grips with . . . our failure to recognize the worth and dignity of every human person. . . . Many of you here have heard me preach many times about the vulnerability of the unborn and that the sin of abortion consists in the fact that we are destroying a human life made in the image and likeness of Almighty God. We must extend that argument to every human person.

Everyone has the right to live in dignity and to be treated with dignity. . . .

And the Church, too, must practice the kind of justice it

preaches. . . . I believe so fiercely that our health-care workers, our schoolteachers, all of those others who provide such
services, must be paid a living wage and that they cannot
live on air, prayer, and holy water. . . .

—Labor Day Mass,
St. Patrick's Cathedral,
September 1, 1986

The Abortion Mentality, II

In March 1986, a letter to the editor appeared in *New
Youth Connections*, a magazine geared for youth, especially those in the New York area. The letter was signed by
the coordinator of adolescent pregnancy and parenting services for New York City: "The fact is, any teenager who is
pregnant can get Medicaid coverage for an abortion regardless of her parents' income and without parental notification. . . . The teenager simply has to tell the Medicaid/fi-
nance worker at the clinic that she is applying 'on behalf of
the unborn.' After the abortion, the teenager must cancel
the Medicaid coverage."

Now to me this seems to be a bizarre example of Orwel-
lian language when we apply for funds on *behalf* of the
unborn individual in order to destroy the same unborn individual.

Further, what a strange anomaly is a public policy that
provides public funding for the unborn in light of the 1973
Supreme Court decision (*Roe* v. *Wade*), which denied
standing to the unborn.

How is it that one can apply for Medicaid funding for the

unborn? You can't apply for Medicaid funding for a dog, a rabbit.

[Because of the vigorously negative reaction by the Cardinal and others to New York State's policy of allowing teenagers to get medical coverage for abortion in this way, the policy was discontinued.]

—Havard Law School Forum,
April 15, 1986

The Church Is Not Going to Crash

Is the American Church pulling away from the guidance of Rome? I believe this is an overblown story. Now, these are matters of perspective and judgment. During the private sessions in November on Archbishop Hunthausen of Seattle, for example, I never at any moment on that occasion felt that the Church was about to explode. On a longer-reaching basis, I honestly do feel there is afoot what I call a self-fulfilling prophecy. There are some, whatever their motives, who want to believe that the Church is falling apart at the seams and is going to disintegrate and become completely fragmented. And consequently, they examine every incident from that perspective. They're always looking for this potential for explosion, if you will.

Then that feeds upon itself. A simple, obvious example: if enough people talk about a potential crash on Wall Street, you're going to have a crash on Wall Street. If enough people say the banks can't give you your money if you want to go get it, then you're going to have a run on the banks and the banks won't be able to give you your money.

Now, because we believe the Church has divine life, it's not going to crash, but it can be damaged, it can go through a lot of unnecessary turmoil simply by this constant insistence that the problems are very, very deep, very, very profound, that there is a tremendous tension, that there is a very severe conflict between and among the bishops.

There are bishops with whom I disagree, bishops who disagree with me, perhaps more who disagree with me than I disagree with in turn. I think we are all human beings, we all say stupid things, we all do stupid things. I do more than my share every day. We misinterpret events. We are misinterpreted in turn. And we have our arguments and our debates. And there are some one likes and some one doesn't like. You know you don't have to like everybody; you're supposed to love everybody.

But I think these disagreements are very natural. We have a huge body of bishops in the United States. Every conceivable temperament, background, experience level, age level, sections of the country. It's a big country, a great big country, with such diversity of cultures. Bishops, just like any other group of human beings, speak from this apperceptive mass, this cultural context.

I think there are always tensions between Rome and any other country in the world. There are always tensions between every headquarters, if you will, and any field activities. As the Archbishop of New York, a huge diocese, I would be shocked if every priest, every nun, every lay person agreed with everything I do. In fact, I think they'd be crazy if they did. There'd be something wrong with them. Because I do some dumb things.

So you are always going to have these tensions, but I do not see them in the Church of the United States at this stage as nearly so volatile as some people think.

I may be wrong, but I don't think so.

—"Let's Find Out,"
WCBS Radio, New York,
December 21, 1986

The Man Who Feels I Hate Him

. . . I went to see two young to young-middle-aged AIDS patients, both of whom, I was told, were dying. The two of them were in St. Vincent's Hospital, which has done such a marvelous job for well over a year now in treating AIDS patients, whatever their religion, their attitudes, behavior, or financial condition. Both patients had been residents of our Gift of Love house (formerly St. Veronica's Convent), tended by Mother Teresa's Missionary Sisters of Charity.

I went to encourage and show my support for the AIDS patients, to pray with them or for them, should they desire, and to give them my blessing. . . . Each was beautifully prepared to die, each eager to pray, each filled with praise of the treatment given them. . . .

As I talked with these two probably dying patients, I knew we had taken the right step when we had decided to reach out to AIDS victims, at whatever cost, and whether or not there would ever be financial assistance from government. And I knew our decision to try to open still another major residential facility, outside the city and near another of our Catholic hospitals, was also a right decision.

So . . . I was feeling not only at peace with the world, but not a little smug about it all, indeed bordering on feeling quite noble. "What a fine fellow you are," I'm sure I told myself more than once on the way out of the hospital, "and how lucky New York is to have you."

God writes straight on crooked lines. He's always right there to restore the balance. . . .

I had no sooner set foot on the sidewalk than along came

a small group of young to young-middle-aged men, looking very pleasant and strolling in the American sunshine. I smiled the smile that I'm told does wonders on television. We weren't on television. One of them slowed his pace to detach himself from the others long enough to say: "Take a hike, hatemonger."

Wow! Want to do some quick penance for your sins? Get somebody to say that to you, especially on a wonderful Memorial Day weekend, when you're crazily in love with the whole world and head-over-heels with America and with New York. Does funny things with the sunshine.

All through the years I have castigated myself for many vices, but I had never thought of myself as a hater, or a stirrer up of hatred toward others. Certainly, it was the last thing I had in mind as I expressed my views regarding the famous "Intro 2" legislation [the "Gay Rights Bill," passed by the City Council despite O'Connor's opposition]. So it came as a shocker for real.

But beneath the hurt—and it hurt very much—was the sadness of knowing how much hurt a fellow like that must be carrying around *all the time.*

I believe it's my job as archbishop to teach what the Church teaches: that homosexual behavior is wrong. I believe it's my job as a citizen to express my views about any piece of legislation I believe harmful to society, and to resist its passage, using legitimate means. . . .

I have been taught to do this without hating. . . . I *know* I don't hate, and therefore my hurt didn't last long, although I suspect some people believe I deserved it and wish it would last longer.

The man who honestly feels I hate him, however, undoubtedly hurts all the time, and I can't forget him or the sadness over *his* hurt.

—*Catholic New York*,
May 29, 1986

Catholic Self-Consciousness

Church historian Father Gerald Fogarty considers the Catholic Bishops' pastoral letter on war and peace as evidence of a newfound confidence that we are indeed first-class citizens. That is, we feel secure enough to criticize governmental policy without losing our status as loyal Americans.

Yet there is unquestionably a continuing defensiveness in this regard, a tendency to think two or three times about whether we will be attacked for "imposing Catholic morality" on the citizenry at large. Such a charge always implies un-Americanism.

I am not sure that I have ever heard the same charge against any other religious body. That is, that their efforts to shape public morality, however they may be rebuffed, were somehow un-American . . . Never do *we* indict *other* religious bodies . . . for openly endorsing candidates or for encouraging the use of their pulpits for explicit campaigning. Nor do I believe we should. . . .

None of which is to suggest for a moment that *we* should endorse individuals for election. Father Coughlin should surely have taught us that.

But that we alone, the "Roman" Church, with all the sinister overtones that title conveys, should have to be excruciatingly meticulous about every word spoken, every step taken—this without question imposes on us extraordinary restrictions as we attempt to affect public policy. And the more self-conscious we ourselves are, the more trepidatious we become about what has come to be called "overstepping the line."

—Address before the Catholic Press Association, Columbus, Ohio, June 14, 1986

The Burning of the Rabbi

Let the haunting story of the great prophet of the Apocalypse, Elie Wiesel, keep us ever mindful of who we are as a people of God and why.

I tell that story in his words:

Rabbi Hananiah ben Teradyon was one of the Ten Martyrs of the faith in Roman times. In those days to teach the Torah or to study it meant capital punishment. Rabbi Hananiah decided to teach the Torah not clandestinely but in the marketplace. Naturally he was arrested, and the Romans sentenced him to be burned. They wrapped him in the Torah, in the scrolls, and lit the fire.

"And then comes a very beautiful passage in the Talmud, one that we recite every Yom Kippur," says Elie Wiesel.

As he was burning, his disciples said, "Rabbi, tell us what you see." His answer became a classic. "What do I see? The parchments are burning, the parchments are burning, but the

letters remain, the letters remain alive, the letters are inde-
structable."

—Liberty Weekend Homily,
July 3, 1986

I Cannot Give Stones. . . .

It was the worst dream I ever had. There was a terrible
famine. I was the only one who knew where there was a
huge hollow mountain filled with bread. I told somebody
that if he could get me a big helicopter, I would go to the
mountain, fill the helicopter with bread, fly around drop-
ping it to the hungry people, go back and fill it up again, and
keep doing the same thing. Then somebody got me a helicopter. I flew it myself to save room for bread. I almost hit
the Empire State Building, but somebody moved it out of the
way just in time.

I started toward the mountain, flying very low so I could
call out to the people and tell them I would be back with the
bread. They looked as if they didn't believe me, and I told
myself it was because they had been starving for a long time
and too many people had promised them bread and had
never come back.

It seems to me that it was around Yonkers, because I
believe I passed the gold dome of the seminary—but you
know how dreams are—where I saw what looked like millions and millions of little round loaves of bread, gleaming
in the sunlight. I circled a few times. Yes, that's what they
were. "Wonderful," I said to myself, "exactly what the peo-

ple need, and so much closer. Why should I fly to the mountain for bread?" Down I went.

I landed and was shocked to see that what looked like little round loaves of bread from a distance were really shiny, round white stones. Great. Much better for the people. They'll appreciate them a lot more.

They can look at them in the sunlight, throw them around, play games with them, even pretend they're bread. I piled so many stones in my helicopter I could hardly take off. In only a few moments I saw a crowd of starving people looking up to me and crying: "Give us bread." I threw them some stones and woke up, freezing and shivering and feeling more depressed than I had ever felt in my life.

The dream is by no means the reason, or even the smallest part of the reason, why I have virtually an obsession about my responsibility for teaching and preaching the truths of our Catholic faith. But every once in a while, when I reflect on the deep hunger for such teaching that characterizes our day, the dream comes flashing through my mind as though it were only last night I had gone through it.

I read a piece in the newspaper that tells me of a survey on the question of removing even food and water from certain terminally ill patients. The article tells me that 73 percent of the people surveyed approved removal. This encourages the medical profession, the article says, because it shows they have popular support for their own convictions. Not what's right or what's wrong, but how many vote for it. It's the approach to contraception, to abortion, to extramarital sex, to Mass on Sundays, to confession, to drugs, to the divinity of Jesus, to teaching of the Church on *any* subject. Not what's right or wrong, what the Church teaches or doesn't teach, but how many vote for it.

I read such and I'm saddened. Yet I must ask myself honestly: "How are people to know? Who is teaching them? Where? When?" At most, 25 percent of our youngsters go to Catholic schools. Only a small percentage of the others go to comprehensive religious education programs outside school, on a regular basis, through high school. A huge number of adults in our archdiocese have had minimal Catholic schooling. The average youngster has watched 20,000 hours of television, or 30 hours per week, by the time of graduation from high school, and has seen 16,000 televised murders. Much else of what is seen on TV is indescribable. The damage to family life, the perverted notions given about love, sex, and marriage are incalculable.

Where is the average Catholic exposed to the opposite, the positive, constructive teachings of our faith? Few, very few, do adult Catholic instructional reading, or take adult Catholic educational courses. This means that the average Catholic's formal instruction in our faith is received at Mass on Sunday, with the homily the primary mode of instruction.

I consider no responsibility as Archbishop of New York more serious than that of seeing that all our people, young and old, are given bread, not stones. I can carry out a major portion of that responsibility only by way of the Sunday homilies in our parishes. For this reason, with the concurrence of our Priests' Council, I have asked every priest and preaching deacon in the archdiocese to begin on the first Sunday of Advent a three-year cycle of preaching and teaching in a way that will ensure that over these three years all the basic teachings of our faith will have been presented to our people. I am providing outlines to our priests for each Sunday of the year, based on the Church's formal liturgy and the Sacred Scriptures assigned by the Church for each Sunday, together with a specific doctrinal theme or fundamental Church teaching.

I have not asked any of our preachers to use these outlines slavishly. On the contrary, everyone must preach in accordance with his particular personality and temperament, tell his own illustrative stories, and so on. The only requirement is that the basic doctrinal theme be explained, within the context of the Scriptures and the liturgy of the day.

Why am I publicizing this effort here? Only to alert Catholics of the archdiocese to the fact that we are launching

heat. When an officer deftly snipped the wires, the threat was over, and the investigation was about to begin.

With 15 sticks of dynamite, the bomb was powerful enough to have collapsed the front of the building at 380 Second Avenue and to have shattered windows one-quarter mile away. With a blasting cap, timer and battery, the bomb showed its architect to be someone of sophistication. And one last component, nestled amid the sticks of dynamite, caught the officers' eyes: a medal of St. Benedict.

The dynamite and the medal ultimately led to Dennis John Malvasi. In late February 1987, with 300 Federal agents and city detectives drawing closer, Mr. Malvasi surrendered to face charges of bombing four abortion clinics in the city. . . .

The four abortion-clinic bombings of which he stands accused are the only such attacks in New York City history. They are among the most severe of the 59 cases recorded nationally since 1982, Federal agents say, because they were not the work of any amateur with gasoline and matches, as is the usual scenario, but of a professional capable of locating and assembling high explosives.

—*New York Times,* May 7, 1987

Cardinal O'Connor yesterday pleaded for the surrender of suspected abortion clinic bomber Dennis John Malvasi, calling such attacks "completely contradictory to the fundamental teachings of our Catholic faith."

As cops combed the metropolitan area in search of Malvasi, 37, O'Connor, in a television interview, offered the suspect religious counseling and appealed to him to turn himself in.

"If you have been involved, I pray, God willing, you will not do anything of this sort again." O'Connor said in an interview on WNBC-TV's evening news program.

He told Malvasi, whom police have called a dangerous religious zealot, that he would make a priest available to him at the office of Police Commissioner Benjamin Ward, "or you can call one of my priests." The cardinal broadcast two telephone numbers—(212) 759-1918, for his aide, Msgr. Peter Finn, and (212) 374-5430, a 24-hour police number.

"If you are a Catholic," O'Connor said, "as your archbishop, it is essential that you do this.

"If you are not a Catholic, I appeal to you as a human being, I appeal to you as a citizen to turn yourself in to the police. Get this all over with and certainly do not engage in anything of this sort in the meanwhile."

Malvasi, a Marine veteran and licensed pyrotechnician with knowledge of fireworks and explosives, is named in a federal complaint in the Oct. 29 bombing of the Eastern Women's Center on E. 30th St. and the bombing of the Margaret Sanger Pavilion of Planned Parenthood, on Second Ave., Dec. 14.

—*Daily News*,
February 24, 1987

Responding to a plea from Cardinal O'Connor, suspected abortion clinic bomber Dennis John Malvasi surrendered yesterday, ending a terror spree that began when the ex-Marine allegedly detonated a bundle of dynamite at a Manhattan clinic last October.

Malvasi, a licensed pyrotechnician, believed to be at the core of a small, violent antiabortion group, surrendered to federal agents here after a brief phone conversation with Msgr. Peter Finn, one of O'Connor's top aides.

As Malvasi was led to Manhattan Federal Court in handcuffs about an hour after his surrender, he told reporters he had surrendered "because the cardinal said to." . . .

Malvasi, 37, described as a religious zealot, is charged with the bombing of two abortion clinics and linked in a criminal complaint to the bombing of a third between Oct. 28 and Dec. 14.

More than 50 federal agents had been closing in on Malvasi since he was identified Feb. 5 as the prime suspect in the clinic bombings.

Malvasi called the offices of the Archdiocese of New York about 11:15 A.M. yesterday.

"He was very calm, not hysterical or upset," said Finn. "He said he had seen the cardinal on TV and that he would come in within one or two hours. We didn't talk about the bombings. He seemed quite resigned."

Finn said Malvasi, a Catholic, told him he had decided to give himself up after hearing O'Connor's appeal on WNBC-TV Monday night.

Finn said his conversation with the suspected bomber lasted less than two minutes. "I was trying to support his intention [to surrender] as strongly as I could," Finn said. "I didn't want to mess things up." . . .

Malvasi was arrested as he entered the Federal Bureau of Alcohol, Tobacco and Firearms office at 90 Church St. in lower Manhattan about 2:15 P.M. Dressed in corduroy pants, a plaid shirt and a brown jacket, he also was wearing an eyepatch and sunglasses and walked stooped over—apparently in an attempt at disguise. . . .

—*Daily News*,
February 25, 1986

A 37-year-old fireworks expert was sentenced yesterday to seven years in prison for his role in the bombing of abortion clinics in New York City.

In a two-hour hearing, the man, Dennis J. Malvasi, said he would not take part in such bombings again because of his loyalty to the Roman Catholic Church and to John Cardinal O'Connor.

"The Cardinal is my shepherd," Mr. Malvasi told Judge Thomas P. Griesa in Federal District Court in Manhattan. "If he tells me I cannot, that's an order. I cannot do it because that would get me in trouble with the Almighty."

Earlier, Malvasi had explained: "Cardinal O'Connor is a

prince of the Church. If the Cardinal says something and you don't listen, then when you stand before the magistrate in the celestial court, you got problems. And I got enough problems without God being mad at me."

. . . "I only have one question to ask," Mr. Malvasi said. "Is abortion murder?"

"That under no circumstances is in my province to comment on," Judge Griesa responded. . . .

Later Judge Griesa said Cardinal O'Connor had "respect for the laws of the United States" and asked whether Mr. Malvasi did also.

"What the Cardinal says is the word," Mr. Malvasi replied. "If he says not to do it, I cannot do it. That supersedes man's law. Whether it's right or wrong, that's his problem."

—*New York Times*,
September 3, 1987

As the World Has Hated Me, So the World Will Hate You

NATIONAL CATHOLIC REGISTER: At a time when the Pope is attempting to restore a respect for Christian truth and Church authority, the lack of education [in the faith among American Catholics] seems especially problematic. The disciplining of dissident theologians, for example, is viewed as undemocratic and uncharitable.

CARDINAL O'CONNOR: Catholics living in a pluralistic society have confused political pluralism with theological pluralism. In our political affairs and many other things we do, we're accustomed to voting. Not maliciously, but unconsciously, we transfer this experience to the moral and spiritual order. . . .

NATIONAL CATHOLIC REGISTER: Since you arrived in New York, you have been sharply attacked for your stands against abortion, homosexual activity and municipal efforts to restrict the operating standards of Catholic institutions. When you preach at St. Patrick's Cathedral, representatives of gay rights groups stand in protest. When you distribute communion, some opponents spit in your face. Is this what a disciple of Christ must expect today?

CARDINAL O'CONNOR: The maxim I live by is the simplest in the world. The disciple cannot be greater than the master. If there is any meaning at all to the fact that a bishop is an apostle of Christ, it is this: Our Lord said, "As the world has hated me, so the world will hate you."

The Archdiocese of New York is not the most important in the United States, but it is the most visible because it's in the communications center of the country. No one could be archbishop of New York without attracting attacks.

Honestly, I have no sense of being personally abused. The attacks are not really directed against me. Of course, I could escape a considerable amount of criticism if I went along with what most anybody and everybody wanted. But then some people would say the archbishop of New York is betraying the Church and the reasons he was appointed archbishop—and they would be right.

I have another theory about controversy. Of course, I don't like to be attacked or criticized, but if the attacks help spread the teaching of the Church, that's the price you pay. . . .

NATIONAL CATHOLIC REGISTER: Someone once called you a warrior-bishop.

CARDINAL O'CONNOR: There are many bishops in the United States who think and feel as I do. They write to me, I write to them. I don't criticize others who have a different approach, but one reason why I'm happy to have St. John Fisher as a patron saint is that he was the only bishop who refused to cave in to the demands of Henry VIII.

I don't want to have my head cut off, I am the least noble in the Church. I am basically a coward. But it's ludicrous to say that everyone can be right. Two and two is four, and that can't be changed.

In moral and spiritual matters I didn't create the truth. It is inherent in the nature of things.

> —"The Task of Saving Souls,"
> Joan Frawley Desmond's
> interview with
> John Cardinal O'Connor in
> the August 9, 1987,
> *National Catholic Register*

Time Passes and We Shall Soon Laugh No Longer

You may recall how Belloc ends his *Path to Rome*:

So let us love one another and laugh. Time passes and we shall soon laugh no longer. Meanwhile, earnest men are at siege upon us all around. So let us laugh and suffer absurdities, for that is only to suffer one another.

> —From a letter,
> partly in contrition,
> by John Cardinal O'Connor
> to a friend who had criticized
> the Pope and, accordingly,
> had received a previous
> furious letter from
> the Cardinal

INDEX